LATE KANT

Fenves is one of the most innovative and brilliant thinkers now writing in the field of German philosophy and literature ... [He] makes a compelling case for the importance and undeserved neglect of the "late" Kant; and suggests new ways in which Kant's work is relevant to the present. Fenves has the rare gift of combining scrupulous historical scholarship, a finely tuned literary ear, and an extraordinary analytic mind.

Susan Shell, Boston College

Immanuel Kant spent most of his life working on what would eventually become his masterpieces: the three *Critiques*. But his work did not stop there: in later life, under political pressure and complaining of oppressive "brain cramps," he undertook a number of new and surprising adventures in thought.

In *Late Kant: Towards Another Law of the Earth*, Peter Fenves explores for the first time Kant's post-critical writings as a philosophical and political project in its own right. In his opening chapters, he investigates the precise manner in which Kant invents, formulates, and complicates the thesis of "radical evil" – a thesis which serves as the point of departure for all his later writings. *Late Kant* then turns towards the counter-thesis of "radical mean-ness," which states that human beings exist on earth for the sake of another species or race of human beings. The consequences of this startling thesis are that human beings cannot legitimately divide and claim possession of the earth, but must rather prepare the globe for its rightful owners.

Late Kant: Towards Another Law of the Earth is the first book to develop the "geo-ethics" that issues from Kant's critical philosophy and to examine the unprecedented proposal that human beings must be prepared to concede their space to another kind of humanity. It is essential reading for anyone interested in the thought of Immanuel Kant.

Peter Fenves is Professor of German, Comparative Literature, and Jewish Studies at Northwestern University. He is the author of *A Peculiar Fate: Kant and World History* (1991), *"Chatter": Language and History in Kierkegaard* (1993), *Arresting Language: From Leibniz to Benjamin* (2001), and the editor of *Raising the Tone of Philosophy: Late Essays by Kant, Transformative Critique by Derrida* (1993).

LATE KANT

Towards another law of the earth

Peter Fenves

Routledge
Taylor & Francis Group

NEW YORK AND LONDON

First published 2003
by Routledge
29 West 35th Street, New York, NY 10001

Simultaneously published in the UK
by Routledge
11 New Fetter Lane, London EC4P 4EE

Routledge is an imprint of the Taylor & Francis Group

© 2003 Peter Fenves

Typeset in Garamond by
Florence Production Ltd, Stoodleigh, Devon
Printed and bound in Great Britain by
MPG Books Ltd, Bodmin, Cornwall

Library of Congress Cataloging in Publication Data
Fenves, Peter D. (Peter David), 1960–
Late Kant: towards another law of the earth/Peter Fenves.
p. cm.
Includes bibliographical references and index.
1. Kant, Immanuel, 1724–1804.   I. Title.
B2798.F355 2003
193–dc21   2002045489

British Library Cataloguing in Publication Data
A catalogue record for this book is available from the British Library

ISBN 0–415–24680–6 (hbk)
ISBN 0–415–24681–4 (pbk)

FOR INBO

. . . kurz, laßt den Menschen spät erst wissen, daß es
Menschen, daß es irgend etwas außer ihm giebt . . .
– Hölderlin

CONTENTS

vii

CONTENTS

CONTENTS

NOTE ON TRANSLATION

Except in the case of the *Critique of Pure Reason*, where references are to the 1781 edition ("A") and the 1787 revision ("B"), all parenthetical references are to Immanuel Kant, *Gesammelte Schriften*, ed. Königlich-Preußische [later Deutsche] Akademie der Wissenschaften zu Berlin, 29 vols to date (Berlin: Reimer; later, De Gruyter, 1900–). Other abbreviations used in this book are: MDT (Hannah Arendt's *Men in Dark Times*); PA (Jacques Derrida's *Politiques de l'amitié*); and VM (Hannah Arendt's *Von der Menschlichkeit in finsteren Zeiten: Rede über Lessing*). Unless otherwise indicated, all translations are my own.

INTRODUCTION

Lateness

Theodor Gottlieb von Hippel, who later became the first mayor of Königsberg, wrote a one-act comedy in 1765 entitled *Der Mann nach der Uhr; oder, Der ordentliche Mann* (The man by the clock; or the orderly man).[1] The central character of the play, as the title emphasizes, lives by the clock – so much so that any delay is unbearable. The day is rigorously scheduled from the first moment of waking to the last moment of consciousness. And lateness is almost a form of criminality. One of the models that has been suggested for the character of Herr Orbil, the "orderly man," is Hippel's long-time friend, Immanuel Kant, and if the model is not Kant himself, then – so the suggestion goes – it may be his closest friend, Joseph Green, from whom he learned how he could bring order to his life.[2] Heine's depiction of Kant's later punctuality is among the most famous portraits of his double-sided character, which remains loyal to a strict daily regiment while at the same time executing a revolution in thought:

> He lived a mechanically ordered, almost abstract bachelor-life in a quiet, out of the way little street in Königsberg, an old city at the northeastern border of Germany. I do not think that the great clock of the local cathedral performed its daily routine less passionately and more regularly than its countryman Immanuel Kant. . . .
> Strange contrast between the outer life of the man and his destructive, world-crushing thought! Indeed, had the citizen of Königsberg suspected the full significance of this thought, they would have felt a far more ghastly aversion for this man than for a hangman, since a hangman executes only human beings. But the good people saw in him nothing more than a professor of philosophy, and when, at the appointed hour, he walked by, they gave him a friendly greeting and adjusted their watches accordingly.[3]

Yet, despite all the legends of punctuality that formed around him, Kant could be extraordinarily unreliable in at least one respect: he would announce

1

the near completion of his manuscripts but would then, for whatever reason, fail to deliver them to the press as promised. This is true of every aspect of the philosophical project to which he devoted the last half of his life. In a famous letter to Marcus Herz of February 1772, which first elaborates the idea of critique, Kant writes:

> I am now in a position to bring forward a critique of pure reason, which contains the nature of theoretical as well as practical knowledge insofar as it is merely intellectual; of this [critique] I will first elaborate the first part, which contains the sources of metaphysics, its method and limits, and thereafter I will elaborate the pure principles of morality; as far as the first part is concerned, I will publish it within around three months.
>
> (10: 132)

The first *Critique* appeared nine years later. And as far as the second part of the original plan for a critical enterprise is concerned, the delay is much longer: as early as 1765 Kant had told Johann Heinrich Lambert that he had already "elaborated" the contents of a few projects that he soon intended to publish, including one entitled "Metaphysical Foundations of Practical Philosophy" (10: 56). Such promises of prompt publication are not limited to private correspondence, moreover. At the close of the Preface to the *Critique of Judgment* Kant makes a similar announcement to the public at large: "Thus with this I bring my entire critical enterprise to an end. I shall proceed without fail to the doctrinal element in order, wherever possible, still to snatch from my increasing age a modicum of time favorable for that purpose" (5: 170). Some seven years later, more than a generation after the original letter to Lambert, the *Metaphysics of Morals* finally appears – only in truncated form, as Kant indicates in the Preface to its first part, the *Doctrine of Right*: the sections on "public right" remain in sketchy shape, since a "decisive judgment" (6: 209) on matters of such great importance, which have generated so much heated discussion of late, can be rightfully postponed.

The central chapters of this study of late Kant are concerned with the intricately devised texts that Kant wrote in the meantime. Aware that only a limited amount of time was still granted him, he nevertheless distracts his attention away from the project that he announces: the development of the "doctrinal" dimension of the critical system of philosophy. The first of these distractions – "On the Failure of All Philosophical Attempts at Theodicy" (1791) – sets the tone for many subsequent ones. In the middle of the essay, having already shown that all philosophical attempts at theodicy fail, as though he were beginning anew, Kant introduces the distinction between "doctrinal" and "authentic" interpretation (8: 264): whereas the former depends on learning, the latter does not, since it consists in the interpretation of a legal document by the one who instituted the legislation in the first place. As a manner of disposing with a "doctrinal" undertaking, "authentic interpretation" is the original enterprise of the late Kant. Overtaken by this enterprise, his first post-critical essay shows that philosophical "attempts" or "essays" (*Versuche*) uniformly fail, and yet this failure of philosophy grants access to the success of a wholly non-philosophical text, namely the biblical Book of Job, which is supposed to contain "authentic interpretation" in allegorical form. The success of Kant's own "philosophical essay" then depends on departing from philosophy – not only from Leibnizian-inspired metaphysical systems, moreover, but also from his own "critical enterprise." Whereas he begins the first *Critique* by resolutely refusing any "sovereign sentences [*Machtsprüche*]" (A: xii), he interrupts "On the Failure" so that he can wholeheartedly welcome one. This departure from the explicit promise of the first *Critique* to do away with all appeals to sovereign sentences doubtless corresponds to a development within the "entire critical enterprise," but it is a departure nonetheless. By attending to certain interpretative distractions of Kant's late years, this study seeks to plot the direction of this departure.[4]

The conclusion of "On the Failure" directly leads to Kant's next and perhaps most famous late writing, "On the Radical Evil in Human Nature" (1792). Reflection on the failure of straightforward attempts at theodicy reveals in a particularly stark manner, according to Kant, the general disposition of human beings toward falsifying the assertions they make in the court of their own conscience – a self-falsification that results in lying to others as well. From this "sad remark" (8: 270) to the thesis of radical evil is only a slight step. And although Kant may have needed to take few precautions in making this step – why not publish an essay on "radical evil," especially since it accords in certain respects with Lutheran doctrines, which have recently been revived in the royal court? – it is a step on which he soon had to reflect with the greatest of caution. For at the very same time as Kant finally fulfills the promise announced in the Preface to the *Critique of Judgment* and publishes the "doctrinal" element of the critical system, he comes close to breaking a solemn promise to do the very opposite: *not* to publish his work. In a letter of 1794 to Friedrich Wilhelm II, which responds to the king's demand that his "obstinate" subject apply his professorial "respect" and philosophical "talents" to "our sovereign purpose" (11: 525), Kant promises to desist from lecturing or publishing anything "touching on religion" (11: 530). Soon after the death of the king in 1797 Kant not only publishes an extensive essay on the conflict between the theological and philosophical faculties of the university but also includes his correspondence with the king in the Preface to this publication. In a footnote to the reproduction of the correspondence he offers the following sentence by way of explanation: "Also this expression" – the expression in question is "as a *most loyal subject* of Yo[ur] Roy[al] Maj[esty]" – "I chose carefully, so that I would not renounce *forever* my freedom to judge in this trial of religion [*Religionsprozeß*], but only as long as H{is} Maj{esty} would still be alive" (7: 10).

Had Kant included this footnote in the original letter – which would accord with his general advocacy of openness and his patent aversion to the "Jesuitical" policy of *reservatio mentalis* (8: 384) – it is unlikely that Friedrich Wilhelm II would have recognized him as his *most loyal* subject: a promise of silence is still a promise, regardless of whether the one to whom one has made this promise has passed into eternal silence. This study does not seek to resume the "trial of religion" by accusing Kant of dishonesty in his dealing with the king; still less does it set out to determine the precise chronology of these dealings in order to acquit him of the same charge.[5] Rather, it accepts that Kant held a "little saving clause" (8: 343) in reserve and seeks to read some of his writings not so much from the perspective of this particular reservation – under the assumption that they were all written with the threat of royal censure in mind – as from the perspective of its underlying possibility. The author says exactly what he means to say; but a footnote can always be added later, which says, in effect, "I said something other than I seemed to say." No wonder Kant's post-critical publications begin by introducing the term "authentic interpretation," which then turns into one of the principal terms for the adjudication of the conflict between the theological and philosophical faculties: only the author – be it God alone or Immanuel ("God with us") – can belatedly say what was originally said in the text.

Inconsistency

And no wonder Kant effectively concludes his independent philosophical publications, in the last year of the century, with an acrimonious attack on Johann Gottlieb Fichte, who was then even more vulnerable to the threat of his sovereign's censure than Kant had been a few years earlier. Having addressed Fichte as "treasured friend" (12: 219), Kant – with the ferocity of the ailing Job – decries him in public as a pernicious enemy, whose pretence of friendship serves only his own sly purposes. At stake in Kant's Open Letter against his "hypercritical friends" (12: 207) is not so much the success or failure of the various attempts to go beyond the letter of the *Critiques* as the presumption that the letter of the text does not capture its spirit – a presumption that late Kant vigorously denies. The point of this study does not lie, once again, in judging his conduct with respect to Fichte, nor does it seek to trace the chronology of his dealings with his erstwhile adherents. Rather, it takes Kant at his word and seeks to make a case for its very inconsistency – a case that he "himself" begins to formulate by repeatedly quoting, both in private and in public, the dictum attributed to Aristotle: "My friends, there is no such thing as a friend." The friend, for Kant, is not one. Which is to say: friendship exists only as a plurality, and this plurality cannot be ordered into a consistent class of elements, each of whom could in all honesty identify him- or herself as a friend – or, indeed, taken to the limit, identify him- or herself as *a* self at all. Kant's "hypercritical friends" sought to formalize the standpoint or position of absolute self-consciousness. Without saying so, and against some of his own intentions, Kant moves in another direction altogether: toward a self that is not one.

At the same time as he begins to formulate a case for inconsistency with reference to the Aristotelian dictum "My friends, there is no such thing as a friend," he starts to personify precisely such a case as well. The last part of *The Conflict of the Faculties*, which is oriented toward medical matters, concludes with Kant's concession that he cannot keep his line of thought straight: the illness from which he begins to suffer around the time of Friedrich Wilhelm II's death robs him of the capacity to maintain the "unity of consciousness" (7: 113) whenever he sets out to develop his thoughts in both speech and writing. The more strongly he tries to hold onto a partic- ular line of thought, the more distracted he becomes – to the point where, as he tells a trusted friend, he suffers from something akin to "brain cramp" (12: 294). Freed from the oppression under which he lived during the last years of the king's life; able once again to publish his matters "touching religion" without fear of royal disfavor and without the more devastating threat of his own conscience, Kant is ironically overcome by another form of oppression: "oppression in the head" (7: 112), which prevents him from elaborating precisely those theoretical dimensions of the critical system in which the king, for one, had absolutely no interest.

Rigorously loyal to the constitutive inconsistency of his own illness, Kant publicly takes responsibility for its severity – the fault lies with his own philosophical technique of mastering ill feelings by sheer resolution – while he privately tells his friends, to their dismay, that an atmospheric revolution is wholly responsible for his inability to maintain a consistent line of thought: "That I have been so powerless stems from a revolution in the air, which has been in place for several years."[6] The point of this study is not to delve into the details of Kant's arrested thought; still less does it seek to identify its source either in his body, in his mind, or in the air. Nothing will be said of "senility." Rather, the study seeks to take Kant at his – divided – word: the "oppression" from which he suffers when he is finally released from an oppressive king, whom he subtly identifies with the Antichrist, is his own doing; but this "oppression" at the same time demonstrates a singular recep- tivity to a terrestrial revolution, the significance of which he himself cannot as yet decipher: "The most common topic of conversation by far was the origin and nature of an electric property of the air, which, according to his own admission, he did not comprehend."[7] The aging Kant alters in tune with the earth, whose "aging" he had diagnosed as a young man.[8]

A late-coming kind

Beginning with a passing reference in the second part of the *Critique of Judgment* to a "revolution" (5: 419) of the earth that first set the stage for the "regime" (*Reich*) of plants and animals, Kant becomes progressively more concerned with the epochal transitions of the planet from archaic chaos to higher degrees of organization. Not only did a revolution draw the earth out of its original chaos by establishing the stable conditions for the vegetable and animal kingdoms; another revolution did away with this regime, so that it could be replaced by the current regime of human beings, who, taken together, can rightly claim to possess the entire surface of the globe. But the last revolution may not be the last, after all. As Kant indicates in a footnote to the concluding section of the *Anthropology from a Pragmatic Point of View* (1798), as a result of another terrestrial revolution, "the orangutan or the chimpanzee" (7: 328) may raise themselves to a position where they, too, can claim a part of the earth as their own. In a subsection of *The Conflict of the Faculties* entitled "Soothsaying History of Humanity" Kant even envisages – for the purpose of denying its moral significance – a terrestrial revolution that would play "the very same game" (7: 88) with the regime of human beings as the previous revolution did with the reign of plants and animals. And in a draft of the so-called *Opus postumum*, which has been dated around the winter of 1799, Kant goes further still: "human beings, as rational beings, exist for the sake of other human beings of a different species (race)" (21: 214). Of this late-coming kind of human being Kant claims to know almost nothing – not even whether they are a different species or a different race. All that is known – although this little can be known a priori – is that human beings exist for the sake of something else: not something altogether different, to be sure, much less for the sake of either an abstract idea or a concrete concept but, rather, for the sake of something strangely familiar – a kind of human being that is, nevertheless, different from us.

As long as nature alone makes a place for this late-coming "species (race)," there are, as Kant insists in *The Conflict of the Faculties*, no consequences to be drawn from the knowledge that human beings exist for the sake of another kind of human being. Only in a single passage, to my knowledge, does Kant indicate otherwise: it appears in a complicated clause that, according to the various editors who prepared the Akademie edition of the *Opus postumum*, Kant ultimately deleted, and it is therefore placed in the editorial apparatus. The passage runs, in part, as follows: "although rational creatures neverthe-less preferably make a place [*Platz zu machen*] for other, still more perfectly organized ones – not merely [*de*] *facto* (with respect to their political exist-ence) but rather [*de*] *jure* because of their now innately greater specific perfec-tion, so that it would be organized after the earlier ones have conceded them their place [*nachdem die vorige ihnen ihren Platz geräumt haben*]" (21: 214). Nature makes a place for the other kind of human being; its arrival on earth is definitely not the result of any human planning. Yet human beings still have a duty: conceding them their place. Such concession has nothing to do with the calculation of respective magnitudes of power, on the basis of which the existence of another political body is either acknowledged for the sake of self-preservation or annihilated for the sake of self-aggrandizement. Conceding that others have a right to divide the earth is the right thing to do, although, as Kant implicitly concedes, the mere prospect of this rightful division jeopardizes one of the principal foundations of the *Doctrine of Right*: the claim, namely, that human beings, taken together, have a right to possess the planet. Making way for an epochal making place follows in turn. Only those who are already divided – by themselves, by the earth – are in a position to concede the division of the earth to others. Whoever has done so is no longer one but is, instead, a constitutively inconsistent plurality. Late Kant leads the way.

1

THE PLEASURES OF
FAILURE

Toward an unnumbered "Remark"
in the *Critique of Judgment*

The spirit of Epicurus

The last of three *Critiques* sets out to accomplish at least three tasks: complete the "entire critical enterprise" (5: 170), as Kant announces in the concluding paragraph of its Preface; develop the idea of a philosophical system, as he proposes most extensively in its original Introduction; and give both the "power to judge" (*Urteilskraft*) and the feeling of pleasure their due, as he emphasizes in both the original and the published Introductions. These tasks are intimately related: showing the immediate relation of pleasure to an a priori principle of the power to judge is a condition for the completion of the critical enterprise, which, in turn, makes possible the articulation and exposition of philosophy as a system of rational knowledge. But the philosophical system as such has no place for pleasure – nor the power to judge, for that matter. Both the faculty of feeling and that of judgment are without any doctrinal dimensions but are, instead, solely matters of critical self-reflection on the sources of human knowledge and the projective structure of finite rationality. As philosophy lays itself out in a systematic fashion, the feeling of pleasure no longer plays any role, and the same is true of the power to judge. This is the case not only for Kant, who says little about pleasure in the doctrinal treatises he composed after completing the third *Critique*; it is equally true of the great systems that took their inspiration from the *Critiques*. In his *System of Transcendental Idealism* of 1800, Schelling – for all the talk of his supposed "romanticism" – scarcely considers the phenomenon of feeling, much less the nature of pleasure, and in the first part of the "System of Science" that Hegel publishes under the title *Phenomenology of Spirit*, pleasure comes into play only as the initial moment of the self-realization of rational self-consciousness, soon to be superseded by the "law of the heart."[1] "Beyond the pleasure principle" – this is not only the title of Freud's speculative inquiry into the "death drive" but is also an apt description of the late-born idea of philosophy as a systematic science.

Pleasure cannot, however, enter into the project of critical reflection on its own — as a raw datum of sensation or a sweet sensation of well-being. Only under the condition that pleasure should not be wholly *mine* – or, more exactly, under the condition that I can legitimately demand of all other similarly constituted beings that they feel the same feeling as I do – can the feeling of pleasure play a role in the "critical enterprise." For this reason, although Kant had announced his intention to write a "critique of taste" long before he completed the first *Critique*, the inquiry into this faculty is a late offspring of earlier inquiries into the a priori principles on the basis of which human beings can gain knowledge of an external world and act in spite of their knowledge.[2] Only a pleasure that consists merely in the act of judgment – "*bloß in der Beurteilung*," as Kant repeatedly says – can be demanded of all others, including those who share little else in common. Such is the immensely difficult problem around which the *Critique of Judgment* revolves. Only insofar as philosophers can legitimately suppose that such a pleasure is something other than a *fata Morgana* can they further propose that there might be an *immediate* relation between the faculty of feeling and the power to judge. Without this proposition, pleasure would have to be mediated by a purpose, and this purpose would bring it into the sphere of practical philosophy, from which it could escape only on the basis of another, much older philosophical proposition that Kant, for his part, could never seriously entertain – the proposition, namely, that the activity of philosophy, understood as the contemplation of things-in-themselves, amounts to the highest pleasure. Since the *Critique of Pure Reason* denies that human beings can know such things, this classical conception of the relation of philosophical reflection to pleasure holds no promise. And since pleasure, like all modifications of the faculty of feeling, is, for Kant, a sheer fact, an indisputable but non-referential *datum* of consciousness, incapable therefore of being "pure," perhaps even devoid of "intentionality" in the sense that Edmund Husserl would later develop from scholastic sources, it cannot be conceived in "ethical" terms either: it does not pertain to the comportment of the agent. Which is to say: pleasure is not grounded in, or an expression of, good or bad modes of life. The feeling of pleasure with whose help Kant seeks to complete the "critical enterprise" – a feeling immediately related to the power of judgment – cannot be considered morally superior to a pleasure that invites no such claim. Or, more exactly, its superiority can be discovered only in retrospect – as a bonus, so to speak, which allows for the successful completion of the "critical enterprise" but which does not earn any additional moral credit. Unlike Aristotle, whose thought is perhaps never more tortured than when it seeks to account for *hedonai*,[3] Kant has no intention of establishing an axiomatics of pleasure by drawing attention to the difference between those activities that good human beings enjoy and those in which their wretched counterparts indulge. Such a distinction makes no sense in a context where pleasure is understood to be a modification of the faculty of feeling, which, in turn, consists in the ability of the finite subject to be receptive to, and therefore aware of, its inner states. Only in this way, however, can the faculty of feeling enjoy a certain independence from the other higher faculties, especially that of desire. And only insofar as the faculty of feeling achieves such independence can it enter into a genuine relation to an a priori principle of judgment through which the other two higher faculties of the mind – understanding and reason – can be brought into a mediate relation, the development of which constitutes the basis for the systematic unity of philosophical science.

Just as the modification of the faculty of feeling that can legitimately be demanded of all others cannot be represented as morally superior to the pleasures about which this claim cannot be made, it cannot be understood in accordance with an equally ancient distinction through which pleasures have been divided – the distinction between mental and corporeal pleasure. The pleasure in the mere act of judgment is, of course, a matter of the mind; but so, too, are those modes of "satisfaction" that are in each case non-generalizable modifications of particular subjects. This is not to say, however, that nothing of the traditional opposition between mental and bodily pleasures occupies Kant's attention in the *Critique of Judgment*; on the contrary, it enters into the discussion at the precise point where Kant, having concluded his Critique of Aesthetic Judgment prepares to turn to its teleo-logical counterpart, draws attention to the philosopher who, more than any other, is associated with the word *pleasure*, namely Epicurus. The appearance of Epicurus at a crucial juncture in the "critical enterprise" is all the more surprising in retrospect, for in the next section of the *Critique*, which considers teleological judgment, the laughing philosopher is judged to be the most failed philosopher of all: his pretence of doing away with teleological judg-ment is revealed to be just that – pretence, perhaps even perfidious deception. All of the tensions that enliven Kant's inquiry into the faculty of feeling come to a point of crisis when it touches on the doctrine of life ascribed to the scandalous "materialist" whose name is synonymous with a life dedicated to pleasure.

From its inception, Kant's thought is engaged with the spirit of Epicurus. The engagement does not take the form of acceptance, of course; still less does it make Kant into a champion of Epicureanism.[4] Nothing could be more unacceptable to the author of the *Critique of Practical Reason*, which criticizes Epicurus by name and denounces the so-called "principle" of pleasure. The principle of pure practical reason, according to which actions ought not to be grounded on the presence or prospect of pleasure or pain – or, to cite a more authentic Epicurean doctrine, the attempt to be released from the constraints of both – can never be represented in terms of pleasure. The Kant of the *Critiques* also wants nothing to do with the physiological speculation through which Epicurus seeks to secure a modicum of equan-imity in the face of life's inescapable vicissitudes: the proposal, namely, that the cosmos is composed entirely of atoms and the void. *The Metaphysical Foundations of Natural Science* (1786) dismisses all forms of atomism. And in the second part of the *Critique of Judgment* the rejection of Epicurean doctrine is even more devastating: of all the "systems" that try – and fail – to explain "natural purposes" (*Naturzweck*), none is a greater failure and none is closer to outright deceit than the "system" proposed by the ancient atomists: "nothing is explained, not even the illusion in our teleological judgments" (5: 393), as Kant announces, with a certain degree of outrage.

Nevertheless, regardless of his immense failures as a moral and natural philosopher, Epicurus is not to be despised. On the contrary, Kant associates his own "critical enterprise" with the careful, methodical reflection on the limits of human cognition that distinguished Epicurus among ancient philosophers. To the extent that Epicurus' method of inquiry consists in a rigorous reticence to overstep the bounds of possible experience, "he showed," as Kant notes in the first *Critique*, "a more genuine philosophical spirit than any other philosopher in antiquity [*zeigte er daran echteren philosophischen Geist, als irgend einer Weltweisen des Altertums*]" (B: 500), which is to say, a spirit that serves as a *prolepsis* of the critical mind – to cite the only philosophical doctrine of the ancients that finds its way into the exercise in "first philosophy" that Kant undertakes in the Transcendental Analytic of the first *Critique*.[5] Just as the ancient philosopher refuses to overstep the bounds of experience and thus allows for things that no philosopher will ever know, so, too, does his modern successor. And this critical stance, which consists in cheerful reticence, cannot fail to appear as a general assault on all those who indiscriminately apply theological and teleological principles. Philosophical spirit, in other words, consists in wanting nothing to do with the "dreams of spirit-seers." Even if the idea of prolepsis is itself implicated in spirit-seeing – future and present being exchanged for each other, as simulacra communicate themselves throughout the cosmos – the implication nevertheless does no harm: understood in a critical manner, prolepsis is only the ghost of the spirit supposedly seen by "spirit-seers," a *Geist* to the second power that can legitimately be called, for this reason, "philosophical spirit."

The remarkable peon to Epicurus in the *Critique of Pure Reason* is safely tucked away in a footnote. The opposite is true of Kant's first major natural-scientific enterprise, *Universal Natural History and Theory of the Heavens* (1755). Just as the young Marx greets Epicurus as a friend to all those who wish to liberate themselves from servile social relations,[6] so, too, in his own more cautious, less untroubled way does the young Kant. And so, too, does the young king whom Kant seeks to serve both in body (as a professor) and in spirit (as a philosopher), namely Friedrich II. The young philosopher is so impressed by the king's Epicureanism that the *Critique of Judgment*, many years later, memorializes a half-dozen lines from one of the poems Friedrich composed "in imitation of Lucretius."[7] And it is not difficult to see why Kant would be impressed long before he began the critical project:

"Epicurus," the king writes in a letter of 1759, "is the philosopher of humanity, Zeno that of the gods."[8] Only a single circumstance prevents the pleasure-loving king from following Epicurus' principal prescription for healthy living and retreating, *sans souci*, into a garden with a group of friends: his public duties, which is to say, the requirement that he be supremely visible.

The young Kant, who does not have the luxury of this option, goes in the opposite direction, as he throws himself into the world of publication. The most ambitious of his earliest publications – and the only one dedicated to the "Most Illustrious, Most Magnificent King, Most Gracious King and Lord" (1: 217) – announces in its Preface a Promethean imperative that gives direction to everything else Kant placed into print: "Give me only matter, and I will build a world out of it for you" (1: 229). Prometheanism is not, however, the name of the threat under which Kant finds himself as he – unsuccessfully – publishes his *Universal Natural History*: it is, rather, Epicureanism. For the bold treatise is suspiciously close, on the one hand, to a theoretical philosophy that allows only atoms and the void and, on the other, to a practical philosophy that takes its principle from the prospect of pleasure. As Kant announces – or confesses – in the Preface, "I enjoy the satisfaction [*genieße das Vergnügen*] of seeing a well-ordered whole generate itself on the occasion of fixed laws of nature without arbitrary fictions [*Erdichtungen*], a whole that looks so much like the one we have before our eyes that I cannot refrain from considering it the same" (1: 226).

Just as Kant does not have the luxury to retreat into a private garden, however, he cannot enjoy another of his king's privileges: exemption from legal proceedings. Even when the king, as a would-be Epicurean, makes irreligious remarks, he cannot be brought into a court of law. Kant, by contrast, is very much at the mercy of the courts for the remarks he publishes. As a precaution against the threat of legal proceedings – which issues from his close association with the spirit of Epicurus – Kant produces a prolepsis of the very forum from which he wishes to escape; he subjects *himself*, in other words, to an improvised legal process and arraigns, as a result, his first tribunal of reason: "Since I know that these reflections are free from all criminalities, I will loyally present what well-meaning as well as weak minds might find objectionable, and I am prepared to subject it to the rigors of the orthodox [*rechtgläubigen*] Areopagus, which is the mark of a sincere disposition" (1: 222). The "orthodoxy" of this new Areopagus does not consist in its allegiance to any articles of faith but, rather, in its desire to separate right from wrong by distinguishing the rational from the irrational. By subjecting himself to the decision of a tribunal of his imagination, the young philosopher hopes to immunize himself from a *real* courtroom and thereby achieve something like a simulacrum of the royal privilege: freedom from every law other than those to which he subjects himself. The idea of autonomy has its origin in this Areopagus of the scientific imagination. Its origin, in

12

turn, is the barely concealed accusation of orthodox theologians that the lines of inquiry Kant pursues so closely parallel those of Lucretius' *De rerum natura* that his work threatens to unleash a new Epicureanism. If this were indeed the case, then the young Kant would ironically turn into a reborn atomist – ironic, of course, because Epicurean doctrine, much to the chagrin of the Church fathers, runs counter to the Platonic conception of the soul in which the idea of rebirth takes hold. And since the crux and crisis of the *Universal Natural History* will be a wholly non-Christian idea of rebirth – nature as a "Phoenix" (1: 321) that restores itself from its own ashes, without the intervention of extra-mundane intervention – the accusation carries a certain degree of urgency:

> If the structure of the world with all its order and beauty is only the effect of matter abandoned to its own universal laws of movement ... then the proof of the divine author that one draws from gazing at the beauty of the cosmic architecture is completely undone; nature is sufficient unto itself; divine governance is unnecessary, Epicurus lives again in the midst of Christendom [*Epikur lebt mitten im Christentume wieder auf*], and an unholy world-wisdom [*Weltweisheit*] tramples on the faith that offers a light to illuminate philosophy.
>
> (1: 222)

Such are the words of the "attorney for the faith," who, by speaking in these terms, ironically indicts himself – not of Epicureanism, to be sure, but of being under the unconscious influence of its teachings. For the image by which he seeks to cast suspicion on the author of the *Universal Natural History* is drawn from some of the most famous lines of *De rerum natura*: "*Quare religio perdibus subiecta vicissiml obteritur, nos exaequat victoria coelo* [Religion has been hurled down and trampled underfoot, And victory has raised us to the heavens]."[9] Kant, however, cannot rest content with this not-so-subtle allusion. He defends himself from the charge of Epicureanism by presenting himself as the unambiguous champion of reason. The ancient atomists, by contrast, fail to be fully rational, and the sign of their failure is their reliance on the *clinamen* or "swerve" for the explanation of two scenes of origination: that of the cosmos as a whole and that of the living bodies that find their home therein.

The young Kant is more successful in showing that he diverges from the Epicureans in his explanation for the origin of life than in his explanation for the origin of the cosmos, for in the latter case, despite his protests to the contrary, he proposes no intra-mundane reason for the initial stirrings of the mechanical forces from which the universe then develops. In the case of life, by contrast, Kant can acquit himself of the accusation that he represents the revival of Epicurus in the midst of Christendom by insisting that the principles on which all living bodies are based cannot be understood in terms of the mechanical principles that he used to project the cosmos. The purposiveness exhibited by even the tiniest living creature – a "blade of grass" (1: 230) is Kant's example both early and late – cannot be explained in terms of mechanical principles. Kant's defense against the charge that he seeks to revive the doctrine of Epicurus thus revolves around the proposition that his conception of life cannot be reconciled with theirs. And this defense receives subtle support from the account of *his own life* that he slips into the Preface: the fact that the world conforms to its projection in his imagination guided by reason, that he can project a world on the basis of two merely mechanical principles and discover, upon comparison, that this project is exactly like the world that appears to observant eyes during a clear night, demonstrates that our cognitive powers are fit for nature, and this fitness, recognized only in reflection, is comparable to the fitness that living beings demonstrate both in their internal composition and in their interaction with one another. And what is more: this reflective recognition of fitness is not only pleasurable; it "redoubles" (1: 226) the pleasure that comes from perceiving the beautiful order of things.

"The attainment of every intention"

Something similar is also true of the old Kant, whose *Critique of Judgment* regularly revisits scenes from the *Universal Natural History* and repeats almost *verbatim* the sentence from its Preface concerning the inexplicable nature of a mere "blade of grass" (5: 400). That Kant remembers a "redoubled" pleasure of his youth in his last *Critique* cannot be simply attributed to chance, moreover, for an odd but incontestable lesson of its Introduction is precisely this: pleasures such as those he felt when he rewrote *De rerum natura* on the basis of Newtonian principles are unforgettable, even if it happens that they are again and again repressed. With certain changes in terminology – *Lust* (pleasure) for *Vergnügen* (satisfaction) – the central section of the second Introduction to the third *Critique* can even be understood as an amplification and extrapolation of the earlier genealogy of pleasure. Discovering to our surprise that our mental capacities correspond to those of the cosmos is, for the early Kant, the source of his own redoubled satisfaction; for the later Kant, it is a source of pleasure that can legitimately be attributed to everyone. In the sixth section of the Introduction he chose to publish – the title of which, "On the Connection of the Feeling of Pleasure with the Concept of the Purposiveness of Nature," could easily have been incorporated into the overall design of the *Universal Natural History* – Kant points out certain features of the feeling of pleasure, and the delineation of these features allows him to bind together the two seemingly disparate "critiques" he wishes to capture under a single title. The integrity of the project as a whole, in other words – not only that of the *Critique of Judgment* but also the "entire critical enterprise" – comes to rest on this connecting section of the published Introduction.

The line of argument Kant pursues in the sixth section proceeds in the following direction: aesthetic judgment is, by definition, bound up with the faculty of feeling; but the same cannot be said of teleological judgment, nor, in a wider sense, of those "logical" reflective judgments by means of which the faculty of cognition lends itself a principle for the ordering of the empirical laws of nature; and yet, unless such applications of the power to judge can be directly linked to the faculty of pleasure, the unity and integrity of the *Critique of Judgment* is severely compromised. Reflective judgment in its "logical" dimension should, in short, *also* be related to the ability to feel pleasure, even if its own peculiar pleasure – that of cognitive success – must later be distinguished from the pleasure taken in the mere act of judgment. Whatever their differences, both pleasures can be legitimately attributed to all those who share the same cognitive faculties. The grounding of this attribution secures the unity and integrity of the third *Critique*, which, in turn, makes way for the completion of the "entire critical enterprise":

> In fact, we do not find the concurrence of our perceptions with the laws governed by universal concepts (the categories) has the slightest effect on our feeling of pleasure; nor can there ever be any such effect, because the understanding proceeds with these laws unintentionally, by the necessity of its own nature; by contrast, when we discover that two or more heterogeneous empirical laws of nature can be unified under one principle that comprises them both, the discovery gives rise to a very noticeable pleasure [*einer sehr merklichen Lust*], frequently admiration, even an admiration that does not cease when we have become fairly familiar with its object. To be sure, we no longer detect any noticeable pleasure [*spüren wir . . . keine merkliche Lust mehr*] that results from our ability to grasp nature in terms of its particular laws; but this pleasure was doubtless there at one time [*zu ihrer Zeit*], and it is only because even the commonest experience would be impossible without it that we have gradually come to mix it with mere cognition and no longer take any special notice of it [*nicht mehr besonders bemerkt worden*]. – It therefore requires something to make [us] attentive to the purposiveness of nature for our understanding in judging it, a study [*ein Studium*] that brings heterogeneous laws of nature, if possible, under higher, although still empirical laws, in order that, when successful, in view of this accord of such laws for our faculty of cognition, which we regard as merely contingent, pleasure be felt. By contrast, a representation of nature that foretold [*voraus sagte*] that even in the most minor investigation of the most common experience we would stumble on a heterogeneity in its laws that would make the unification of its

15

particular laws under universal empirical ones impossible for our understanding would thoroughly displease us, for this would contradict the principle of subjective-purposive specification of nature in its genera and our reflecting power of judgment with respect to the latter.

(5: 187–88)[10]

The complexities of this passage are immense, and an exhaustive treatment of them would require a *Studium* not unlike the one it discusses. Nevertheless, this much is simple enough: Kant proposes that the mind holds hidden treasures of pleasure. In everyday life – and perhaps this is, for Kant, one of the defining features of "everyday life" – the pleasure of subordinating lower empirical laws under higher ones goes unnoticed, and yet it is still "feelable," although not generally felt, until we undertake a *Studium* that consists in bringing to consciousness something inseparable from its constitution. Kant proposes, in short, that we search for an archaic pleasure and struggle against an equally archaic anestheticization. *An* aesthetics – not, however, the one Kant develops either in the opening section of the first *Critique* or the first part of the third – is subtly suggested in this exposition of primordial anestheticization. The imperative of this unexplored aesthetics would be "pay attention" – attention, above all, to those pleasures of which we have lost consciousness because of our immersion in everyday concerns. By obeying this imperative, our pleasure would be literally *redoubled*: the original pleasure would be felt again and the remembrance of this pleasure would be another, added pleasure.

In contrast to this redoubled pleasure stands the desolate vision of a nature that does not allow its empirical laws to be subsumed under higher ones – a nature that cannot, in other words, be brought into a system. Kant rarely, if ever, entertains such a vision of nature. He does, however, do so in terms of human nature. Melancholia takes hold of those who, for all their thoughtfulness, are unable to discover higher laws under which the chaos of human affairs can be brought into order. Epicureans are often associated with such a melancholic atmosphere – not because they are subject to his humor but, on the contrary, because their doctrine of the *clinamen* expresses their own random, unsystematic, thoughtless, even silly ways. Withdrawal from the public realm is the only reasonable option. The "Abderiten hypothesis" (7: 82) – Abdera, home of ancient atomism, became a byword for silliness – saves reflective souls from their own inherent tendency toward melancholia, but no one who was thoughtful would entertain this hypothesis in the first place. With this thought, although not precisely in these terms, Kant concludes his "Conjectural Beginning of Human History" (1786):

The thinker feels a grief that the unreflective do not know, a grief that can well lead to moral ruination: this is discontentedness with the providence that governs the entire course of the world; and he feels such grief when he thinks about the evil that so greatly oppresses the human race, leaving it without (apparent) hope for something better.

(8: 120–21)

In more muted language, a similar grief – Kant only calls it "displeasure" – clouds the vision of whomever "prophesizes" (*voraussagt*) that the project of organizing the contingent laws of nature under ever-more general ones would someday prove impossible. The remedy for this ominous threat remains the same throughout Kant's critical work and reaches its culmination in the concluding section of the *Critique of Judgment*: trust in the principle of natural purposiveness. And this trust, as the work seeks to show, is justifiable insofar as the principle has no other purpose than providing a basis for our own reflection on the systematic ordering of nature.

Everything in the last *Critique*, if not the critical project as a whole, thus revolves around the thesis through which the sixth section of the published Introduction secures the basis of its demonstration: "The attainment of every intention is connected with the feeling of pleasure [*Die Erreichung jeder Absicht ist mit dem Gefühle der Lust verbunden*]" (5: 187). This thesis certainly does not exhaust Kant's attempt to make sense of pleasure; indeed, it may not even be completely reconcilable with other accounts of pleasure that make their way into the *Critique of Judgment*.[11] The centrality of the thesis lies, rather, in the place of its articulation: as a point of commonality for the "aesthetic representation of natural purposiveness," which is the topic of discussion in the seventh section of the Introduction, and the "logical representation of natural purposiveness," which comes into consideration in its eighth section. That all cognitive acts are "connected," "combined," or "bound up" (*verbunden*) with the feeling of pleasure connects, combines, and binds the volume as a whole, making it into *a* single, unified book. One might even go so far as to say: on the basis of this thesis, for which Kant makes no argument, the logical and the aesthetic dimensions of reflective judgment are so tightly bound together that the power to judge can be considered *an* ability – "one force" (*eine Kraft*) rather than a potentially inconsistent multitude.

And, of course, nothing could be more familiar, nothing less objectionable than this thesis: "The attainment of every intention is bound up with the feeling of pleasure." It draws strength from a long-established conception of the relation between feeling and willing, according to which pleasure is a direct result of – or even equivalent to – the fulfillment of a desire. Although this conception of pleasure doubtless lends Kant's thesis its undeniable plausibility, he slightly yet decisively changes its terms: instead of using *desire*, he employs *intention*: "the attainment of *every* intention" – and not simply those intentions that can be attributed to the faculty of desire – "is bound up with the feeling of pleasure." Pleasure, in other words, is not

17

simply a function of the will; cognitive intentions, which have nothing to do with volition, not only have some relation to pleasure; they have a potentially direct relation. Unless the traditional association of pleasure with fulfilled desire is severed, moreover, none of the third *Critique*'s ambitions can be fulfilled: aesthetic judgment cannot be made independent of practical interest; a transcendental exposition of taste is inconceivable; and the intricate articulation of the higher faculties of the mind – cognition, desire, and feeling – collapses into incoherence. Or, more exactly, the book turns into a disconnected, unbound series of remarks. If, however, the third *Critique* turns into a series of remarks, so, too, does the "entire critical enterprise" – which is to say that it can no longer be considered an "entire" enterprise but only, at best, a remarkable one. The success of Kant's life work is therefore contingent on demonstrating that the successful accomplishment of *every* intention is necessarily connected with the feeling of pleasure. And something like "transcendental success" turns into Kant's explicit theme, as he delineates the dimensions and consequences of the initial thesis of pleasure:

> If the condition of reaching the intention is an *a priori* presentation, as in this case it is a principle for reflective judgment in general, then there is a basis that determines the feeling of pleasure *a priori* and validly for everyone. And the feeling of pleasure is determined *a priori* and validly for everyone merely because we refer the object to the faculty of knowledge; in this case the concept of purposiveness does not in the least concern the faculty of desire and hence is quite distinct from any practical purposiveness of nature.
>
> (5: 187)

Whatever else may be said of this argument – the point of which is to secure the possibility that one can legitimately demand of all human beings that they take pleasure in something besides the morally good – it neither explains nor justifies the thesis from which it departs; on the contrary, it takes the thesis for granted, as if it were self-evident, in need of no further ground of demonstration, a thesis of equivalent status to his definition of "being" in the *One Possible Ground of Demonstration for the Existence of God* (1763). Yet the validity of the thesis may be even less perspicuous: it cannot be simply a matter of empirical generalization, and it does not appear to be an a priori principle either. And even if the thesis seems to be an innocent remark, made almost in passing, it still expresses a claim that must be adjudicated in a tribunal of reason. For the term *every* is an expression of universality, which, in turn, implies necessity. What is at stake in this thesis is a "necessary connexion," as Hume would say, between pleasure and success. If some versions of success yield something other than pleasure; if some – or only one – accomplishment of an intention were felt in another manner, then the connection between the two parts of the third *Critique* would be severed, and the "entire critical enterprise" could not be successfully completed – or not completed in the manner that Kant himself intends. It is *either* part of the concepts of "intention" and "pleasure" that the attainment of the former is necessarily bound up with the latter, in which case an attained intention not connected to pleasure is either not, in truth, an intention or the true intention is not, in fact, attained; *or* a third term must be posited through which the others are connected. In Kant's own terms, the proposition "every attained intention is connected with pleasure" expresses either an analytic judgment or a synthetic judgment a priori, and in either case, as a universal and therefore necessary claim, it should be treated in the same manner that Kant treats other such propositions. Or – and this is the crux of the matter – the thesis is itself an expression of the power to judge in its reflective capacity, valid for Kant at this very moment, a claim on all those who are the same cognitive circumstance, a "subjective universal" rather than an objectively valid proposition. Kant, for his part, never even hints at this solution to the puzzle that he poses with his unsubstantiated, unsupported thesis. Never does he undertake an exposition of the relation between feeling and intentionality (in both senses of the term). Perhaps for this reason his unusually unambiguous thesis – which is one of the clearest statements in the entire third *Critique* and arguably the least demanding sentences in either of its two Introductions – could not resist editorial refinements: with no basis in any of the editions published during Kant's lifetime, Wilhelm Windelband, editor of the official Akademie edition, adopted Gustav Hartenstein's "correction" of the word *jeder* (every) by *jener* (the former); one of the recent English translators drops the word *every* altogether;[12] and a well-respected commentator renders the thesis as follows: "The attainment of an aim is always accompanied by a feeling of pleasure."[13]

"The attainment of every intention is connected with pleasure." So says Kant, and who would dispute him? Every time he attained an intention he may have felt pleasure; indeed, he may have felt pleasure when he wrote the sentence "The attainment of every intention is connected with pleasure," for on the basis of this highly plausible thesis he could attain the intention that he had just expressed: that of completing his "entire critical enterprise." But even if this sentence were true of Kant, it could not be immediately ascribed to anyone else, nor would it then be justified if he were to have asked all his friends about this matter, or even, *per impossibile*, everyone who ever lived, past and future. And even if the thesis expresses in its own way something like a "subjective universality," this makes it valid only for those who transpose themselves to the cognitive stance of Kant around 1790 – on the verge of completing the critical project by connecting the two critiques of the power of judgment. For all my efforts to transpose myself into this position, I cannot say whether the thesis is true from my own experience, and if I were to do so, if I were to say, "Yes, every attainment of an intention has been connected with pleasure and promises to be so in the future," such a statement would be less a straightforward assertion than a potentially deceptive confession – which is what it is perhaps for Kant: a round-about confession of his preferred manner for gaining pleasure, namely, attaining his intentions.

Nowhere in the third *Critique* does Kant contradict his initial thesis; he never mentions, much less discusses, the possibility that an attained intention might be bound up with displeasure. But two passages run counter to the thesis: pleasure in these cases is connected with *failure*, more exactly, the collapse of a cognitive intention. And in both of these passages, with a certain reluctance, perhaps even with a trace of embarrassment, but not perhaps without its own treasures, Kant undertakes a study of the corresponding pleasures. Both times he places his reflections under the unsystematic title "Remarks." And both times he lets himself be led by the failed critical philosopher par excellence, namely Epicurus. The late-born atomist may not live again in the critical enterprise – quite the contrary – but the non-teleological character of his conception of life gives Kant a chance to make sense of those pleasures that are connected to what, by all rights, should be wholly unpleasant: the failure of the mind to grasp what it wishes to secure for itself. This situation is all the more remarkable, since, according to the second part of the third *Critique*, Epicurus is the philosopher least capable of explaining the phenomenon of life. A failed account of life, in short, accounts for the pleasures of failure. And the success of this failure provides for the material that binds together the two parts of the third *Critique*.

The two passages of the third *Critique* in which failure is connected with pleasant feelings are the Analytic of the Sublime, particularly its opening and closing remarks, and the analysis of laughter, which brings the Analytic of Aesthetic Judgment to a close. These remarks will be considered in the order of their appearance.

Whole life

The Analytic of the Sublime takes its point of orientation from the experience of cognitive failure. In this regard, it is distinguished from the Analytic of Beauty – not because beauty is the function of success but, rather, because the proleptic premise on the basis of which judgments of taste can be justified consists in a basic "mood" or "attunement" (*Stimmung*) that favors the success of cognition in general:

> this attunement of the cognitive powers [the understanding and imagination] varies in its proportion in accordance with the varia-tions in the objects that are given. But there must nevertheless be one mood in which this inner relation is most conducive [*zuträg-lichste*] for the enlivening [*Belebung*] of the two mental powers (one

20

by the other) with an intention toward cognition (of given objects) in general [*in Absicht auf Erkenntnis (gegebener Gegenstände) überhaupt*].
(5: 238–39)

The contrary is true of those representations that are judged sublime: not only are they unfavorable to the enlivening of the mental powers in view of empirical cognition in general; they are also positively counter-conducive to this intention. If the attainment of every intention is connected with the feeling of pleasure, then it seems implausible that the failure to attain an intention should *also* be connected with the same feeling. Yet this implausibility is the thesis for which Kant must argue when he makes room for an Analytic of the Sublime as a supplement to the Analytic of Taste. Only by making reference to life in the form of "enlivening" (*Belebung*) can the implausible be initially justified.[14]

The idea of life haunts the *Critique of Judgment* – as if it were one of those ideas that cannot escape critical analysis but does not wholly submit itself to any specific analytic exposition either. Every section of the last *Critique* has something to do with life: beauty enlivens the soul; teleological judgments concern themselves with living things; and the very principle of the power of judgment – that of natural purposiveness – serves as the principle of everything "organic." Yet, nowhere does Kant take issue with life as such. Of course, he does propose definitions of life, one version of which receives a particularly bold exposition at the opening of the *Critique of Practical Reason*:

> **Life** is the faculty of a being to act in accordance with laws of the faculty of desire. The **faculty of desire** is an *ability to be the cause of the reality of the objects of its representations by means of these representations*. **Pleasure** is the *representation of the agreement of an object or an action with the* **subjective** *conditions of life*, that is, with the faculty of the *causality of a representation with respect to the reality of its object* (or with respect to the determination of the powers of the subject toward action in order to produce the object). For the purposes of critique I have no further need of concepts borrowed from psychology; critique itself performs the rest.
>
> (5: 9)

Far from forgetting these definitive statements, the third *Critique* explicitly recalls them, as it explains in a footnote why the critical enterprise rejects every attempt to reduce the three "faculties or capacities of the soul" to a "common ground" (5: 177). Yet the exposition of the idea of life in terms of the faculty of desire makes it into an entirely *practical* matter – unsuitable for a critique that mediates between this faculty and that of cognition. If, however, the idea of life is supposed to be of some use in solving the problem around which the *Critique of Judgment* revolves – the problem of

21

bridging the "gulf" between the legislation of the understanding (or theory) and the legislation of reason (or practice) – it cannot be entirely ascribed to the faculty of desire. And yet, it cannot be subsumed under the categories of the understanding either. Which is to say: the idea of life reproduces in miniature the puzzle that the last *Critique* is supposed to solve. Nowhere in Kant's *Critiques* does this puzzle find a more exacting shape than in those passages of the Analytic of the Sublime where "living forces" return from their momentary inhibition.

As an introduction to his analysis of the judgment "such and such is sublime," Kant delineates that feature of this mode of the power to judge in a purely reflective manner that distinguishes it categorically from those concerned with beautiful things. The latter promotes life, whereas the former – for a moment at least – goes in the opposite direction: "The two delights are very different. For the one delight (the beautiful) carries with it directly a *feeling of life's being furthered* . . . But the other delight (the feeling of the sublime) is a pleasure that arises only indirectly: it is produced by the feeling of a momentary inhibition of the living forces followed immediately by an outpouring of them that is all the stronger" (5: 244–45). Rarely is Kant clearer. Or he would be so, if only one could say without ambiguity what "living forces" means, for this well-worn term surely cannot be understood simply as "the faculty of a being to act in accordance with laws of the faculty of desire." The term "living forces" functions here as the expression of an idea *faute de mieux*. More exactly, it comes into play at the moment when intentionality falls into a crisis: when, in particular, the feeling of pleasure not only disentangles itself from the attainment of an identifiable intention – this is already true of the beautiful and is, indeed, one of its defining features – but is also released from any association with the *attainability* of cognitive intentions in general. At the point of this crisis, which eludes critical exposition, the idea of life comes to the rescue in the form of a revived Epicurus. "Nor," Kant writes in an unnumbered subparagraph entitled "General Remark on the Exposition of Aesthetic Reflective Judgment," as if his afterthoughts, by virtue of a self-reflexivity internal to the *Critique* itself, would make up for what the previous paragraphs had missed, without thereby doing damage to what they had proposed:

> Nor can it be denied that all presentations in us, no matter whether their object is merely sensible or instead wholly intelligible, can in the subject still be connected with satisfaction or pain, however unnoticeable these may be (because all of them affect the feeling of life, and none of them can be indifferent insofar as it is a modification of the subject). It cannot even be denied that, as Epicurus maintained, *satisfaction* and *pain* are ultimately always bodily [*körperlich*], whether they come from the imagination or even from presentations of the understanding, because, without the feeling of

a bodily organ, life is merely consciousness of his existence, and not a feeling of being well or unwell, that is, of the furtherance or inhibition of living forces; for the mind taken by itself is wholly living (the life principle itself), whereas any obstacles or furtherance must be sought outside it and yet still within the human being itself, and hence in the connection with its body.

(5: 277–78)

"It cannot be denied" – this repeated use of litotes, which signals a certain reluctance, if not downright repression, gives voice to the convoluted relation of the mind to the body, on the one hand, and both mind and body to life, on the other. According to the account of life that Kant takes over from his ancient precursor, the body is outside of the dimension of the "wholly living" (*ganz Leben*); it is, in every sense of the word, an *Ergänzung*, an "addition" to a life that is altogether itself, without the need of, or the desire for anything else. The mind, as the *principle* of life, is so wholly itself, however, that it can be aware of itself *as* living – and therefore as *itself*, the principle of life – only under the condition that it be connected with something that is itself, only less so. The name of this unprincipled element of internal otherness is the body, which, for this reason, cannot be considered "wholly" alive but must, instead, be understood as an ensemble of instruments or "organs" that the mind, devoid of everything mechanical, can use for its own sake. In the Critique of Teleological Judgment Kant will explicitly reject this conception of the part-whole relation of "organic" life – and reject both Aristotle and Epicurus, in turn.[15] For now, however, in the space of a "General Remark," the organs of the body – neither wholly alive nor wholly dead – serve the principle of life, which, as mere consciousness of existence, may be fully aware of itself but cannot be aware of itself *as* life, *as* different from the less-fully-alive internal otherness of its organs. An awareness of this otherness, otherwise known as "feeling," resides neither in the body nor in the mind but, rather, in the "binding" (*Verbindung*) of the two – a binding that reflects the "connection" (*Verbindung*) between the attainment of an intention and the feeling of pleasure, on the one hand, and the binding together of the two parts of the third *Critique*, on the other.

All of these complicated connections and convulsions of mind and body, "the life principle itself" and the organs of the body are cast in terms of Epicurus' lived experience – *without* any mention of the principal term of everything associated with Epicureanism: *pleasure*. Instead of using the terms "pleasure" (*Lust*) and "displeasure" (*Unlust*), Kant prefers the pair "satisfaction" (*Vergnügen*) and "pain" (*Schmerz*). At the beginning of the Critique of Aesthetic Judgment, without any further explanation, Kant speaks of "the feeling of life under the name of the feeling of pleasure and displeasure" (5: 204). *Under this name* only up to a point, however: when Kant resumes his exposition of the term *life*, it is as though pleasure and displeasure,

23

Lust and *Unlust*, are no longer suitable names for the feeling of more and less life. By casting his reluctant concession to Epicurus in terms of "satisfaction," which under no condition can claim general validity, Kant cuts himself off from the very line of argument by which he first accounts for the "negative pleasure" of the sublime. To quote once again the introductory remarks: "a momentary inhibition of the living forces followed immediately by an outpouring of them that is all the stronger."

Laughter

At the end of the analysis of taste, as Kant makes way for its corresponding dialectic, he inserts another remark – not a "general" one this time: a remark, his last,[16] which is so isolated from its surroundings that it should not even be counted among the numbered paragraphs of the *Critique*. Kant, at any rate, does not do so: between paragraphs 53 and 55, he adds a paragraph entitled "Remark" (*Bemerkung*) and fails, forgets, or decides not to assign it a number. It is as though he had experienced his own cognitive failure, a subtle or inadvertent parody of the mathematical sublime: skipping the number 54 testifies to the failure of his own comprehensive capacity, which must make the elements of a series into a whole, to keep up with his apprehensive power, which effortlessly enumerates any series. After counting up to 53, one cannot so effortlessly bring the objects enumerated into unity, with the result that the fifty-fourth is a loose element – or unnumbered, unnamed, and "nongeneral" remark. Perhaps the resulting section does not deserve the dignity that numbers confer on the discrete sections of an extended argument; perhaps Kant simply failed to notice that he had forgotten the number and failed again to notice his error upon reading over the proofs of the second edition. In any case, whether as parapraxis or mechanical error, the absence of a number mirrors the absence toward which the "Remark," for all the diversity of its contents, is generally oriented: toward nothingness; more exactly, toward the nothingness that the mind presents to itself as the basis for the laughter that convulses its body. With a dry wit of his own – and in opposition to a long-standing topos of the eighteenth century, which places wit alongside judgment as two aspects of the same mental capacity[17] – Kant may even encourage the suggestion that the appropriate number of the last "Remark" of the Critique of Aesthetic Judgment is not 54 but, rather, 0. Or, more radically still, a constitutively inconsistent "number" that acknowledges the incompetence of numbers at certain points:

> Whatever is supposed to arouse lively, convulsive laughter must contain something absurd [*Widersinniges*] (hence something that the understanding cannot like for its own sake). *Laughter is an affect that comes from the sudden transformation of a tense expectation into nothing* [Das Lachen ist ein Affekt aus der plötzlichen Verwandlung einer gespannten Erwartung in nichts]. This very transformation, which

24

is certainly not enjoyable for the understanding, is nevertheless for a moment indirectly enjoyable in a very lively manner [*erfreuet doch indirekt auf einen Augenblick sehr lebhaft*].

(5: 332)

Under the sign of "laughter" Kant treats an experience that he would otherwise consign to the sphere of madness: total cognitive collapse. That this failure of the mind is only momentary does not sufficiently distinguish it from various "sicknesses of the head" he had analyzed in a much earlier essay of this name, for the collapsed mind can as little determine the length of the "moment" (*Augenblick*) as it can devise strategies for its restoration. Jokes are not the only sign under which Kant treats such an experience. Music is similarly structured: "music and material for laughter [*Stoff zum Lachen*] are two kinds of play with aesthetic ideas or even with representations of the understanding by which in the end nothing is thought [*am Ende nichts gedacht wird*]" (5: 332). Yet the constitutively indeterminate "material for laughter" enjoys a dubious privilege over music in this regard, for the cognitive collapse it occasions is not only unexpected; it also derives from "representations of the understanding" (*Verstandesvorstellungen*), which, unlike aesthetic ideas, make no allowance for conceptual indeterminacy. For both music and laughter, the problem remains the same: how to understand the pleasure bound up with cognitive failure?

Epicurus once again comes to the rescue. In the name of the laughing philosopher the unnumbered "Remark" can be seen to be written. If, as Kant famously proposed, it is vital to understand Plato and Leibniz better than they understand themselves,[18] the same is true of their mutual antagonist and, by understanding Epicurus against his own intentions, not only can the pleasures of failure be understood; this understanding of misunderstanding may itself be the source of immense satisfaction:

Remark

Between that which pleases merely in the act of judging and that which satisfies (pleases in the sensation) there is, as we have often shown, an essential difference. The latter is something that one cannot, like the former, require of everyone. Satisfaction (even if its cause happens to lie in ideas) always seems to consist in a feeling of the furtherance of the complete life [*des gesamten Lebens*] of the human being, consequently also the furtherance of bodily well-being, that is, his health; so that, when Epicurus claimed that all satisfaction is at bottom bodily sensation, he was perhaps not mistaken but only misunderstood himself when he counted intellectual and even practical pleasures among the satisfactions [*wenn er das intellektuelle und selbst praktische Wohlgefallen zu den Vergnügen zählte*].

(5: 330–31)

Epicurus miscounted, in other words. More exactly, he counted every element of the set of pleasures as though each one was a member of the same class. Kant, by contrast, wants to demonstrate that there are fundamentally two distinct kinds of pleasure; such is the starting point for the third *Critique*, and the distinction corresponds to a series of similar ones that give structure to the "critical enterprise." The apparent fact that both kinds of pleasure consist in the promotion of human life, however, tends to blur the distinction: all pleasure, regardless of its source, lends support to life. And the sudden, even surprising appearance of the term "intellectual pleasure" – to say nothing of "practical pleasure," which has the undeniable tendency to compromise "respect for the law" insofar as it makes purely rational practice sound pleasant – renders the entire "Remark" rather dubious. What is the "intellect" in the term *intellektuelle* if not the Latin term that Kant translates as *Verstand* (the understanding)? And what could an intellect enjoy other than the intelligible world? In either case – or any other circumstance through which one could understand *intellektuelle* – the *Critiques* say "no": "all feeling is sensible" (5: 75). Understanding this passage means, therefore, understanding its own misunderstanding of the function of the understanding in the "critical enterprise." Of course, Kant *means* by "intellectual" the adjectival form of *Gemüt*, whatever he may have written, and he means to say that the ground of the pleasure has nothing to do with any body. Understanding "intellectual" in this way makes the passage once again *gemütlich* – and this, too, is a powerful pleasure.

By presenting his argument in terms of the distinction between intellectual and corporeal pleasure, Kant draws back from the radicality of his initial point of departure. But this step backward, which hollows out the ground of the "critical enterprise" by suggesting that the intellect can enjoy its own objects, is motivated by an otherwise irresolvable puzzle: the failure of the intellect to secure any content for itself can be, strangely enough, great fun. The source of this pleasure must obviously lie in the body or, more exactly, in the apparently pre-established harmony between the body and the mind. In his earliest forays in metaphysics Kant cautiously distanced himself from the Leibnizian doctrine of pre-established harmony between soul and body; but it returns, altered, in the last *Critique* as a psycho-physical hypothesis on the basis of which the "satisfaction" in mental breakdown can be made comprehensible:

> For, if one assumes that some kind of movement in the organs of
> the body is at the same time harmoniously connected [*harmonisch
> verbunden*] to all of our thoughts, then one grasps rather well how
> to that sudden displacement of the mind [*plötzlichen Versetzung des
> Gemüts*], first to one and then to another standpoint for considering
> its object, there can correspond a reciprocal tension and relaxation
> of the elastic parts of our viscera, which communicates itself to our

diaphragm (like that which ticklish people feel), so that the lungs expel the air with rapidly succeeding breaks [*mit schnell einander folgenden Absätzen*] and thereby produces a movement that is conducive to health, which alone – and not what takes place in the mind [*was im Gemüte vorgeht*] – is the real cause of a satisfaction in a thought that at bottom represents nothing [*einem Gedanken ist, der im Grunde nichts vorstellt*].

(5: 334)

Nine years earlier, at the beginning of the critical program, Kant had famously announced that "thoughts without content are empty" (A: 51; B: 75), and at least one reason for such emptiness can now be identified: the sudden, unexpected, and unpremeditated movement of the mind from one standpoint to the next. Such mental "displacement" (*Versetzung*) corresponds to the rapid "breaks" (*Absätzen*) in the routine operations of the body. With this hypothesis, which gives life to a moribund Leibnizian doctrine, pleasure can be reserved for mental success – if not reserved for actual success in any particular intention, then at least, and indeed for the most important pleasures, possible success in cognition. The failure of the mind to make anything of its rapid alteration of perspectives, its inability to turn its standpoints into solid grounds upon which it can launch its projects, does no damage to the thesis, according to which "the attainment of every intention is bound up with pleasure," for the motility of the body is the *sole* source of the pleasure. And why suppose otherwise, given the fact the mind is, so to speak, out of service, broken down, perhaps incapable even of maintaining the unity of consciousness? The body in convulsions keeps the mind, as this principle, as life itself, from being *wholly itself* – so completely alive that, having disburdened itself of content, it floats free, even free of itself *as* mind. Kant, for one, cannot conceive of this freedom as in any sense pleasurable.

No wonder Epicurus returns at this juncture, for his failed explanation of the teleological order of organic substances does not suppose that the organs of the body are ordered in an "organic" manner, each existing for the sake of the others. Only an out-of-joint body is capable of corresponding to a mind in default. And so, after a dash and a paragraph break – or, to use the German expressions, a *Gedankenstrich* (stroke of thought) and an *Absatz* (break) – Kant promotes the spirit of Epicurus one last time:

– Voltaire said that heaven has given us two things to counterbalance the many hardships in life: *hope* and *sleep*. He might have added laughter, if only the means for arousing it among those who are rational [*bei Vernünftigen*] were so close at hand, and if wit or the originality of humor needed for it were not just as rare as the talent is common to poeticize, like a mystical ponderer, in a *head breaking* manner, or like a genius, in a *neck breaking* manner, or like a sentimental novelist (and also indeed sentimental moralists) in a *heartbreaking* way [kopfbrechend, *wie mystische Grübler*, halsbrechend, *wie Genies, oder* herzbrechend, *wie empfindsame Romanschreiber (auch wohl dergleichen Moralisten), zu dichten*].

It seems to me, therefore, that Epicurus may certainly be granted that all satisfaction, even if it is prompted by concepts that arouse aesthetic ideas, is animal (i.e. bodily) sensation. For granting this does not in the least rupture [*Abbruch tun*] the *spiritual* feeling [*geistigen Gefühl*] of respect for moral ideas, which is not satisfaction but self-esteem (of the humanity within us) elevating us above the need for satisfaction, nor does it even rupture the less noble feeling of taste.

(5: 334–35)

If Kant had been asked to respond to the question that Hölderlin famously poses in "Bread and Wine" – "what are poets for?" (*wozu Dichter?*) – his answer may well have been: to cause breaks. This is what it means to poeticize (*dichten*): break heads, break necks, and break hearts. Granting this carnage causes no break, however, with the noble feelings of respect or taste, and for good reason: nobility breaks with commonality. So, too, do wit and humor, *Witz* and *Laune*, the uncommonness of which means that they cannot be counted among heaven-sent gifts, each of which, like laughter, gives us nothing. Such is the sardonic point of Voltaire's wit: heaven gives us nothing. For this reason alone, it is best to cultivate our own gardens. And there is no better proof of the uncommonness of jovial genius than Kant's own attempt to compete with Voltaire and make a joke about the rarity of the capacity to make jokes. This would-be witty remark is even less successful than the various witticisms recounted earlier in the "Remark" – and far less coherent, since, although it is fairly clear why a deluded mystic should crack open heads and a bad novelist break open hearts, it makes little sense to say that a failed genius breaks anyone's neck. Unless, of course, the neck can be understood as a metaphor for the connection between mind and body. Under this condition the genius *manqué* gives the lie to the unsubstantiated hypothesis through which Kant had secured an explanation for the pleasure taken in jokes that clears the mind of any association with such pleasure. And so something of Kant breaks – if not his neck, then at least a connecting joint of "my entire critical enterprise." Broken by all-too-common geniuses, broken even by his own unsuccessful attempt to compose a joke worthy of Voltaire, Kant takes a break, starts a new paragraph (*Absatz*), and assures his readers that there are no breaks *where it counts*: in "spiritual feeling." Not only does he fail to define this surprising term, however; it is as difficult to understand in terms of the critical program as any of the sentences invented by mendacious mystics, bad novelists, and would-be geniuses.[19]

28

The inner "jokester"

The last "Remark" could have ended where it began – with Epicurus recti-
fied, if not precisely revived. But something breaks up this tidy outcome: a
sudden and unexpected outbreak of unlikely uprightness. The last break is
the sudden break-up of the very artifice of culture to which the *Critiques* seek
to provide a secure and lasting foundation. The unconscious agent of this
break-up is the naïf, and the sign of an impending collapse is the combination of the two feelings that Kant had, throughout the Critique of Aesthetic
Judgment, sought to keep apart:

> Something composed of both is found in naïveté, which is the
> outbreak of the uprightness that is originally natural to humanity
> against the art of deception that has become another nature [*Etwas
> aus beiden Zusammengesetztes findet sich in der Naivität, die der Ausbruch
> der Menschheit ursprünglich natürlichen Aufrichtigkeit wider die zur
> andern Natur gewordenen Verstellungskunst ist*]. One laughs at the sim-
> plicity that still does not understand how to deceive and yet also
> enjoys the simplicity of nature that here puts a stitch through this
> art. One expects the everyday mores [*alltägliche Sitte*] of artificial
> expression carefully prepared for beautiful illusion [*schönen Schein*];
> and lo and behold! it is uncorrupted, innocent nature, which one
> did not at all expect and in which the one who allows it to be seen,
> never intended it to be disclosed [*zu entblößen auch nicht gemeinet war*].
> That the beautiful but false illusion, which usually means so
> much to our judgments, is suddenly transformed into nothingness
> [*hier plötzlich in Nichts verwandelt*], so that, as it were, the jokester
> in ourselves is laid bare [*gleichsam der Schalk in uns selbst bloßgestellt
> wird*], produces successive movements of the mind in two opposing
> directions, which at the same time shakes the body in a healthy
> manner. But [the fact] that something infinitely better than all
> assumed mores, namely purity of the mode of thought [*Lauterkeit
> der Denkungsart*] (at least the disposition to it), has not been entirely
> extinguished from human nature adds seriousness and high esteem
> to this play of the power of judgment.
>
> (5: 335)

Whereas, according to Kant's original explanation of laughter, it is only
the expectation of a gain in cognition that is suddenly transformed into
nothing, here it is the entire edifice of "beautiful illusion." The naïf unin-
tentionally brings to light the illusory character of *schöner Schein*, showing it
to be what it wishes to conceal: not a dimension of nature but, rather, of
"another nature," which hides everything natural to human beings. For this
reason, as Kant notes, "an art of being naïve is a contradiction" (5: 336), and

for the same reason he may have capitalized *Nichts* here: everything in everyday life turns into – or, more exactly, turns out to be – nothingness. This disclosure of nothingness, as a function of reflective judgment, is simultaneously a self-disclosure of the nothingness of our acculturated selves: a laying bare, disrobing, or undressing of what Kant here calls the "jokester [*Schalk*] in ourselves."

Upon encountering a naïf, the inner jokester becomes the butt of the joke, for he, whose existence consists in the pretence that he is something, discovers that he is, after all, nothing. So it is a good thing that the jokester is bound to a body, for otherwise the encounter with the naïf would be a strange adventure indeed: it would amount to the discovery that the self does not quite exist. Under these troubling conditions, against which philosophy since Descartes has sought to secure itself, a good corporeal convulsion can only be considered "healthy," "wholesome," or even "holy" (*heilsam*), for it shakes the self back to life. All of us who play host to this jokester can thus resume our previous enterprises, as if the naïf – not ourselves – were the object of all the raucous pleasure. The structure of what might be called "authenticity" reveals itself in this convulsion: the insincere self comes to recognize itself as such – not "itself" but always only given over to the assessment of others – by exposing itself to a sincere self, which, by virtue of its naïveté, cannot recognize itself as such. And the "outbreak of uprightness" enacts the failed joke that Kant invents: it breaks heads by confounding expectations, breaks necks by severing the connection between nature and "other nature," and breaks hearts by eliciting feelings of "tenderness [*Zärtlichkeit*]" (5: 335).

The jokester asks, however, in reflection: can a naïf ever be encountered? Is not the naïf a creature of clever invention rather than reality? Kant, for his part, provides no answer; instead, he simply emphasizes the possibility – but also the rarity – of fictional representations of naïveté: "An art of being naïve is a contradiction; but to represent naïveté in a poeticized person [*in einer erdichteten Person*] is certainly possible and is a beautiful but rare art" (5: 335). Another task of poetry can therefore be identified: create naïve characters who, by breaking into the "other nature," interrupt the consistency and continuity of "beautiful illusion." Kant gives no example of such characters – which is hardly surprising, given the paucity of literary references in the third *Critique*. Perhaps he has in mind a character invented by Wieland, one of the two "geniuses," along with Homer, whom he mentions in passing (5: 309). He certainly does not suggest what Schiller will soon explicitly propose: that Homer is the naïf. Who, then, might be? If human beings are evil by nature, then the answer to this question is unambiguous: no one. Not only is it impossible for the naïf to recognize him- or herself, it is impossible for anyone to recognize anyone else as a naïf – outside of fiction. And this is precisely what Kant, having completed his *Critiques*, will propose: that human beings are evil by nature. His first post-critical venture, "On the Failure of All Philosophical Attempts at Theodicy" (1791), prepares for the positing of the explicit thesis of radical evil by turning his attention to a well-known naïf: Job, who, unlike his "so-called friends" (23: 85), says exactly what comes to mind, without the interference of an inner jokester, whose function would otherwise consist in making sure that his pronouncements are cleverly tailored to his audience. Job, as poeticized naïf is, therefore, the emblem under which Kant begins his late work.

2

THE SOVEREIGN
SENTENCE

From the Preface to the first edition of the
first *Critique* to the *Doctrine of Right*

Infallibility

Sovereigns have at their disposal an uncommon form of speech: sovereign
sentences. By means of such sentences a sovereign can arrest legal processes
and dismiss cases from the arena of judicial competence. Sovereign sentences
remain outside of the legal order, even though they possess the force of law.
By virtue of their extra-legal status, they cannot be considered generally
applicable rules, much less universally valid principles. Each sovereign
sentence is applicable only to a single case and applies only once. The singu-
larity of the sentence corresponds to the uniqueness of the sovereign who
pronounces it. Sovereignty can even be understood as the power to issue
sovereign sentences, which, for their part, recreate the condition of their own
accomplishment: the condition, namely, of sovereignty as exemption from
legal processes and judicial procedures. In other words, only a sovereign
can pronounce a sovereign sentence; it does not belong to common forms of
discourse. Once such a sentence has been pronounced, however, no word can
be spoken in response; arguments are in vain, discussion at an end. Whatever
has been sentenced must be enacted, and this "must" cannot be gainsaid, for
if a sovereign sentence were not immediately enacted – without delay and
without appeal to a law by means of which it would be legitimated – it
would prove to have been something other than a sovereign sentence. Success,
in other words, is one of its constitutive criteria. Sovereigns can falter,
of course, but sovereign sentences cannot. Any apparent failure of such a
sentence is only evidence of a faltering sovereign. To this extent, sovereign
sentences are infallible. By virtue of their infallibility, moreover, they cannot
be counted among common forms of "speech acts." However much misery
they may bring, their enactment cannot be "infelicitous."[1] Because they
cannot fail, however, they cannot be judged successful either – regardless of
how much felicity they may bring. For the same reason, and despite their
incomparable power, it is doubtful whether sovereign sentences can be

32

considered one form of "speech act" among others. Just as sovereigns remain outside the legal order over which they dispose, sovereign sentences escape the category into which they obviously fall.

"Sovereign sentence" is not among the technical terms of Anglo-American juridical discourse – which is not to say that the phenomenon of an infallible "speech act" is unknown, unrecognized, or insignificant. Yet it does suggest that an exposition of this idea can be more fruitfully undertaken within a context of a juridical discourse that not only recognizes this phenomenon but also accords it a stable name. Such is the case in Prussia, particularly during the decades in which its jurists begin to reflect on its newly acquired status as a kingdom. The name for a "sovereign sentence" is *Machtspruch*: the "saying" (*Spruch*) in which "power" (*Macht*) expresses itself without recourse or reference to the processes and procedures of the "legal order" (*das Recht*): "The propositions '*Princeps legibus solutus*' and '*Quod principi placuit legis habet vigorem*' stand in close connection with each other. Advisors and attendants of the king already found these sentences in the *corpus iuris civilis* and thereby forged a theory, according to which law in its entirety is subject to the sovereign."[2] Retranslation of *Machtspruch* into the Latin legal lexicon from which this newly devised theory develops might yield phrases like *decretum principis* and *sententia definitiva*; but a better interpretation of the word, which has no exact Latin or English equivalent, would be captured by two other terms: *fatum* and *fiat*.[3] Because a *Machtspruch* has the power to make what it says come true, it corresponds to *fatum* in the original sense of the word: "what has been said" – and comes true for this very reason. Only those who can immediately create the conditions for the truth of their speech escape the sphere of fate, fortune, and fallibility. Because a *Machtspruch* is immediately enacted, moreover, its force is equal to that of the original jussive of *Genesis*: *y'hi or*, which is to say, in Latin, *fiat lux* or, in English, "let there be light" (Gen. 1: 3). No word can be said in response to this command, for nothing precedes its enunciation. The first word is in this sense also the final one. Every subsequent *Machtspruch* – if any *Machtsprüche* can be called "subsequent" – remains like the first: at once first and last.

Although the term *Machtspruch* suggests a stark exercise of unprincipled power, its use in specific legal circumstances moves in the opposite direction: toward justice, more exactly, toward a sphere of justice that frees itself of cumbersome, confusing, and often conflicting legal procedures and processes. Whenever the outcome of a juridical process appears unjust – or is unjustly delayed – the sovereign may choose to pronounce a *Machtspruch* as an extralegal remedy. According to the principal jurists in the court of Friedrich Wilhelm I (the first Prussian king), a sovereign may reject any legal decision that he deems unjust; considerations of equity require nothing less. Defined as an indispensable means "*ex plenitudine potestatis principis jus subditis quaesitum auferre*,"[4] the *Machtspruch* enjoyed a secure position in Prussian juridical discourse until the middle years of the eighteenth century, at which time its validity as a solution to mishandled civil suits began to come under increasing scrutiny for two reasons: some poorly planned sovereign sentences caused even greater confusion than the decision of the courts they over-ruled, and certain principles of *Aufklärung*-inspired administration took hold of royal jurists and royalty alike. In 1765, Philipp Joseph von Jariges, Friedrich II's high chancellor, anonymously published a treatise modeled on Montesquieu's *L'Esprit des Loix* (1755), in which the alteration finds an apt expression. The sole German term that makes its way into the French pamphlet is *Machtspruch*, which serves as a translation of the phrase around which the entire endeavor revolves: "décision arbitraires et immédiates du sovereign." Jariges concludes his pamphlet by firmly rejecting sovereign sentences, regardless of their underlying motive or overall intention: "sover-eign sentences, even the most equitable, are illegal and contrary to the constitution of the state."[5] In 1780, Friedrich the Great himself echoes his former high chancellor's opinion and goes one step further: "I am very far from presuming to render immediate decisions. That would be a sover-eign sentence [*Machtspruch*], and you know that I abhor them."[6]

By the last decade of the eighteenth century, Friedrich II's antipathy achieves a well-articulated conceptual framework. During the time in which Carl Gottlieb Svarez sought to convince the Prussian royal family to bring into effect the massive codification of Prussian law he co-authored under the title *Allgemeines Landrecht*,[7] he also held a series of lectures on juris-prudence for the crown prince. For Svarez, nothing is more important for the edification of princes than the following lesson. Instead of retaining the prerogative to pronounce *Machtsprüche*, according to Svarez, the sovereign should resolve to accept under all conditions the *Rechtsprüche* (legal decisions) of his courts:

> The regent who wants to nullify or alter the verdicts of his courts by sovereign sentences [*Machtsprüche*] acts in opposition to one of his first duties, the protection of everyone in his domain. . . . Sovereign sentences produce neither rights nor obligations. . . . As a result, there is no wiser principle for the security of property and for the freedom of Prussian subjects than the following highly benefi-cent one: that the juridical circumstances of these subjects only be investigated and decided according to those laws of the State that derive from the courts established by the State; that sovereign sentences never have a juridical effect; and that the sovereign himself never want to issue such sentences, nor allow his ministers to do so.[8]

From the perspective of a *Rechtspruch* – and the jurists who guard the inde-pendence of juridical principles and procedures – every *Machtspruch* appears wholly arbitrary, even tyrannical, for each one depends on the "magisterial right" of the prince to present himself as the highest master of the land.

From the perspective of the *Machtspruch*, by contrast, the *Rechtspruch* appears insufficient, if not outright impotent, for the strength of its pronouncements are ultimately dependent on the ability of the sovereign to exert his power. The antinomy between "might" and "right," *Macht* and *Recht*, plays itself out in terms of their respective modes of speech – with the proviso that "might" in this case presents itself as the guardian of that unformalizable quality of justice which "right" is prepared to forfeit so as to preserve its continuity, coherence, and integrity: "Only in the eighteenth century did anyone dare maintain that the *Rechtspruch* of a court could not be nullified and declared invalid by a *Machtspruch* of the sovereign."[9] If Svarez can be understood as a representative voice of legal reasoning, then one can say that the *Machtspruch* had entirely relinquished its "rights" by the end of the eighteenth century. *Rechtsprüche* alone are justifiable from the perspective of enlightened jurists, lawmakers, and princes. Whatever sovereigns may represent in relation to their own states and whatever they may do in relation to other ones, they have no say in the legal order, whose "potentate" they are – which is to say that the legal order can operate safely, without concern for the threat of unprincipled, case-by-case interventions of princely power.

Echoing the king

As long as the threat of a *Machtspruch* has not been fully extinguished, no legal process can be sure that it will have the last word, and if the legal process cannot be sure of having the last word, it cannot be certain that it will have the first one either. Investigations can be suspended, trials interrupted, and outcomes revoked. The mere acceptability of a *Machtspruch* menaces legal proceedings and juridical processes from start to finish. Only by doing away with this threat can the legal order secure itself as an order in its own right. In his lectures to the crown prince – to say nothing of the general code of law he helped prepare – Svarez presents himself as an uncompromising proponent of the *Rechtspruch*. The legal order must dismiss from its midst the menacing prospect of an internal agent of judicial disintegration and legal incoherence. A decade earlier, as if in anticipation of Svarez, Kant had done the same. So completely does Kant cast himself into the role of enlightened jurist that the treatise upon which he hopes to secure a sure path for the science of metaphysics not only begins with a critique of such sentences but justifies its now-famous title by demonstrating the degree to which this critique is the point of departure for a philosophico-juridical review of finite – and therefore eminently fallible – reason. No sentence can be allowed to escape the jurisdiction of an "Areopagus" (1: 222) that Kant, repeating the gesture that opens the *Universal Natural History*, institutes under the rubric "critique of pure reason." Since sovereign sentences, by definition, are exempt from legal reasoning, they must be silenced from the start. If the "court of reason" were to accept any *Spruch* other than a *Rechtspruch*, it would immediately cease to be an autonomous tribunal in which it sets out to investigate cases, "deduce" rights, and pronounce decisive verdicts.[10]

Sometimes Kant indicates that the chaos of war is the disastrous alternative to the court of reason that he is in the process of establishing; but at other times – less famously, although more closely in line with the legal reasoning of a Jariges or a Svarez – he insists that the alternative to the court of reason is an unstable court of justice menaced by the threat of uncivil sentences issued by unstable sovereigns. Under this lamentable condition, war becomes a civic affair: reason, which champions the *Rechtspruch*, comes into irresolvable conflict with power, which expresses itself in *Machtsprüche*. Nothing is more important for the vast project of philosophical review and doctrinal codification that Kant first begins to outline in the *Critique of Pure Reason*, therefore, than the dismissal from its inception of the danger posed by, to cite Jariges again, "décision arbitraires et immédiates du souverain." A few months after Friedrich the Great makes known his profound distaste for sovereign sentences, his "most loyal servant" (1: 219) does the same. Echoing the king, as the king echoes his counselors, Kant makes an antipathy to *Machtsprüche* into the basic mood of a philosophical project that seeks to show the means and manner by which all of us – princes and subjects alike – give laws to nature:

> However much they may think to make themselves unrecognizable by exchanging the language of schools for a popular tone, these so-called indifferentists, insofar as they think anything at all, always fall without fail back into metaphysical assertions, which they yet professed so much to disdain. Yet, this indifference, occurring amidst the flourishing of all sciences and directed precisely at those sciences whose cognitions, if there were any, we could least do without, is a phenomenon deserving our attention and reflection. It is obviously the effect not of the thoughtlessness of our age, but of its ripening *power of judgment*, which no longer puts up with illusory knowledge, and it is a demand addressed to reason to take over once again the most difficult of all its occupations, namely self-knowledge, and to institute a tribunal [*Gerichtshof*], by which reason may secure its legitimate claims [*gerechten Ansprüchen*] while at the same time dismissing all groundless presumptions – not by sovereign sentences but, rather, according to its eternal and immutable laws, and this is none other than the *critique of pure reason* itself [*dagegen aber alle grundlose Anmaßungen, nicht durch Machtsprüche, sondern nach ihren ewigen und unwandelbaren Gesetzen, abfertigen könne, und dieser ist kein anderer als die* Kritik der reinen Vernunft *selbst*].
>
> (A: xi–xii)

In these well-known words of the first Preface to the first *Critique*, Kant expresses himself with exceptional lucidity: the philosophico-juridical review of reason that he has just initiated will not accept any sovereign sentences. No *dictum*, in other words, that, by fiat, constitutes irrevocable *fatum* will enter into the halls of metaphysical jurisprudence. The integrity of philosophical discourse, like that of its juridical counterpart, thus rejects sovereign sentence outright. To do otherwise would be to open the tribunal of reason to an alien power that would also have the air of strange familiarity. Such is the paradoxical character of the *Machtspruch*: it defies the legal order for the sake of what this very order is supposed to establish, protect, and represent – namely, justice. In the same way, the *Machtsprüche* that Kant rejects in the opening gesture of the first *Critique* would defy the court of human reason for the sake of a "higher" reason. Whereas sovereign sentences are infallible inasmuch as they create the conditions for their own accomplishment, the sentences whose source lies in human reason are not. On the contrary, these sentences are highly fallible, so much so that they demand vigilant self-critique. The sole space in which the "peculiar fate of human reason" (A: vii) can be heroically borne – which is not to say, "overcome" – is a closed courthouse. By proclaiming "no sovereign sentences," Kant encloses the tribunal of reason once and for all.

But the courthouse within which finite reason adjudicates its claims is not absolutely sealed. Twice Kant breaks his promise to forbid sovereign sentences. The first break – which is the subject of the next chapter – takes place in the first publication that appears under Kant's name after the completion of "my entire critical enterprise" (5: 170), namely "On the Failure of All Philosophical Attempts at Theodicy" (1791). The second break – which occupies the rest of this chapter – occurs in the first of the two "doctrinal" works upon which Kant promises to exert all of his quickly waning energy now that he has completed his "critical enterprise," namely the *Metaphysical Foundations of the Doctrine of Right* (1797). Whereas "On the Failure" makes failure into one of its themes, the *Doctrine of Right* begins by conceding that it is, at least in part, a failure. Even after the long delay – publicly promised in 1790, delivered some seven years later[11] – the sections that include the acceptance of a sovereign sentence remain unfinished: "the later sections (concerning public right) are currently subject to so much discussion and are nevertheless so important that they can well justify for some time a delay in rendering the decisive judgment" (6: 209). This postponement is undeniably odd: a "decisive judgment" on matters of great importance will be delayed because they are now under discussion; but there is room for discussion only because a "decisive judgment" has yet to be rendered. As long as discussion continues, "decisive judgment" will be delayed, and as long as a "decisive judgment" about matters of general importance remains outstanding, discussion will continue. Only one kind of sentence can break into this vicious circle – a sentence that neither discusses nor judges but, instead, dismisses both juridical judgments and general discussion: in other words, the sentence of a sovereign.

"The spectacle of a slaughter-bench"

One of the principal components of "public right" is the right of the state to punish those who break its laws. The principle of punishment enunciated in the *Doctrine of Right*, like all of its principles, derives from the application of the categorical imperative to external relations among persons. In this case, punishment can never serve merely as a means − deterrence of crime, for example, or rehabilitation of criminals, as another − but must always also be an end in itself: in particular, the preservation of the moral personality of the condemned criminal. Penal law must therefore operate entirely under the law of retribution (*jus talionis*): "all other principles are fluctuating and unsuited for a sentence of pure and strict justice, for extraneous considerations are mixed into them" (6: 332).[12] Nevertheless, in a single circumstance an exception to the law of retribution is acceptable: when the rigorous execution of the penal law threatens the very existence of the state that it is instituted to protect. In this singular circumstance the sovereign can − and indeed must − arrest the legal process, interrupt the juridical procedure, enter the courthouse, and dismiss its "decisive judgment":

> All those who murder, commit murder, order it, or are also commanded, or participate in it, they must suffer death. Justice as an Idea of judicial power [*richterlichen Gewalt*] wills this in accordance with universal laws that are grounded *a priori*. − If, however, the number of accomplices (*correi*) to such a deed is so great that the state, in order to have no such criminals in it, could soon come to be without subjects; and if the state still does not want to dissolve itself, that is, to pass over into the state of nature, which is far worse because it is then entirely bereft of external justice (especially if it does not want to deaden the people's feeling by the spectacle of a slaughter-bench [*vornehmlich durch das Spektakel einer Schlachtbank das Gefühl des Volks abstumpfen*]), then the sovereign must also have it in his power [*der Souverän in seiner Macht haben*], in this case of necessity (*casus necessitatis*), to make himself into the judge (to represent one) and pronounce a judgment [*den Richter zu machen (vorzustellen) und ein Urteil zu sprechen*], which, instead of capital punishment, recognizes another punishment for the criminals, by which the population is still preserved, such as deportation [*Deportation*]: this cannot be done in accordance with public law, but it can be done by a sovereign sentence [*Machtspruch*], that is, by an act of the magisterial right [*Majestätsrechts*] which, as clemency, can always be exercised only in singular cases.
>
> (6: 334)

Nothing Kant ever published is stranger than this paragraph. The sovereign deports the populace of his state in order to preserve its population, on the one hand, and keep intact the feeling of its people, on the other. It is difficult to imagine the circumstance to which Kant refers, and yet, in its own way, few passages of his work come closer to representing – albeit in an oblique manner – those historical catastrophes that, from the perspective of both sanguine *Aufklärung* principles and their melancholic counterparts, are simply unimaginable: a country becomes so saturated with *correi*,[13] so filled with murderers and accomplices to murder, that the proper execution of well-founded legal procedures would constitute a grave threat to its very existence; the state might even commit suicide by rigorously enacting its principles of justice. This circumstance is so strange, moreover, that the "deportation" Kant recommends even enters into his own formulation. The sovereign does not simply act as judge, he also (in parentheses) *"represents himself"* as one. The parentheses around *vorzustellen* (to represent) indicate at the very least that the act in which the sovereign arrests the juridical process is also *play-acting*. Those before whom the sovereign represents himself as judge – without being one – appear in the previous parentheses: "the people," whose "feeling" would be "deadened by the spectacle of a slaughter-bench."

The deadening of feeling corresponds to mass execution undertaken by the legal authorities. Not only does the sole sovereign sentence Kant accepts into his *Doctrine of Right* serve to preserve the state by deporting its people; it also prevents the people who escape deportation from falling prey to an enigmatic anesthetization. When the feeling of the people is deadened, it does not die; rather, it survives – as something other than itself, as something other than "a" people. For, as Kant emphasizes at the very inception of his *Doctrine of Right*, feeling is an indispensable element of the phenomenon we call "life": "the *faculty of desire* is the faculty to be, by means of one's representations, the cause of the objects of these representations. The faculty of an entity to act in accordance with its representations is called *life*. First, *pleasure and displeasure*, susceptibility to which is called *feeling*, is always connected with desire or aversion; but the converse does not always hold" (6: 211). A people without feeling is no longer either alive or dead; it falls into an indeterminate zone in which the first article of legal reasoning – that distinguishing life from death – is itself moribund. And if the first principle is moribund, so, too, are all the subsequent ones.[14] Once the distinction between life and death comes into question, so, too, does the difference between extra-legal violence and legally sanctioned coercion: "juridical power" may now be indistinguishable from "juridical violence." And even if this is not the case; even if the law can distinguish its violence from the violence it seeks to punish, the execution of its verdicts still appears to the people as a "spectacle of the slaughter-bench," which is to say, as a stark display of state-controlled cannibalism.[15] In strict accordance with the principles of justice, the legal order thus becomes, in effect – regardless of its intention – indistinguishable from the murderous *correi* that it condemns to death.

Only someone outside of, and immune from, the demonic cycle of this potential spectacle can arrest the proceedings. This is the function of the sovereign, who can halt the legal process by virtue of his own internal immunity from its judgments. Even if the sovereign were also a member of the *correi* – and who doubts it? – it would make no difference, for the sovereign is still exempt from judicial rulings. And the sovereign in Kant's strange scenario does not simply arrest these procedures and processes; he does so in the form of a *counter-spectacle* – not the "spectacle of a slaughter-bench," to be sure, but a dramatic display of himself as judge. By casting himself in this inappropriate role, however, the sovereign violates the very separation of powers that, according to Kant, allows a state to make good on the very Idea of legality and thus become the *res publica* toward which all juridical programs and legal philosophies should tend.[16] There is, therefore, a choice of spectacles: either a show of legally sanctioned mass slaughter or a display of the sovereign coming on stage in – borrowed or stolen – legal attire.

Kant chooses the latter. The choice does not go without saying, however, for everywhere else in his reflections on legal principles, he not only insists on the strict separation of powers but also advocates the merciless enforcement of the law of retribution. He thus writes a short essay "On a Supposed Right to Lie Out of Philanthrophy" (1797) in which he strenuously argues for the proposition that everyone must always tell the truth, under every conceivable circumstance, even when murderers knock at the door and demand to know the whereabouts of their enemies. The prospect of a friend's murder, according to Kant, does not generate any right – not even an "emergency right" to mislead homicidal interrogators.[17] The prospect of mass slaughter under the direction of legal authorities, by contrast, generates such a right; more exactly, it gives rise to a supposed right: not a "real" right that could be unambiguously pronounced, but only the right of an exceptional figure to represent himself as someone else in the exceptional circumstance of potential civil war. The sovereign may not be precisely lying when he represents himself as judge, but he is still mendacious, for he has no right to be what he presents himself as. Only a few paragraphs after his approval of a sovereign sentence, Kant concedes this very point:

> Of all the rights of a sovereign, the *right to grant clemency* to a criminal (*ius aggratioandi*), either by lessening or entirely remitting punishment, is certainly the slipperiest: in order to show the splendor of his majesty and yet, thereby, to do injustice to a high degree [*um den Glanz seiner Hoheit zu beweisen und dadurch doch im hohen Grade unrecht*]. – With regard to crimes of subjects against one another, it is absolutely not for him to exercise his right, for here the absence

of punishment (*impunitas criminis*) is the greatest injustice against his subjects. He can make use of it, therefore, only when a wrong is done *to himself* (*crimen laesae maiestatis*). But not even then, if lack of punishment could endanger the people's security. – This right is the only one that deserves the name *magisterial right*.

(6: 337)

So slippery is the right to grant clemency that Kant himself almost slips up. In this paragraph, which explains the idea of "magisterial right" invoked in the previous one, the exercise of an uncommon right is acceptable only in those circumstances where the life of the sovereign has been endangered. In the earlier discussion, however, the sovereign is allowed to commute the legally valid decision of the court under completely different conditions: when crimes have been committed by subjects against one another – and indeed committed on an unprecedented scale. If every exercise of magisterial right is "unjust to a high degree," then the supreme degree of injustice is reached in this instance. The exercise of this right is outright wrong. Drawing on Prussian legal tradition, without indicating so, Kant proposes a sovereign sentence as the remedy for a legal situation in which the unchecked juridical process would give rise to injustice: the people in this case would be sickened by the sight of so great a slaughter. But Kant does not – and cannot – present the sole *Machtspruch* that he accepts into his *Doctrine of Right* as an interruption of the juridical process for the sake of a higher justice; on the contrary, the pronouncement of this sentence must still be considered wrong, perhaps even as wrong as the wretched crime committed by those revolutionaries who, according to a footnote of the *Doctrine of Right*, carried out the "formal execution" of their sovereign – one of those mysterious crimes that "cannot be forgiven either in this world or the next" (6: 321).[18] Unforgivable and yet acceptable in the same stroke: such is the paradox of the sovereign sentence that preserves the population and spares the feelings of the people by deporting a sizable portion of the populace.

The pronouncement of the sovereign sentence is not done for the sake of justice, only for the sake of its appearance. By pardoning criminals who commit crimes *lèse majesté*, a sovereign "demonstrates the splendor of his majesty," which is to say: he reveals the extent to which he remains exterior to the sphere of law from which judge and judged cannot escape except on pain of death. When the sovereign pronounces a sovereign sentence that commutes the sentence of subjects who have done harm to other subjects, he, too, enters into this sphere – as both judge *and* judged. This "and" marks the absorption of civil divisiveness into the person of the sovereign, who, for his part, cannot fail to appear (even to himself) as a split personality. Because the crimes in question are against his subjects, not himself, the sovereign cannot even appeal to the dubious right of majesty as the basis

41

for the commutation. Casting himself into the legal sphere, the sovereign appears as outlaw – but only under the condition that this self-casting produces a spectacle in which the sovereign plays all parts of the drama. The resolution of this spectacle demands *real* outcasts. Such outcasts cannot be produced at will, however. The earth must be divided in a very special manner in order for the drama to resolve itself. The state in question must have at its disposal certain zones that are both inside and outside its legal order. Drawing on the Roman legal tradition, Kant calls such zones "provinces." Outside of a country's legal jurisdiction and yet, nevertheless, within its executive power, provinces express, consolidate, and confirm the "split personality" of the sovereign. As judge and outlaw, the sovereign transposes the condemned into places where the juridical authorities can be arrested under any conceivable circumstance – where, in other words, the "doctrine of right" ceases to function. The obverse of the highly conspicuous tribunal of reason at the opening of the *Critique of Pure Reason* is the equally inconspicuous "province" that makes its way into those sections of the *Doctrine of Right* that, as Kant concedes in its Preface, shy away from a "decisive judgment."

Colonialism

None of the three *Critiques* says anything about provinces of the critical enterprise. The introduction to the *Critique of Judgment* lays out the "domain of philosophy in general" by delineating the spaces into which the "field" of concepts is divided into "territories," "domains," and "domiciles" – without any provinces or colonies. In a passage of the *Prolegomena to Any Future Metaphysics* Kant does, to be sure, describe pure mathematics as "the most valuable province" in the "whole field of *a priori* cognitions" (4: 272); but this curious remark, which casts some light on the sovereignty of philosophy, remains undeveloped. Only in the *Doctrine of Right* – and only after allowing for the pronouncement of a deportation order as a "sovereign sentence" – does Kant pay any attention to the concept of province. Yet, even here the attention is not so much directed toward the complexities of this concept as toward the usefulness of provinces for the resolution of conflicts in the homeland. A province, more exactly, is the destination of deportees. As opposed to exile, in which the "lord of the land withdraws all protection" (8: 338), deportation requires certain ambiguous but by no means vague geographic zones in which subjects are removed from the juridical authorities of a state without escaping the exercise of its power. The following three passages from Kant's *Doctrine of Right*, taken together, comprise his scattered account of provinciality:

A country (*territorium*) whose inhabitants are citizens of one and the same common wealth [*eines und desselben gemeinen Wesens*] already through its constitution, that is, without having to perform any juridical act (therefore by birth), is called a *fatherland* [Vaterland]; a country of which they are not citizens apart from this condition is called a *foreign land* [Ausland]; and this is called a province [*Provinz*] (in the sense in which the Romans used this word), if it makes up a part of the country's dominion [*Landesherrschaft*]; because it does not constitute an integrated part of the realm (*imperii*), a place of *residence* for fellow citizens, but only its possession as an under-house [*als eines Unterhauses*], the province must honor the dominant country as a motherland [*Mutterland*].

(6: 337)

In the case of a crime committed by a subject which makes all community with his fellow citizens harmful to the state [the lord of the land] also has a right of *banishment* to a province outside the country [*das Recht der Verbannung in eine Provinz im Auslande*], where he will not participate in the rights of a citizen, that is, *deportation*.

(6: 337–38)

A colony or province is a people that has its own constitution, its own legislation, and its own land, on which those who belong to another state are only foreigners, even though this other state has supreme executive power [*oberste ausübende Gewalt*] over the colony or province. The state having that executive authority is called the mother state [*Mutterstaat*]. The daughter state is dominated by the latter but nevertheless governs itself (by its own parliament, possibly with a viceroy presiding over it) (*civitas hybrida*). This was the relation Athens had with respect to various islands and that Great Britain now has with regard to Ireland.

(6: 348)

By virtue of its relation to the provinces over which it exercises executive authority, the fatherland turns into a motherland: it can give birth – not to a son-land, of course, which might challenge the fatherland but, rather, to a daughter-land, which cannot. Nor can the daughter-land give birth to its own daughter-lands, for, as a hybrid, it remains barren. An island is a particularly propitious place for a *civitas hybrida* because it is de facto isolated, and its intercourse can therefore be effectively controlled. The constitutions of such places are not "mixed," as this term is traditionally understood in political philosophy; rather, each has its own constitution, its own legislation, and its own "land" (*Boden*), but they all remain subject to a "supreme executive power" that can at any moment and under any pretense interrupt its legal processes and arrest its juridical procedures. In other words, the spatiality of the provinces corresponds to the language of the sovereign sentence. In still other words – those of Hannah Arendt – its spatiality corresponds to "government by decree."[19] And "government by decree" operates in reverse as well: returning from the daughter-land to fatherland, as the sovereign sends his subjects to the provinces by means of a sovereign sentence. In order for the exceptional pronouncement of a sovereign sentence to be issued inside the fatherland, therefore, sovereign sentences must already serve as the rule (in both senses of the term) within its daughter-lands. Kant could not have appealed to a sovereign sentence in the catastrophic circumstance he describes unless he could assume that the sovereign who makes this pronouncement had at his disposal an "outlandish" place where the issuing of sovereign-like sentences goes without saying.

By pronouncing the sovereign sentence in which the condemned are deported, the sovereign imports the spatiality of the province into the "fatherland." "Imported" may not be the right term, however, for the sole sovereign sentence Kant authorizes *realizes* the general condition of sovereignty: *everyone* in the state is *in principle*, if not in fact, deported to the provinces, for everyone is, after all, subject to executive decree – except the sovereign, who, in reverse, casts himself as a judge. Those inside the legal order, in short, are cast outside, and the sole outsider casts himself as one of the insiders. And the country as a whole is transported – not in the sense that all "fellow citizens" are shipped off to some island, but insofar as the fatherland turns into a territory where "government by decree" is in any circumstance acceptable. Neither legally valid nor otherwise legitimate, still less just, but acceptable all the same. And the same can be said of the colonial condition about which Kant writes in the sections on "public right," for he unambiguously condemns their existence in the earlier – and more fully developed – sections on "private right":

> Lastly, it can still be asked whether, when neither nature nor chance but simply our own will brings us into the neighborhood of a people that holds out no prospect of a civil union with it, we should not be authorized to found colonies by force, if necessary, in order to establish a civil union with them and bring these human beings (savages) into a legal condition. . . . But it is easy to see through this veil of injustice (Jesuitism), which would sanction any means to good ends. Such a way of acquiring land is therefore to be repudiated.
>
> (6: 266)

Not so conclusively repudiated, however, as to disappear entirely from the sphere of "public right."

Accordingly, an otherwise unimaginable "under-house" (6: 337) becomes the dominant model of legal architecture; its counter-image is the slaughter-bench. Kant, whose architectonic power perhaps expresses itself nowhere more subtly, does not quite say that the fatherland turns into its own "under-house," without any home, properly speaking, but he comes very close. For the acceptability of a *Machtspruch* depends on the prospect of progressive depopulation. This prospect comes from two apparently conflicting sources: the conspiratorial *correi* and the juridical power that condemns them to death. As an extra-legal remedy – and as a show of might – the sovereign substitutes his own sentence for that of the courts. Yet, this substitution also reveals the condition under which the *Machtspruch* can be pronounced: the motherland must be divided into a fatherland, where the powers are rigorously separated, and daughter-lands, where sovereign sentences – under whatever name – can be issued by self-concealing agents of "public right." The condition for the possibility of an acceptable sovereign sentence, in other words, is a separation of the state into two rigorously divided zones: one in which "executive decrees" are everywhere acceptable and another in which a sovereign sentence is acceptable for the purpose of thwarting the spectacle of mass slaughter. On the basis of this division of the earth into heterogeneous zones of "public right" Kant goes against the demand that he issues at the very beginning of the "critical enterprise." The cost of this concession is high: no longer is the sovereign alone able to pronounce sovereign sentences; on the contrary, anonymous administrators of the provinces can do so – and indeed can, without saying anything, make sovereign sentences with a regularity and ease that would be unacceptable for any sovereign who wants to maintain the appearance of being sovereign. The infallibility of these decrees alters in turn: no longer are they infallible because they, like the command *fiat lux*, recreate the conditions of their accomplishment but, on the contrary, because no one – not even the sovereign who represents himself as such – is in a position to say that they have failed. Or, for that matter, succeeded. Instead of either success or failure, sovereign sentences appear in the guise of fate, as sheer "natural" force.

Another historical sign

Kant's inconspicuous acceptance of a single – and singularly weird – *Machtspruch* can be understood as something like an "historical sign" (*Geschichtszeichen*). In a contemporaneous account of the conflict between the philosophical and the juridical faculties of the university, Kant explicitly identifies such a sign: the distant spectators of the Revolution in France. By publicly expressing their sympathy for one party in the conflict – a sympathy that "closely borders on enthusiasm" (7: 85) – these spectators courageously expose themselves to the danger that emanates from the regimes in which they live. There is only a single conceivable reason they would universally do something so contrary to their self-interest: out of respect for the mere Idea of right.[20] Whatever horrors the Revolution may bring – and Kant does not deny that it, too, may turn into a "spectacle of a slaughter-bench" – the state founded on the Idea of law appears to its foreign spectators as a genuine

45

res publica, that is, as a fatherland in which executive and legislative powers are rigorously separated. Since a "public thing," by definition, grants the legislature the right to decide who is an enemy and who a friend, its declarations of war are no longer *Machtsprüche*. The inevitable result of this transformation of executive *Machtspruch* into legislative *Rechtspruch*, according to one of Kant's more famous political-historical theses, is a gradual elimination of aggressive warfare, at least among fellow "republics."

By contrast, in the *other* historical sign – the acceptance of a sovereign sentence into the philosophico-juridical forum that began by excluding sovereign sentences from its midst – the executive power does not supplant the legislative; rather, the sovereign enters into the legal sphere as judge and thereby makes himself into an internal outlaw. The condition for this counter-spectacle is the rigorous division of the earth into zones where the rule of law alone governs legal procedures and zones where it does not. Whereas the historical sign Kant explicitly identifies indicates constant progress of the human species toward the realization of the immanent Idea of legality,[21] the latter points toward the potential *condition* of such progress: the establishment of zones outside the reach of the legal order and yet inside the sphere of executive power. The strangeness of the sole circumstance for which Kant proposes a sovereign sentence as an extra-legal remedy, moreover, determines the time that corresponds to these "outlandish" zones: when states threaten to destroy themselves by executing their laws; or, less dramatically, when unchecked legal processes and automated juridical procedure threaten to deaden the feeling of the people, and thereby make "the people" into a remnant of itself.

46

3

THE OTHER SOVEREIGN SENTENCE

"On the Failure of All Philosophical Attempts at Theodicy"

"Without fail"

Reason, according to Kant, accepts no sovereign sentences. By contrast, the earliest attempt to proceed along the lines that Kant draws in the *Critiques* and develop an integrated system of philosophical science prominently announces "a sovereign sentence of reason [*ein Machtspruch der Vernunft*]."[1] The appeal to such a sentence appears in the opening part of Fichte's *Foundation for the Entire Wissenschaftslehre* (1794), which delivers the first definitive response to the post-critical predicament. The "sovereign sentence of reason" is indicative of a constitutive failure of "first philosophy" to present itself as a continuous chain of inferences, each of which could be considered a *Rechtspruch* (legally valid decision). It is impossible, as Fichte explains, to produce a "deduction" of the last of its three "basic principles" (*Grundsätze*), which is generally expressed as the "principle of reason" (*Satz des Grundes*). Unless this last principle is somehow authorized, however, the doubts concerning the foundation and validity of human knowledge, which *Critique of Pure Reason* set out to dispel, will inevitably return. "Deduction" still retains the legal sense to which the first *Critique* draws attention (B: 113). The interruption of the legal procedure, for both Kant and Fichte, takes the form of a *Machtspruch*, which invests itself with the power to accomplish immediately what it says – without means, without ground, without reason. Such is the irony of the "sovereign sentence of reason" proclaimed in Fichte's *Foundation*: arriving at the point where the process of valid inference collapses, it issues a groundless command that nothing be without a reason. Its formulation consists in a double negation of the original jussive of *Genesis*: not "let there be light" but, rather, "let there be no non-light," which is to say, "there shall be no not I."[2] *Nicht-Licht* (non-light), as the symbol of *Nicht-Ich* (not I), is – so says Fichte, who, as a philosopher, is only supposed to be the medium for the expression of the *Spruch* – to be dismissed. And this original dismissal of darkness and otherness then poses the "task of action,"[3] which consists in the infinite project of doing away with darkness

47

and otherness. Surpassing the critical claim that practical reason is primary, the "sovereign sentence of reason" sets aside all irrational claims and demands, in turn, that practice be the very foundation of theory.

Such, in miniature, is the reasoning of Fichte's *Foundation*, and it provides a retrospective explanation for those supposedly un-critical residues in the critical enterprise that appear under the rubrics of "sensibility" and "thing-in-itself": the letter of the *Critique of Pure Reason* fails to capture its spirit. A philosophical hermeneutics is, therefore, an indispensable ancillary to the development of transcendental idealism.[4] And Fichte could easily find a retrospective justification for this hermeneutics in the *Critique*s themselves, for, as Kant writes in connection with his reinterpretation of the Platonic term *idea*, "I note only that, by comparing the thoughts an author expresses about some subject, it is not unusual to find both in common conversation and in writing that we understand him even better than he understood himself, since he may not have determined his concept in a satisfactory manner and therefore sometimes spoke or even thought contrary to his own intention [*seiner eignen Absicht entgegen*]" (A: 314; B: 370).[5] Although Kant does not himself invoke the distinction between spirit and letter, it is in the spirit of this "remark" (*Bemerkung*), which says, in effect, that speakers not only can fail to say what they mean, but they can also fail to mean what they do in fact mean. An apt place for Fichte to draw on the distinction between letter and spirit would be in his bold use of announcement of a "sovereign sentence of reason" in the first part of the *Foundation*, for it not only represents an explicit violation of a critical *dictum*; it also consists in the sovereign dismissal of rational argumentation for the sake of fulfilling its spirit.

Fichte does not, however, invoke the distinction between letter and spirit at this point in his exposition. And for good reason: in using the term "sovereign sentence," he follows Kant *to the letter* – not, of course, the letter of the first *Critique*, which rejects sovereign sentences root and branch, but, rather, the letter of the first text Kant publishes after the completion of his critical enterprise: "On the Failure of All Philosophical Attempts at Theodicy" (1791). Fichte may even have chosen the term "sovereign sentence" in response to this essay – as a homage to late Kant, who begins his post-critical career by breaking a promise he makes in the concluding paragraph of the Preface to the *Critique of Judgment*: "Thus with this I bring my entire critical enterprise to an end. I shall proceed without fail [*ungesäumt*] to the doctrinal element in order, wherever possible, still to snatch from my increasing age a modicum of time favorable for that purpose" (5: 170). With death fast approaching, Kant fails to do what these prominent lines promise: he does not bring the "doctrinal" element of the "critical enterprise" to completion "without fail." Instead of getting to the serious business at hand – "business" (*Geschäft*) is Kant's own word – he engages in games. This failure, omission, or neglect (*Versäumnis*) lasts almost seven years, until the *Doctrine of Right* is published in fragmentary form in the winter of 1797. In the meantime, he writes a series of essays, at least two of which he explicitly describes as "playing with ideas" (8: 333; 23: 155). And the first of these post-critical essays concerns nothing less than failure – not his own failure to make good on a promise, to be sure, but the failure of "philosophical essays" (*philosophische Versuche*) to do what they promise to accomplish: justify God in relation to the world or, in reverse, justify the world from the horizonless perspective of a god.[6] For Fichte, this failure indicates that now is the time for something other than philosophy. Its name is the "doctrine of science" (*Wissenschaftslehre*). What the failure of philosophical essays means for Kant is far less easy to divine.

An inside joke

"On the Failure" is organized around the term "sovereign sentence." The first part of the essay explicitly rejects all appeals to sovereign sentences, whereas the second part unexpectedly welcomes a *"divine sovereign sentence* [göttlicher Machtspruch]" (8: 264). Between the dismissal of all sovereign sentences and the acceptance of a divine one lies a third alternative, moreover, which consists neither in accepting sovereign sentences nor rejecting them entirely but, instead, tolerates a "morally believing" one: "this possibility [that the end of earthly life is not the end of life altogether] cannot be considered a justification of providence but is, rather, merely a sovereign sentence of morally-believing reason [*ein Machtspruch der moralisch-gläubigen Vernunft*] through which the skeptic is referred to patience but is not satisfied" (8: 262). Reason cannot immediately extend our lives beyond their earthly end by saying that such is the case; but it can cut off discussion about the end of life by saying that, in order to secure the final purpose of life, it shall not end here on earth. From this passage, which serves as the fulcrum of "On the Failure," Fichte can find explicit warrant in the letter of Kant's late writings for the otherwise unjustified pronouncement of a "sovereign sentence of reason."

Three sovereign sentences punctuate the essay, then, each of which is evaluated differently: one sentence is rejected, another is neither accepted nor rejected but reluctantly tolerated, and still another is welcomed as "divine." Instead of speaking of *an* essay, therefore, it is better perhaps to speak of at least two, the first of which concerns the failure of philosophical essays, the second non-philosophical success. In line with the origin of the term in Prussian legal reasoning, all references to sovereign sentences concern the conditions under which a sovereign can dismiss the outcome of a legal procedure. The procedure in this case is that of God, who, however, as sovereign, cannot in principle be brought to trial. The trial can then be understood to be about precisely this issue: whether there is a legal process in the proper sense of the term or, instead, merely a mock, feigned, figural, or even hypocritical trial. After defining the term *theodicy* and indicating that it is by no means certain that this, the last case tried in the tribunal of reason is a case properly speaking, Kant recalls the original moment in which he convenes the tribunal by banning sovereign sentences:

> By a "theodicy" one understands the defense of the highest wisdom of the world-author against the charge that reason brings against it from the counterpurposiveness [*Zweckwidrigkeit*] in the world. – One calls this "defending God's cause" [*die Sache Gottes*], even though the cause may be at bottom no more than that of our presumptuous reason failing to recognize its limits; this surely is not the best cause, but it can nevertheless be accepted insofar as (putting aside that of self-conceit) the human being, as a rational being, is justified in testing all assertions, all doctrine that imposes respect on him, before he subjects himself to it, so that this respect may be upright [*aufrichtig*] and not hypocritical [*erheuchelt*]. . . .
>
> The author of a theodicy therefore agrees on this: that this juridical action [*Rechtshandel*] be brought before the tribunal of reason; and he consents to represent the accused side as advocate through the formal refutation of the plaintiff's complaints; he is therefore not allowed to dismiss the legal proceedings by a sovereign sentence [*Machtspruch*] of the incompetence of the tribunal of human reason (*exceptionem fori*), that is, he cannot dismiss the complaint with an admission, imposed upon the plaintiff, of the highest wisdom of the author of the world, which immediately explains away, even without examination, all doubts that might arise.
>
> (8: 255–56)

This dismissal of sovereign sentences is clear enough, and it is far from unexceptional in the context of eighteenth-century theodicical reasoning. Although Leibniz would, on rare occasions, gesture toward "the bathos of Paul," which defies human understanding, he accepts – and indeed establishes – the basic juridical conditions that Kant delineates.[7] It is less clear, however, why Kant, in 1791, decides to renew the debates surrounding theodicy, especially when there are obviously so many more urgent questions of the day. To be sure, "lawyers for the faith" (1: 222) had not simply faded away, even if the fortunes of "essays in theodicy" suffered a notable decline in the latter half of the eighteenth century.[8] Witness the reaction to "On the Failure" in the journal where it was published: the editor of the *Berlinische Monatsschrift*, Johann Erich Biester, responds to the essay by reasserting an inaccurate version of Leibniz's argument according to which "a perfect being (i.e. God) can create only the most perfect possible world,"[9] and G. L. Spalding, in the same journal, concurs with this assessment, as he describes the "sources" of theodicy.[10] And Leibnizism as a whole was far from vanquished: Kant's acrimonious response to Johann Peter Eberhardt, which he published in 1790 under the sarcastic title "On a Discovery, According to Which All New Critique of Pure Reason Can Be Replaced by an Older One" is proof of its persistence. But of all the various remnants of a Leibnizian spirit, none is perhaps more troublesome for Kant than the question that the Académie Royal des Sciences et Belles-Lettres in Berlin posed for its prize contest of 1791: "What are the real steps forward [*les progrès reel*] of Metaphysics in Germany since the time of Leibnitz [*sic*] and Wolf [*sic*]?"[11] In the very words of this question there is a not-so-subtle presumption that, at least in Germany, metaphysics has made "unreal" steps forward. And who could doubt that the author of the *Critiques* stands silently accused by the Prussian Royal Academy of having made false steps?

The notes Kant wrote in response to the prize contest, which were first published in the year of his death, indicates the degree to which he felt accused. Some thirty-five years earlier, as he may well have remembered, the Royal Academy had made a similar attack on Leibniz. Suppressing the name of the philosopher whom it wishes to discuss, the Royal Academy calls for an assessment of "essays in theodicy" for its prize contest of 1755: "examine the system of Pope, contained in the proposition: All is good [*Tout est bien*]."[12] Whereas in the 1750s the Royal Academy names Pope in an effort to evaluate Leibniz, in the 1790s it names Leibniz when it takes aim at Kant. And Kant responds in kind: he answers in the 1790s the question that the Royal Academy posed in the 1750s. The much-belated response to the prize contest a far younger Kant had intended to enter amounts to an inside joke, the butt of which is the Royal Academy, which cannot bring itself to identify the authors of the propositions it wishes to examine.[13] The various notes that Kant belatedly wrote for the prize contest of 1791 confirm the joke. According to these notes, the possibility of any "real progress" in metaphysics begins with the institution of the tribunal of reason in the first *Critique*. Without the slightest trace of modesty, Kant makes "real progress" his own invention. Others steps have gone astray. The verdict he renders on *all* essays in metaphysics – not simply those in theodicy – is therefore unequivocal: "the total failure of all attempts in metaphysics [*das gänzliche Mißlingen aller Versuche in der Metaphysik*]" (20: 263). "On the Failure of All Philosophical Attempts in Theodicy" performs in miniature what the response to the prize essay would have done on a grander scale: it demonstrates the total failure of all previous philosophical attempts – without ever mentioning "Leibniz," "Wolff," or the "Prussian Royal Academy of the Sciences and Fine Arts." If the Royal Academy can indirectly indict him, in other words, he can do the same in return.

For all the solemnity of its proceedings – and what could be more solemn than trying the judge of the world? – the essay is something of a joke. As anyone familiar with the results of the first *Critique* would know, including even those in the Academy who posed the question concerning "les progrès reel de la Metaphysique," no one can be sure that the defendant in this case really exists. It would be wrong to say that the defendant is thus tried *in absentia*, since he may be altogether absent. Only his surrogates can "really" enter the courtroom; but they can do so only as long as everyone pretends that they could successfully argue in the same forum that their client exists. Little wonder, then, that Biester responds to "On the Failure" by reasserting the ontological proof: as the editor of the journal, he must have vaguely realized that, without such a proof, the whole thing assumes the air of an elaborate inside joke. For those familiar with Kant's explanation for the pleasure derived from jokes, which he had published only a year before, the title alone suggests an intimate link to laughter: "So we laugh," Kant writes, having told a joke about a colonialist whose wig turns white: "we treat our own failure to grasp [*Mißgriff*] some object that is otherwise indifferent to us, or rather the idea we had been pursuing, as we might a ball: we knock it back and forth for a time, although we merely intended to grab it and hold onto it" (5: 333–34). Such is the "failure" (*Mißlingen*) about which Kant writes – or such *would be* the failure if the object in this case could, indeed, be indifferent to us; if, in other words, we could treat issues around God as though they were equivalent to mere games. If, as Kant asserts, "we laugh" after hearing the story of a merchant's fake hair turning white, how much funnier would be the account of a trial that is similarly fake, that arrives at no final verdict, and that concerns a defendant who, for all we know, may not even exist.

Laughter

A burst of laughter, moreover, is heard during the course of the last trial Kant stages. Neither he, who acts as the judge, nor the defenders of "God's cause" laugh, of course, but the wicked do. And their laughter serves as evidence that the defenders of the faith have failed to make their case. Of all the charges brought against God, Kant emphasizes, none is more devastating and none needs a more compelling defense than the accusation that he is an incompetent judge, for the punishments he imposes do not fit the crimes in question. What is worse: the punishments generally miss the criminals and strike their victims. The other two charges leveled against God – which concern his holiness as law-giver for the presence of evil in the world and his goodness as ruler for the predominance of pain over pleasure – may be equally serious; but the accusation that, in his capacity as judge, God fails to distribute the proper amount of pain to those who have committed the appropriate degree of evil reproduces the elements of the trial as a whole. If God cannot be acquitted of this charge, the trial may not have reached a final verdict, but the defendant nevertheless appears guilty: the supreme judge of the world authorizes the suffering of the innocent and the careless enjoyment of the guilty.

When the lawyers for "God's cause" present their defense against this charge, they refrain, as required, from Biblical exegesis, but they invoke a mythic image of divine retribution: "The pretension that the depraved go unpunished in the world is ungrounded, for by its nature every crime already carries with it its due punishment, inasmuch as the inner reproach of conscience torments the depraved even more harshly than the Furies" (8: 261). To this invocation of the Furies, who pursue murderers in the absence of the Areopagus with which the *Universal Natural History* associates its legal procedure, Kant replies in the following manner: "wherever this mode of thinking [of the virtuous] and its accompanying conscientiousness are entirely missing [*gar fehlt*], the tormenter of the crimes committed is likewise missing [*da fehlt*]; and the vicious one, if only he can escape external floggings for his heinous acts, laughs at the anxiousness of honest people who inwardly plague themselves with self-rebukes" (8: 261). This burst of laughter presumably has the same etiology as any other: "Whatever is supposed to arouse lively, convulsive laughter must contain something absurd [*Widersinniges*] (hence something that the understanding cannot like for its own sake)" (5: 332). The absurdity in this case is called "conscience": it goes against sense, *wider-sinnig* in a literal sense, since the depraved cannot sense its appeal. Conscience, for them, is as mythical as the Furies. To speak of it, much less to show signs of being tormented by it, is risible: "Laughter is the affect that arises if a tense expectation is transformed into nothing" (5: 332). The tense expectation in this case is that of corporeal punishment; the transformation of this threat into nothing results in corporeal convulsions. Not only are these convulsions *not* painful; they are positively enjoyable, and, as Kant repeatedly emphasizes, they even contribute to one's health. The laughter of the depraved is, from this perspective, Satanic: wickedness makes one *more* fit to inhabit the earth than does conscientiousness. The world, in other words, is made for – or, to use Kant's term, "purposive" in relation to – the wicked. Kant is no Schopenhauer, to be sure, but the inconspicuous burst of laughter that resounds throughout "On the Failure" gives credence to the thesis that human beings inhabit one of the worst possible worlds.

Kant does not conclude his demonstration of the failure of all philosophical attempts at theodicy with Satanic laughter, but it signals that the defense of "God's cause" is effectively over. What remains is a "sovereign sentence of morally believing reason," which commands that, for the sake of the final purpose of the world, death shall not be the end. But even this sentence, which Kant can tolerate solely because it does not interfere with the juridical procedure, is the subject of subtle ridicule: "unless reason, as a faculty of moral legislation, enacts a sovereign sentence [*einen Machtspruch tut*] in accordance with its interest, it must find it probable, according to the mere laws of theoretical cognition, that the course of the world, according to the order of nature, will determine our fates elsewhere as it does here. For what else does reason have as a guiding thread for its theoretical conjecture but natural law?" (8: 262). Bursts of laughter again, for the tense expectation that life in another world will be fundamentally different from life here on earth is suddenly transformed into nothing. And nothing, as a result, comes of the trial. *Non liquit* is the verdict – not because the case must be brought before a higher instance of legal authority but, rather, because the trial could never secure its own reality. The lawyers have not successfully made their case, but the defendant has not been judged unequivocally guilty either: the existence of moral evil runs counter to divine holiness; the persistence of pain speaks against divine goodness, and the disproportion between "the impunity of the vicious and their crimes" makes a mockery of divine justice. Even if the defendant cannot be properly defended, however, he cannot be properly condemned either. With this, the case is interrupted without a proper decision, and the efforts of philosophy are judged a total failure: "Now the outcome of this juridical process before the forum of philosophy is this: Every previous theodicy has failed to accomplish what it promised" (8: 263).

Instead of acquitting God, his lawyers ironically commit a civil crime of their own: breach of promise. With reference to the basic ontological distinction for which the *Critiques* argue and whose consequences they explore in detail – the distinction between the sensible and the intelligible – Kant halts the proceedings, and the first part of the essay, which makes good on the title, comes to an abrupt end: "The proof of the world-author's moral wisdom in the sensible world can be found only in this insight [into the supersensible, intelligible world] . . . and that is insight to which no mortal can attain" (8: 264). Any attempt to gain insight into the intelligible world is doomed to fail. Of course, with this single remark Kant could have saved himself the trouble of refuting theodicical reasoning point by point. Instead of making his belated reflections on theodicy into an independent essay, he could have appended them to the final sections of the *Critique of Judgment*, perhaps as a concluding remark to the long footnote to section 84, "On the Final Purpose of the Existence of a World, that is, of Creation itself," where he poses an eminently theodicical question: "why did human beings have to exist [*Wozu haben Menschen existieren müssen*]?" (5: 436). "On the Failure" removes any suspicion that the Critique of Teleological Judgment is supposed to be interpreted as a new philosophical attempt at theodicy. But then, again, such an interpretation would only prove that the interpreter was incapable of understanding the "critical enterprise" from the start. The entire exercise of refuting the specific claims of dogmatic theologians has been, from the beginning, beside the point. The *Critiques* have done away with theodicy in the same stroke that crushed rational metaphysics. Bursts of laughter from those in the know, which is to say, those who know the limits of human knowledge. At this point, the temptation is to say "enough already": the point has been made, and in any case it did not have to be made after the publication of the *Critiques*, since the *Critiques* already make it sufficiently well themselves.

But Kant does not stop. Nor does he go forward and make "real progress" on the exposition of his own doctrine during the few remaining years left to him. Rather, he begins the essay anew, and this new beginning can be understood as the inception of a post-critical Kant – a Kant who does not, of course, disavow anything in the "critical enterprise" but who seeks to understand what else the failure of philosophy might mean. Having concluded the first part of his essay by showing that all "philosophical essays" fail, he begins the second by indicating that a *non-philosophical* essay has succeeded. Beyond the title of the essay lies an implicit coda: "and On the Success of a Non-Philosophical Attempt at the Same." Instead of going forward to develop something like a meta-philosophy in light of philosophy's failure to justify the world from a extramundane perspective, Kant turns away from philosophical modes of argumentation and returns to a text that, for all its argumentation, comes closer to poetry than philosophy: "the ancient holy book [of Job]" (8: 264). This is the last joke: Kant, the great *Aufklärer*, appears as the champion of the Bible.

"Authentic interpretation"

Before Kant ventures a new interpretation of the Book of Job, however, he interprets interpretation anew. The opening sentences of "On the Failure" assign the definition of Leibniz's neologism to a neutral and anonymous "one" (*man*): "By 'theodicy' one understands [*versteht man*] the defense of the highest wisdom of the world-author against the charge that reason brings against it for whatever is counterpurposive in the world. – One calls [*Man nennt*] this 'defending the cause of God'" (8: 255). Having shown that one cannot defend this cause in the first part of the essay, Kant starts again by stipulating what ought to be understood by the term *theodicy*: "All theodicy should, properly speaking, be an *interpretation* of nature, insofar as God announces the intention of his will through it [*All Theodizee soll eigentlich Auslegung der Natur sein, sofern Gott durch dieselbe die Absicht seines Willens kund macht*]" (8: 264). Although this sentence is set off from the previous ones only by a few asterisks, it is a world apart, for the second part of the essay frees itself from the discourse of "one." Whenever "one" understands the term *theodicy* simply as the "defense of God's cause," "one" does not understand the word – or oneself. If the talk of a "one" who does not understand itself sounds more like Kierkegaard or Heidegger than the author of the *Critiques*, this is hardly surprising, since the term he unexpectedly introduces into his discourse for the first time in the second part of "On the Failure" is very familiar to anyone who has read Kierkegaard or Heidegger in English translation, namely "authentic" (*authentisch*): "Now every interpretation of the declared will of a legislator is either *doctrinal* or *authentic* [doktrinal *oder* authentisch]. The first reasons out [*herausvernünftelt*] the will from the utterances of which

55

the law-giver has made use, in conjunction with his otherwise recognizable intentions; the law-giver himself makes the second" (8: 264).[14]

Instead of "proceeding without fail to the doctrinal [*zum Doktrinal*]" (5: 170), as he promises, Kant heads in the opposite direction: *zum Authentischen*. On the basis of the distinction between doctrinal and authentic modes of interpretation Kant begins the second part of the essay, which is so completely distinguished from the first part that it could even be said to be an entirely new essay. At the very least, the title "On the Failure of All Philosophical Attempts at Theodicy" no longer describes its content. This "nouveau essai de théodicée" is less interested in the case per se than in the process in which all legal cases are decided: by interpreting the text of the law. Whatever Kant may mean by *doctrine* as a technical term, it retains its original sense: "what is taught." Doctrinal interpretation is learned; by contrast, authentic interpretation requires no education. Legal pedagogy consists in learning what legislators meant to say by studying what they wrote. Only the law-giver is exempt from this process of learning. Authentic legal interpretation is defined accordingly: it is the interpretation of the law by its giver. But for this reason, as Kant soon makes clear, authentic interpretation is not genuinely interpretative. Having begun the second part of the essay by declaring that "every theodicy should, properly speaking [*eigentlich*], be called an *interpretation* of nature," he proceeds to define the "genuine" or "authentic" (*eigentlich*) use of the term: "Philosophical attempts of this kind," he writes, referring to "essays" (*Versuche*) that claim to discover the intentions of the world-author by interpreting his works, "are doctrinal and constitute theodicy proper [*eigentliche Theodizee*], which one can therefore call the doctrinal ones" (8: 264). "Authentic" (*authentisch*) interpretation of nature, in other words, is "inauthentic" (*uneigentlich*) theodicy. The "impropriety" (*Uneigentlichkeit*) of authentic interpretation undoes – or outdoes – the impropriety of authentic attempts at theodicy, which, as the essay has already shown sufficiently well, can only stage the exoneration of the divine sovereign, legislator, and judge. At this point in the argument, where the authentic depends on a certain inauthenticity and vice versa, Kant inserts a dash that serves as both the sign of a sovereign stroke of thought and the mark of a hitherto unacknowledged infallibility:

> – Yet one cannot also deny [*man kann nicht versagen*] the name of "theodicy" to the mere dismissal [*Abfertigung*] of all objections against divine wisdom, if it is a *divine sovereign sentence* [*göttlicher Machtspruch*] or (which in this case comes down to the same), if it is a pronouncement of the same reason through which we form our concept of God, necessarily and prior to all experience, as a moral and wise being. For through our reason God then becomes himself the interpreter of the will as announced through creation; and this

interpretation we can call an *authentic* one [*diese Auslegung können wir eine* authentische *nennen*].

(8: 264)

By welcoming a sovereign sentence, Kant appears inconsistent, for he establishes the principles of the trial when he denies the lawyers for God's case this privilege. But the appearance of inconsistency is slightly deceptive, since Kant never barred the defendant himself from entering into the courtroom and declaring, by the mere force of his presence, a halt to the proceedings. And this is precisely what takes place with the announcement of the "divine sovereign sentence": the sovereign himself speaks immediately, without surrogates, and thus brings an end to the discussion. It is no longer necessary to determine what the law-giver wished to say, since he can now simply say so. And we, according to Kant, are legislators. Such is the point of the "Copernican hypothesis" (B: xvi): we give laws to nature for the purpose of knowledge, laws to ourselves despite our knowledge, and laws to the power of judgment for the purpose of regarding nature as purposive. Something unforeseen in Copernican turn is new here, however: interpretation of a given law, which, as such, is extra-legislative, a supplement to legislation, without thereby being illegal, properly speaking. The structure of this interpretative supplement to legislation is similar to that of the supplementary "postulates" of pure practical reason delineated in the second *Critique*, and indeed the two sovereign sentences that Kant deems acceptable in "On the Failure" can be understood as versions of these postulates: whereas a "sovereign sentence of morally believing reason" derives from the postulate of an afterlife, the "divine sovereign sentence" articulates the postulate of a divinity. Even here, however, there is something new, for the divinity postulated by pure practical reason, in a gesture that would be called "condescension" in other contexts, now uses *us* as the medium of its immediacy: "For through our reason God then becomes himself the interpreter of the will as announced through creation, and this interpretation we can call an *authentic* one." Kant takes leave of the "one" (*man*), and "we" begin to call things by the names we choose, and we can authorize ourselves to pronounce an interpretation authentic because "our reason" is the medium for the pronouncements of the divinity whose concept we ourselves – without the need for divine condescension – form. "One cannot deny" (*man kann nicht versagen*) the "we" its ability to pronounce a sentence that "cannot fail" (*nicht versagen kann*).

And what the "divine sovereign sentence" (*göttlicher Machtspruch*) cannot fail to say is: I am in power. It goes without saying that this power needs no further justification. Might is not simply right in the case of this voice; it is the very basis of right. And might is, for this reason, entirely immune from juridical review: its speech cannot be justified, since it is just, by definition. Even more succinctly, the "divine sovereign sentence" simply says: "this is a sovereign sentence." It is, in other words, its own meta-speech.

If it were translated into the language of theoretical speculation it might read: "I = I." And if Fichte did indeed draw the term "sovereign sentence of reason" from "On the Failure," it demonstrates the carefulness with which he read his master's writings. For Kant, the name of that which is the basis of all juridical review and is therefore immune from any juridical process is "practical reason." Since the "divine sovereign sentence" refers only to itself; since it is a tautological act, it can gain content only if it is understood as something other than a "divine sovereign sentence." And since this "as" cannot depart from the tautological structure of the sovereign sentence, it can be understood only as the very structure of the "as" – as, in other words, interpretation pure and simple. Or in Kant's own terms, as "authentic interpretation," which is not interpretation, as it is generally understood. And one could hardly recognize sovereign sentence as interpretative:

> This [authentic interpretation] is not an interpretation of a rational-izing (*vernünftelnden*) reason but of a practical reason *having power* [einer *machthabenden* praktischen Vernunft], which, just as in legis-lating, it commands absolutely without further grounds, so can it be viewed as an unmediated explanation and voice of God [*Erklärung und Stimme Gottes*] through which he gives sense to the letter of his creation [*durch die er dem Buchstaben seiner Schöpfung einen Sinn gibt*].
>
> (8: 264)

Dem Buchstaben, a single letter, not *den Buchstaben*, which refers to many. In an illuminating passage of the *Prolegomena* Kant compares the work of the categories to the act of differentiating letters for the purpose of uniting them into meaningful words: "if the pure concepts of the understanding try to go beyond objects of experience and be referred to things in them-selves (*noumena*), they have absolutely no meaning [*Bedeutung*]. They serve, so to speak, only to spell out appearances, so that we may be able to read them as experience [*Sie dienen gleichsam nur, Erscheinungen zu buchstabiren, um sie als Erfahrung lesen zu können*]" (4: 312).[15] Whereas this explanation of the categories, like the explanation of authentic interpretation, depends on the familiar topos of the world as a book, the latter is significantly stranger, for the world of appearances is made up of only a *single* letter. The use of the singular form of *letter* would make better sense if it were contrasted with its Pauline opposite, namely *spirit*. But Kant refrains from making this distinction: the law-giver does not reveal the spirit of the letter; he gives it sense. By giving sense to *a* letter, however, he renders his *other* act of giving – other than lawgiving – senseless. And this senselessness is reproduced in the scenario Kant sketches: the law-giver interprets his own text – to himself. There is no one else on the scene. Of course, it is possible to interpret this crucial passage of "On the Failure" in the following manner: practical reason, regarded as the divine voice, interprets its text for the sake of theoretical reason, which recognizes its status as finite. Such an interpretation is doubt-less valid – and doctrinal: it is based on what Kant must have meant, given a study of his other utterances. The passage, however, says nothing of the kind: the giving-sense of the law-giver has no audience; it teaches no one and is, therefore, non-doctrinal and, to this extent, authentic.

The late Schelling acknowledges something like the madness of reason.[16] Not so Kant – or at least this is a common conception, especially in view of his late writings. The oddities of his late utterances, according to a familiar line of argument, can be understood as private quirks, strictly irrelevant to the "critical enterprise" itself. "On the Failure" is evidence against such interpretations of late Kant, for it discloses a mode of madness internal to reason. The law is interpreted by the law-giver, who is as alone as the letter of the law he gives. Such a scene is, for Kant, a sure sign of madness: "The suspicion that someone is not quite right in the head already arises whenever he *speaks aloud* with himself" (7: 218). The best "subjective test" for madness consists, therefore, in making sure that we do not "isolate ourselves" (7: 219) – which, however, is precisely what the speaker of "the divine sovereign sentence" must do in order to ensure that the spoken sentence is indeed sovereign.[17] No wonder God gives voice to the letter – not the letters – of his creation: the inarticulateness of the letter corresponds to the senselessness of its vocalization. In order for authentic interpretation to *make sense*, someone other than the law-giver himself must be present; otherwise, the act of giving sense to the letter of the law is as meaningless as the isolated letter itself. Authentic interpretation takes place only in a fit of madness, perhaps even a spell of *Wahnwitz* (insanity), which intensifies the arresting of cognitive processes that defines the strange work of *Witz* (wit). This means, however, that authentic interpretation not only cannot be accomplished; it cannot even be *attempted*. Attempts to interpret authentically are doomed to failure by virtue of the very intention to do so. Instead of being attempted, authentic interpretation can only be *found*. And it can only be found in *another form*, which, by virtue of its otherness, makes sense of the mad act of isolated self-interpretation. Kant does not, therefore, attempt an authentic interpretation himself; he only finds one in an allegorical form. And he similarly finds the wherewithal to say – after all the uses of "one" and "we" as grammatical subjects – "I": "Now I find such an authentic interpretation allegorically expressed in an ancient holy book" (8: 264).[18]

Allegorical expression

Kant disavows any interpretative activity of his own. *He* will not interpret the "ancient holy book" but will only display what he finds: that the book expresses an authentic interpretation in an "improper," "inauthentic," or *uneigentlich* manner – as allegory. An allegorical expression of authentic interpretation resolves its irony. Giving sense to a letter that I myself have created solely in my own presence makes no sense otherwise. And Kant charges allegory with the task of presenting whatever is otherwise unpresentable. In a passage of the *Critique of Judgment*, which, like "On the Failure," draws attention to the figure of the Furies, Kant outlines the apotropaic function of allegoresis:

> [O]nly one mode of ugliness cannot be represented in accordance with nature without doing away with all aesthetic delight and thus all artistic beauty: that ugliness which awakens disgust [*Ekel*]. For the following reason: because in this strange sensation, which rests on nothing but imagination, the object is represented as if it insisted [*aufdränge*] that it be enjoyed, which is, however, what we forcefully are striving not to do; and therefore the artistic representation of the object is no longer distinguished in our sensation from the nature of the object itself [*die künstliche Vorstellung des Gegenstandes von der Natur dieses Gegenstandes selbst in unserer Empfindung nicht mehr unterschieden . . . werden*], and it is therefore impossible to consider it beautiful. The art of sculpture, too, has excluded from its creations any immediate presentation of ugly objects from its formations, for in its products art is almost confused with nature, and it has thus allowed, for example, death (in a beautiful genius) and the fever of war (in Mars) to be represented by an allegory or attributes that look pleasant, therefore only indirectly by means of an interpretation of reason [*Auslegung der Vernunft*] and not for a merely aesthetic power of judgment.
>
> (5: 312)

At issue in authentic interpretation is not the ugliness of death, which is in any case an acceptable subject for literary works. Sculpture has to make recourse to allegory only because its representations tend to be taken for the thing represented. An utterance is in a comparable condition only when it speaks of its enunciation, and this enunciation is comparable to death only when it bespeaks the derangement of the speaker, who, by speaking about his or her own speech, makes no allowance for the distinction between the subject of speech and the speaking subject. The vertiginous character of such an utterance demands its allegorization. In order to safeguard it from the madness of isolated self-interpretation, the sole sovereign sentence that Kant wholeheartedly welcomes is accessible only "by means of an interpretation of reason." In his exposition of the "sovereign sentence of reason" Fichte notes that it can only be found; but he would have been closer to the spirit of "On the Failure" if he had also noted that it can only be found in a form alien to its own formulation – and found to be something much less sturdy than the foundation of the principle of reason. By means of an interpretation of reason, an utterance can be interpreted as authentic interpretation: what this utterance "actually" (*eigentlich*) means to say is anyone's guess. The same is true, for Kant, of the Book of Job. Whatever its author actually meant to say has no bearing on its interpretation, which is neither doctrinal nor authentic but, rather, strictly rational. It is not, however, the *self*-interpretation of reason: the mode of interpretation Kant adopts remains distinct from the mode of interpretation that, according to his interpretation, the Book of Job allegorically expresses. In other words, Kant does not interpret the "ancient holy book" as though he had written it. The Book of Job remains the work of someone else, and the otherness of the work guarantees that his interpretation will not demand still another allegorization.

According to Kant, the Book of Job allegorically expresses both authentic and doctrinal modes of interpretation. The former is allegorized in the speech of God, the latter in the arguments of Job's "friends" (8: 265), who are, however, friends in name only. In the preliminary notes to the essay Kant describes them as "so-called friends" (23: 85), since their discussions with Job are meant to curry divine favor. Job's speeches, finally, express neither authentic nor doctrinal modes of interpretation; instead, they represent the negative mode of interpretation, which says again and again, in ever varying formulations, "I am uninterpretable." Instead of making sense of what he himself established – which is what the law-giver who makes sense of his law does – Job insists that no one can make any sense of his life. Four modes of interpretation are therefore in play: the interpretation of reason, by means of which Kant makes sense of the utterances he finds; authentic interpretation in the speech of God; doctrinal interpretation in the arguments of Job's hypocritical friends; and the negative mode of authentic interpretation, which calls for an end to interpretation. The voice of God ratifies Job's claim that the interpretation of his life cannot be accomplished in an appropriately negative manner – by declaring the "friendly" opponents of his negative mode of interpretation false. In a line to which Kant alludes but refrains from quoting, Job asks: "will windy words ever end?" (Job 16: 3) – to which the divine voice suddenly responds, descending from a whirlwind and arresting the chatter of "ratiocinating or hyper-ratiocinating [*vernünftlen oder übervernünftlen*]" (8: 265) argumentation once and for all.

Kant never quotes any voice other than Job's. Nothing of the divine voice appears in direct discourse. Instead of articulating the "divine sovereign sentence" by which God brings an end to the ceaseless argumentation, he paraphrases the voice from the whirlwind in such a way that the author of the world begins to sound very much like the author of the *Critique of Judgment*:

> God honors Job, placing before his eyes the wisdom of his creation, especially from the sides of its inscrutability [*Unerforschlichkeit*]. He allows him glimpses into the beautiful side of nature, where ends

comprehensible to human beings bring the wisdom and the benevolent providence of the world into an unambiguous light; but also,
by contrast, into the terrifying [*die abschreckende*] side, by naming
[*hernennt*] the products of his power [*Produkte seiner Macht*], and
among them also harmful, fearful things, each of which seems to be
purposively arranged for its own sake and that of its species, yet,
with respect to other things and to human beings themselves, is
destructive, counterpurposive [*zerstörend, zweckwidrig*], and incom-
patible with a universal plan ordered by goodness and wisdom; yet,
again, God thereby demonstrates an order and maintenance of the
whole, which proclaim a wise world-author [*Welturheber*], although
at the same time his ways, inscrutable to us even in the physical
order of things, how much more so in the connection of the latter
to the moral order (which is, to our reason, still more impenetrable),
must remain hidden [*verborgen*].

(8: 266)

The two "sides" of creation correspond to the two modes of aesthetic judgment: beauty and sublimity. The beautiful side is purposive with respect to
humanity; the sublime side counterpurposive. Each of the counterpurposive
products can then again be regarded as purposive – not from a human
perspective, to be sure, but from that of "the whole," which, regardless of
the enormous destructive powers of its parts, continually reproduces itself.
That the cosmos does not collapse, in short, gives evidence of a "wise" – not
a good, still less a just – "author of the world." Such is, for Kant, the lesson
of God's speeches from the whirlwind, and this lesson proceeds along the
lines laid out in the last *Critique*: from beauty through sublimity to a guarded
defense of natural theology. Less apparent, however, are the distinct modes
by which the two sides of creation appear: the beautiful "side" comes to light
before Job's eyes, whereas the sublime side is only "named thence" (*hernennt*).
The former belongs to the order of phenomena, whereas the latter inhabits
the order of language. Since, however, the side of creation that appears in
its names alone can be understood *as* an order only from a perspective other
than Job's own, it would perhaps be better to say the following: whereas the
"side" of creation that Job glimpses belongs to the order of phenomena, the
"side" he knows only by name belongs to the disorder of language. And this
disorder corresponds to the disorder of the "divine sovereign sentence" itself:
only a voice appears, and this voice interrupts the many conversations, which,
however unproductive, still follow recognizable rules of procedures.

None of this is surprising, moreover, since these "products of his power"
are the only ones at issue from the beginning of the proceedings: there would
be no charges brought against the Creator if there were not evidence of
"destructive, counterpurposive" creatures that the author of the world "names
hence" – and that the author of "On the Failure" *fails to name*. The absence

of these creatures' names may seem an insignificant omission; but these creatures, as "products of his power [*Macht*]," are inscribed in the "divine sovereign sentence [*Machtspruch*]" itself. Kant's failure to name names, so to speak, indicates the limit of expression: modes of interpretation can be expressed but the subject of interpretation – here called the "products of his power" – cannot. Their names run counter to expression. In themselves, without a corresponding phenomenalization, they are as far removed from the sphere of expression as the isolated letter of creation from articulation. And these names are as destructive to the signifying order as the creatures thus named are to the human species.

Leviathan

Carl Schmitt, who knew much less about taste than about tactics, once wrote in passing: "If only for reasons of taste perhaps, Kant would certainly never have dared conjure up an image like that of Leviathan."[19] "On the Failure" shows that this remark is only half true, for Kant conjures up the *image* of the sea monster without naming its fateful *name*. According to God, as paraphrased by Kant, the presence of inhospitable monsters demonstrates that creation as a whole must be considered wisely designed, for, despite all, it renews itself. The sublimity of the images of counterpurposive creatures may even be the source of "negative pleasure" (5: 245), a compensation for Job's suffering in advance of the full restitution of his estate. Had Kant named the image of the destructive creature he conjures, however, it would be far less clear that it could contribute to the line of argument developed in the Critique of Teleological Judgment, which authorizes – and indeed requires – human beings to judge phenomena on the basis of the principle of natural purposiveness. For, ever since Hobbes published his principal treatise, the name "Leviathan" has served as an emblem of the "*Mortall God*, to whom we owe under the *Immortall God*, our peace and defence."[20] In saying this name, therefore, the state might come to light – as "destructive, counterpurposive." Saying "Leviathan," in other words, is inseparable from the phenomenalization of the sole terrestrial power that can pronounce a sovereign sentence:

> Hitherto I have set forth the nature of Man, (whose Pride and other Passions have compelled him to submit himself to Government;) together with the great power of his Governour, whom I compared to *Leviathan*, taking the comparison out of the last two verses of the one and fortieth of *Job*; where God having set forth the great power of *Leviathan*, called him King of the Proud. *There is nothing, saith he, on earth, to be compared with him. He is made so as not to be afraid. He seeth every high thing below him; and is King of all the children of pride.*[21]

The incomparability of Leviathan to all things on earth is the basis for the comparison between this fearsome fish and the political order that *Leviathan* seeks to secure. Hobbes goes no further in the direction of explaining the peculiar title of his treatise; nowhere does he explore – or even gesture toward – the vast variety of meanings that had accrued to this name in the complicated course of rabbinical, patristic, Kabbalistic, and Christian-Kabbalistic interpretation of Chapters 40 and 41 of *Job*.[22] The monster of the waters that catches and devours those who enter its sphere is also, according to some interpreters, itself caught and devoured in a feast of thanksgiving for the messianic end of its tyrannical domination of the earth: "On that day the Lord with his hard, great and strong sword shall punish Leviathan the flying serpent, Leviathan that crooked serpent; and he shall slay the crocodile that is in the sea" (Is. 27: 1); "You crushed the heads of Leviathan, and gave him for food to the people inhabiting the wilderness" (Ps. 74: 14). Thanks to the paucity of biblical references, the portentousness of the imagery, and the obscurity of the name – allusions to Lotan, the Ugaritic sea-monster, were discovered relatively recently[23] – Leviathan has provided a feast for allegorists. For Kant, allegory is the means by which authentic interpretation finds expression; otherwise, without recourse to the otherness of allegory, it would have to view as something like an outburst of madness in which the lawgiver, solely for his own satisfaction, makes sense of the isolated letter of his creation. And something of this madness would become readily apparent if Kant had indeed named the image of counterpurposiveness that he conjures up, for the "divine sovereign sentence" would consist in something like a "double bind": you must leave the state of nature and enter into a state, but this state, which you have no right to resist, is "destructive, counterpurposive" – so much so that it is the source of the very wrongs represented by the incontestable case of Job.[24]

If, therefore, the name "Leviathan" were to find its way into Kant's paraphrasis of the voice from the whirlwind, God, as the allegorical expression of "power-holding practical reason," could be heard to say: "the state is counterpurposive" – to which Kant would have to add immediately: "and is nevertheless necessary, according to the principles of power-holding practical reason." The command that one depart from the state of nature and enter a civil condition is the starting point of the critical project itself, which demands the establishment of a philosophico-legal authority for the adjudication of metaphysical conflicts.[25] And the same command is also at the center of the reformulation of the Hobbesian Leviathan in the *Doctrine of Right*: one must leave the state of nature and enter into the civil condition, which alone distinguishes sheer violence from rationally sanctioned coercion. One must, in short, deliver oneself into the jaws of the very creature that, as God himself is understood to say, runs counter to human purposes – if it does not destroy us outright. No wonder, then, that the sole sovereign sentence that Kant finds acceptable in the *Doctrine of Right* is an unmistakable response to, and symptom of, a condition approximating that of civil war.[26]

The central section of an essay Kant publishes in the *Berlinische Monatsschrift* a few years later, "On the Common Saying: That May Work in Theory but not in Practice," is subtitled "Contra Hobbes," and the sole quotation drawn from the author of *Leviathan* – "a head of state has no obligation to the people by the contract and cannot do a citizen any wrong (he may dispose over him as he wishes)" (8: 303) – is found to be at once correct and terrifying: correct insofar as the wrongs committed by a head of state give his subjects no right to use violence in return; terrifying only by virtue of its generality. Thus Kant writes, having quoted a line from Chapter 7, paragraph 14 of *De Cive*: "This proposition would be entirely right, if one understands by injustice [*Unrecht*] an injury that concedes the injured party a *coercive right* against the one who committed the injustice; but this proposition, so in general, is terrifying [*aber, so im allgemeinen, ist der Satz erschrecklich*]" (8: 303–04). *Erschrecklich* is the term through which "power-holding practical reason," assuming the voice of God, in the words of Kant, describes that "side" of creation whose creatures it only names: "He allows him glimpses into the beautiful side of nature, where ends comprehensible to human beings bring the wisdom and the benevolent providence of the world into an unambiguous light; but also, by contrast, into the terrifying [*die abschreckende*] side, by naming the products of his power, and among them also harmful, fearful things, each of which seems to be purposively arranged for its own sake and that of its species, yet, with respect to other things and to human beings themselves, as destructive, counterpurposive" (8: 266). Kant makes no mention of the term "sovereign sentence" (*Machtspruch*) in "On the Common Saying [*Gemeinspruch*]," which is understandable, since it is the least common of sayings; but the "divine sovereign sentence" finds an echo in "Contra Hobbes" nevertheless.

Right yet terrifying: these words apply to both Hobbes's principle and the emblematic fish under whose name he sets them forth. And nothing indicates the effects of this coordination of rightness and horror better than the strange phrase by which it comes to expression in "On the Common Saying": "aber, so im allgemeinen, ist der Satz erschrecklich," literally translated, "but, so in general, the proposition is terrifying." What principle, for Kant, is not "so in general"? Indeed, is it even possible for a principle of practical reason to be *too* general, *so* universally applied that it suddenly comes under suspicion? If so, then the cornerstone of the "critical enterprise" – the absolute universality of the principles of pure practical reason – begins to teeter. The destructive power of the counterpurposive creatures that the divine voice names for Job's sake extends, in this way, to the very architecture of the *Critiques*.

That the Leviathan is the principle source of human woe is not a thought foreign to Kant, moreover. On the contrary, after the publication of "On the

Failure," he argues in numerous places for the validity of this very thesis, going so far as to describe the behavior of the current collection of European states as a regression from the condition of cannibals (8: 354–55) – or even worse, as an "overturning of the *final end* of creation itself" (7: 89). The reason for this dismal state of affairs is, for Kant, quite obvious: sovereigns have at their disposal the power to issue sovereign sentences – pronounce not only those sentences that dismiss the outcome of legal proceedings, which some rulers are willing to relinquish,[27] but also those sentences that declare a state of war, which no sovereign would willingly abandon. For a sovereign to say "I cannot declare war" is, in effect, for him to abdicate his sovereignty. The people, for their part, have a right to complain about the actions of their rulers but not to resist their power to transform the populace into slaughter animals. And who, in any case, has a right to complain about a declaration of war, since it is at bottom a declaration of an exceptional condition, which allows the sovereign to enter into every hitherto independent sphere of life. Kant, in short, comes close to saying what, in his paraphrase, God almost tells Job: the state destroys the lives of its subjects so as to preserve its own.

Sadness

God does not quite say this to Job, however. The "destructive, counter-purposive" side of creation is never properly named. It could also be understood along the lines tenuously laid out in the Critique of Teleological Judgment and episodically developed as Kant grew older: terrestrial "revolutions" (5: 419), according to a reasonable conjecture, generated the conditions for the plant and animal kingdoms, both of which were then overthrown in favor of a human regime that, for all we know, could suffer the same fate. As he writes some ten years later, in the *Opus postumum*, in conjunction with a thought that Hobbes invokes as the principal justification for the political order envisaged in *Leviathan*: "*Nature* treats human beings despotically. Human beings destroy one another like wolves. Plants and animals overgrow and suffocate one another. Nature does not attend to the care and tending that they require. Wars destroy what long-standing actions of art [*Kunsthandlungen*] established and cared for" (21: 13–14). The "Concluding Remark" (*Schlußanmerkung*) of "On the Failure" avoids any conjectures concerning the identity of the "destructive, counterpurposive" creature created by a despotic nature. But this is not to say that the "Concluding Remark" is any less bleak than the passage from the *Opus postumum*. On the contrary, it is perhaps even bleaker, since *any* identification of a source of human woe – whether it be natural or human despots – is reassuring in comparison to the foe that Kant identifies as he reflects on Job's friends. Not only do they misrepresent their beliefs in public; they also falsify themselves in the court of their own conscience. The famous dictum attributed to Aristotle, which, according to one of Kant's friends, he adopted as his own – "my friends, there is no such thing as a friend"[28] – is particularly applicable to Job's comforters. At least a despot is easily represented as exterior to the self: regardless of whether it is natural or human, the despot is decidedly other. Not so with friends, and as Kant proceeds to show, no one can honestly say: "I am different from Job's 'so-called friends.'" Only those who are dishonest say "I am honest" – with the exception of Job, whose very honesty merely serves as the basis for the indictment of everyone else.

The "Concluding Remark" sets out, once again, in a new direction – new not only from the perspective of the *Critiques* but from that of philosophical discourse on practical reason in general. The outcome of the "authentic theodicy" allegorically expressed in the "ancient holy book" is that Job, the upright one, regardless of his occasional "failings [*Fehler*]" (8: 265), is in the right, whereas his friends are entirely in the wrong, for they say things about which, as they themselves must know, they are unsure. They are liars, in short, not precisely because they make false statements but because they fail to qualify their statements by conceding uncertainty. Since the *Critique of Pure Reason* had, for the first time, according to Kant, properly circumscribed the "land of truth" (A: 235; B: 294), it makes such concessions more urgent than ever. Saying anything of metaphysical import that runs counter to the arguments of the *Critiques* is tantamount to lying. And such lies are even more insidious than outright falsehoods, for they destroy the very medium in which truth can be expressed. The authenticity of the theodicy Kant finds allegorically expressed reveals the insincerity of those who attempt any other. This insincerity can be attributed not only to Job's friends and those, in turn, who pretend to defend "God's cause" but also to human beings in general:

> The remark [*Bemerkung*] that there is such an impurity [*Unlauterkeit*] in the human heart is not new (for Job already made it); yet one would almost believe that attention to it is new among the teachers of morality and religion: one finds few who make sufficient use of this remark despite the difficulties incumbent upon a purification of dispositions in human beings, even when they *want* to act according to duty.
>
> (8: 267–68)

The theodicical trial was fake from the beginning – as fake as the friends of Job are false. Anyone familiar with the *Critique of Pure Reason* would know this. And the fakeness of the trial, like the falseness of the friends, is rooted in – and evidence of – a particularly pernicious impurity, which tends to hide itself in expressions of piety. The joke, so to speak, is on all of God's spokesmen, for they are shown to be jokesters who, even in the presence of an authentic naïf, fail to recognize themselves as such. *So im allgemeinen* (applied in general), this thought is as sad as Hobbes's principle is terrifying. And the conclusion of "On the Failure" is the compact expression of this sadness. Implicitly conjuring up the image of the naïf who concludes the last "Remark" of the Critique of Aesthetic Judgment, Kant says in the "Concluding Remark" what the "Remark" implies – that it is possible to find a naïf only in fiction and that the inner "jokester" can perhaps be "laid bare" (5: 335) but cannot be expunged. The Hobbesian Leviathan contributes to the development of the inner "jokester" by requiring that its officers swear oaths of allegiance to certain articles of faith, but even apart from such considerations, "the jokester in ourselves" predominates:

> Since a purification of this public mode of thinking [professions of faith for the purpose of gain] must in all likelihood be deferred to a distant future, until some day, perhaps under the protection of freedom of thought, it will become a general principle of instruction and teaching, a few lines may here be turned toward a consideration of that defiance apparently so deeply rooted in human nature [*jener Unart, welche in der menschlichen Natur tief gewurzelt zu sein scheint*].
>
> There is something touching and elevating to the soul in the depiction of an upright character that is distant from all falsehood and positive dissemblance. But, since honesty [*Ehrlichkeit*], as mere simplicity and straightforwardness in the mode of thinking, is the least that one can always demand of a good character (especially if one discounts openheartedness), and it is therefore difficult to see the basis for the admiration we grant to such a character: it must be that uprightness is the property farthest removed from human nature. A sad remark! [*Eine traurige Bemerkung!*] For all the remaining properties, to the extent that they rest on principles, can have a true inner value only through that one.
>
> (8: 269–70)

By the time Kant publishes his next contribution to the *Berlinische Monatsschrift*, "On the Radical Evil in Human Nature," the "seems" in the phrase "seems to be deeply rooted in human nature" will be erased in favor of a – problematic – "is." For this remark is equivalent to the thesis of radical evil. Even apart from the promptings of the state, human beings prefer the policy of deception to the principle of honesty. With this thesis the "Concluding Remark" comes to an end. Kant cites the conclusion of Jean André de Luc, who travels into remote mountains, speaks with their uncivilized inhabitants, and discovers, amid ample examples of benevolence, a "ruinous penchant for fine deceptiveness [*schlimmer Hang zur feinen Betrügerei*]." Without impugning the honesty of de Luc, whose geological and meteorological investigation are among the principal sources for his later lectures on "physical geography," Kant adds in conclusion:

> — a result of the investigation that everyone, without traveling into the mountains, could have encountered among his fellow citizens, indeed even closer, in his own breast [*seinem eignen Busen*].
>
> Königsberg   I. Kant
>
>   (8: 271)[29]

The *Berg* (mountain) in *Königsberg* bears more weight than usual. When it comes to the bad habit of being finely fraudulent, there is no difference between city- and mountain-dweller, civilization and natural simplicity. Such refinement is all-too-general, "*so, im allgemeinen.*"

Yet, the "Concluding Remark" ventures even further into the self-concealing mountains of the human heart. The penchant for deception may be so deeply rooted and so well refined that deceivers are, themselves, deceived about the nature of their deceptiveness, earnestly believing that they remain upright when, in truth, they are seized by this penchant — or vice versa. Entirely new territory thus discloses itself for "teachers of morality and religion," who can now speak of a new mode of lying that can be attributed to all those who insist that they know *for certain* the state of their conscience, including themselves. Saying one knows for certain what cannot under any recognizable condition be securely known — including, for example, matters of faith — is, as Kant emphasizes at the opening of the "Concluding Remark," equivalent to lying. If one of the things that cannot be known with certainty is, however, the state of one's conscience, then, the statement that one is honest *or* deceptive is itself dishonest. Whereas it is logically impossible to say, in all honesty, "I am dishonest," it is morally impossible to say, with good conscience, "I am honest." And this impossibility — which, too, cannot be expressed in all honesty — jeopardizes everything Kant affirms in the second part of "On the Failure," as he welcomes a "divine sovereign sentence" precisely because "power-holding practical reason" can be regarded as "the immediate explanation and voice of God" (8: 264). If practical reason cannot *immediately* explain its absolute commands, if it requires a medium for its mediation, then not only is the authenticity of authentic interpretation in jeopardy; the apodictic and categorical character of the imperative that it formulates is in trouble as well. Even worse, a door is opened for *faith in a mediator* between the voice of God and the practice of human beings. Once this door is opened, mystical ravings begin to obscure the work of the Enlightenment.

Little wonder, then, that Kant explicitly denies that anyone can be wrong about the state of his or her conscience. "Certainty" (*Gewißheit*) is as securely inscribed into "conscience" (*Gewissen*) as *Berg* in *Königsberg*, and even though he refrains from calling on the linguistic relation between certainty and conscience, Kant makes clear that there can be no such thing as an errant conscience. Infallibility is an essential feature of our awareness of the state of our conscience, as if it – rather than truth – were an *index sui*:

> Moralists speak of an "erring conscience." But an erring conscience is an absurdity [*ein irrendes Gewissen ist ein Unding*]; and if there were such a thing, then we could never be certain we have acted rightly, since even the judge in the last instance can still be in error. I can indeed err in the judgment in which I believe to be right, for this belongs to the understanding, which alone judges objectively (rightly or wrongly); but in the consciousness *whether I in fact believe myself to be right* (or merely pretend so) I absolutely cannot err, for this judgment, or rather this proposition, merely says I judge the object in this manner.
>
> (8: 268)

The uncharacteristic self-correction contained in the phrase "or rather this proposition" (*oder vielmehr dieser Satz*) attests to the threat of an infinite regress, whereby a judgment says "I judge . . . ," and the object of this judgment could again be another judgment "I judge . . . ," which, in turn, could have as its object still another judgment of this form, and so forth ad infinitum. In this way, the "Concluding Remark" turns into an addendum to the *Critique of Judgment*, which no longer searches for a principle proper to the merely reflective power of judgment but, in reverse, finds a form of judgment concerning the inner state of the self which is so absolutely certain that it no longer should be qualified *as* a judgment and acquires, instead, the public character of a proposition. But the self-correction is of limited value, for what, after all, distinguishes a proposition from a judgment other than the fact that the former expresses the latter? And by the time Kant nears the end of the "Concluding Remark" the difference between what moralists mean by "errant conscience" and what Kant says, is as minor as the difference between a judgment and a proposition:

> I am here restricting myself principally to the impurity that lies deep in what is concealed, where the human being knows how to falsify even inner assertions before his own conscience [*Ich halte mich hier hauptsächlich an der tief im Verborgnen liegenden Unlauterkeit, da der Mensch sogar die innern Aussagen vor seinem eignen Gewissen zu verfälschen weiß*]. The inclination to external deception should be all the less surprising; this, therefore, must be the reason that, although everyone is informed of the falseness of the coinage with which he trades, it can nevertheless always sustain itself in circulation.
>
> (8: 270)[30]

From the perspective of the *Anthropology from a Pragmatic Point of View*, which likewise discusses the validity of the counterfeit currency that circulates in every transaction among human beings, this remark commits "high treason against humanity," for it sides with the "sarcastic Swift," who says, "'Honesty [is] a *Pair of Shoes*, worn out in the Dirt'" (7: 153).[31] If human beings know how to falsify the assertions they make in the court of their conscience, then conscience may remain immune from error, but this immunity does no good, for its judgments can no longer be trusted. And the judgments rendered by conscience become dubious precisely because one cannot immediately say whether the assertions that one tells oneself in absolute secrecy are expressions of what one in fact believes or what one only says to oneself in order to keep one's conscience clear. The "immediate consciousness" (8: 267) of our own honesty or dishonesty, in other words, is fractured from the start.

This fracture is both the source of sadness and the starting point for allegorical expression. The melancholic character of the "sad remark!" derives from the thought that no one is to be trusted – not even the "one" that is oneself. The elation of this remark, marked by the eruption of an exclamation point in mid-sentence, responds to the possibility that it, too, cannot be trusted and may even mean the opposite: that its speaker is overjoyed. The awareness that one's remarks may mean something other than what they say, even when they are made in the privacy of an inner chamber, is the reason that communication can still take place despite the fact that utterances are generally falsified – or, to use Kant's words, despite the fact that the "coinage" of all intercourse is counterfeit. Everyone pretends that the coinage still carries the stamp of the sovereign authority, although everyone also knows that subjects who give themselves out as sovereigns have arbitrarily stipulated its value. The arbitrary stipulation "this means that" is the starting point for allegorical expression: anything can be said to mean something else; any word can signify something other than it says; and everything can therefore be invested with hidden meaning – for a moment. In contrast to sovereign sentences, which cannot fail to be authoritative, stipulations of meaning make sense only under the condition that the stamp of authority, which allows for no replacements, has been so severely compromised that authenticity cannot be properly distinguished from counterfeit. Hence the sadness: "Every person, everything, every relation can mean something else. This possibility sentences the profane world to an annihilating but just judgment: it is characterized as a world in which detail, in any rigorous sense, is of no importance."[32] A sovereign stipulation begins the second part of the essay and opens the door to the sole sovereign sentence that Kant endorses without qualification. Whatever "one" may say *theodicy* means, it ought to mean – such is the stipulation – "an interpretation of nature, insofar as God announces the intention of his will through it." So says the "I" that "finds" an allegorical expression of "authentic interpretation" and signs itself "I. Kant."

Immanuel

Never before has the *I* of *Immanuel* meant as much. As Kant was well aware, his name means "God [is] with us." By way of antonomasia, the Hebrew phrase came to be a particularly potent name. It serves as one of the principal names for the Messiah: "But that has all happened, so that it would be fulfilled what the Lord said through the prophet, who says (Is. 7: 14): 'See, a virgin will be pregnant and will give birth to a son, and they will give him the name Immanuel,' that means in translation: God with us" (Matthew 1: 22–23).[33] Whereas the *El* (God) of the *Immanuel* about whom the Gospel of Matthew speaks is supposed to save humanity as a whole from sin, the *Immanu* (with us) that takes shape in "On the Failure" acquires almost the exact opposite function: "we" save God from the insanity into which he would otherwise fall. For, if we are with him, he is never alone – not even when he gives meaning to the letter of his creation. From this awkward perspective, all of "On the Failure" – except for its signature line, carelessly omitted from the Akademie edition – assumes the character of a grand inside joke. God is saved as long as "Immanuel" is true, and a certain "I. Kant," in turn, verifies the truth of the proposition "Immanuel" by making himself into a proponent, exponent, and exemplar of uncompromising truthfulness. The first act of this self-transformation consists, moreover, in changing the spelling of his first name: born *Emanuel*, he calls himself *Immanuel*. The letter *I* in "I. Kant," in other words, is not a *datum* but a *factum*, not something given but something made. In the words of "On the Failure," the *I* is nothing less than the isolated "letter of his creation [*Buchstaben seiner Schöpfung*]" (8: 264). And Kant emphasizes its isolation from the rest of his name by consistently signing himself "I. Kant."

No one knows why Kant decided to change the spelling of his name. Perhaps Kant himself was unaware of the reason. He may have been under the impression that *Immanuel* more closely approximates ancient Hebrew; at the very least, it distinguishes him from Ashkanazi Jews, who generally, as he doubtless knew,[34] transcribe עמנואל by *Emanuel*. After all, as he writes in the *Critique of Judgment*, only "during its moral period" (5: 275), did the Jewish people, responding to their prohibition on graven images, feel the sublime affect of "enthusiasm" for their religion. By contrast, contemporary Jews are, almost without exception, inveterate liars: "the Palestinians living among us, because of their spirit of usury since exile, have acquired, as concerns the great majority, a not unfounded reputation for fraud [*Betrug*]" (7: 205). Both of these quotations are from works published late in his life, yet they very likely represent a long-standing conviction that the "Palestinians" of his day were, for the most part, liars and cheats, whereas the ancient Jews, notwithstanding the fact that "Judaism as such, taken in its purity, entails absolutely no religious faith" (6: 126),[35] once displayed a sublime grandeur. By changing the spelling of his "Christian name," Kant perhaps wished to associate himself with the sublime Jews of the past and keep his distance for the mendacious Palestinians of the present.

In any case, regardless of the reason for the alteration of the letter, which captures in miniature Kant's ambivalence toward the Jews-Palestinians, this much is certain: he was given the name *Emanuel*, apparently because the date of his birth (April 22) is associated with the like-named saint in the Old Prussian Calendar; and sometime between his entrance into the university in 1740, when he was listed as *Emanuel Kandt*, and the composition of his first work in 1746, *Gedanken von der wahren Schätzung der lebendigen Kräfte*, when he is called "Immanuel Kandt Stud [=iosus]," he changed the *E* into *I*.[36] Not everyone in Königsberg was aware of this change, however: an article in the *Wöchentliche-Königsberger Frag- und Anzeigungs- Nachrichten* from 1755 describes the public promotion of a certain "Candidato Philosophiae Herrn Emanuel Kant" to the position of "Master" (*Magister*) on the occasion of his dissertation *De igne*, after which the Dean of the Faculty, J. B. Hahn, gave a lecture concerning the honorific titles – "rabh, rabbi, and rabban" – that the ancient Jews conferred to students of the Law on the occasion of their academic promotions.[37] The report does not indicate how Master – which is to say, "rabbi" – Kant reacted to this address. *De igne* was in any case published under the name "Immanuel Kant" (1: 369). It is, therefore, entirely justified to say: *I* is Emanuel Kant's first literary achievement. However slight, it provides the schema of all his subsequent achievements: the *datum* is transformed into a self-fashioned *factum*. The success of this achievement is memorialized in the abbreviation by which he almost always identified himself: "I. Kant." And Kant enjoyed reliving this transformation. Just as the *I* can be considered his first literary creation, the spelling-out of his name for the commemoration of his birth may have been his last: "At his last birthday party (1803)," Johann Gottfried Hasse reports, "he waited anxiously for me, in the presence of his friends, to inscribe into the little collection of remarks he maintained the word spelled out and syllabified (*Im*, 'with,' *Immanu*, 'with us,' *El*, 'God'; thus *Immanuel*, 'God is with us'), so that the remarkable events of the day could be recorded."[38]

"De nobis ipsis silemus" (B: ii), according to the motto Kant added for the second edition of the first *Critique*: "of ourselves we are silent." When, finally, I. Kant refers to himself as "I" in his first post-critical work, he ironically expresses the fracture of his "Christian name" in terms of allegory: "Now I find such an authentic interpretation allegorically expressed in an ancient holy book" (8: 264). Who, however, can believe this statement? Kant clearly invests a book of the Hebrew Bible with allegorical significance by stipulating that it expresses distinctions that he himself had discovered for the first time. Only two letters separate "finding" (*finden*) from "inventing" (*erfinden*) – two letters, however, that mark the difference between an act in which the self is primarily passive from one in which it is fully in charge. Allegorists are adept in doing precisely what Kant does here:

inventing meanings they pretend to find. The better the allegorist, the more successful the pretence – to the point where the allegorist no longer believes that it is pretence but insists, on the contrary, that the allegorical expression is a remarkable find. The most successful allegorists are convinced that they merely come across the meanings that they have arbitrarily imposed on the objects of their contemplation. If Kant means exactly what he says when he claims that he merely finds "authentic interpretation" allegorically expressed in "an ancient holy book," he is doubtless misleading himself and thereby confirming the sad condition that "teachers of morality and religion" have only recently discovered; but in the same stroke he confirms the status of a certain "I. Kant" as among the most successful allegorists of his enlightening age.

4

OUT OF THE BLUE

"On the Radical Evil in Human Nature"

Secrecy

"I am here restricting myself principally to the impurity that lies deep in what is concealed, where the human being knows how to falsify even inner assertions before his own conscience" (8: 270). This self-restriction, which is taken from the "Concluding Remark" of "On the Failure of All Philosophical Attempts at Theodicy," also applies to the next essay Kant publishes in the *Berlinische Monatsschrift*, "On the Radical Evil in Human Nature" (1792).[1] And the self-restriction applies equally well to the book into which the second essay was integrated as a result of Kant's conflict with the Prussian censor: *Religion Within the Limits of Bare Reason* (1793).[2] By restricting himself to "bare reason" (*bloße Vernunft*), he not only cuts himself off from those "parerga" (6: 53–54) – miracles and mysteries – in which religion is traditionally wrapped; he commits himself to the "experiment" (6: 12) of stripping bare (*entblößen*) the only rational animal of which we are familiar. By exposing the root of human nature, he runs the risk of exposing himself: laying bare what he has hidden, even from himself. The perils of self-exposure are greatly heightened, of course, by the ominous threat of the Leviathan called "Prussia," which, after the death of the Friedrich II, gives its subjects even more incentives to conceal themselves; but even in the absence of this monster, the exposure of what lies hidden in human beings is a dangerous enterprise. In a letter to a friend, Kant emphasizes that *Religion* makes no attempt to conceal anything: "I have proceeded conscientiously and with genuine respect for the Christian religion but also with appropriate candor, concealing nothing but rather presenting openly the way in which I believe that a possible union of Christianity with the purest practical reason is possible" (11: 429).

That the four essays of *Religion* conceal nothing does not mean, however, that they – and especially the first, to which each of the other three respond – is not everywhere concerned with secrecy. On the contrary, a certain secrecy is inseparable from the conception of morality that Kant first began to develop in *Laying the Ground for the Metaphysics of Morals* (1785) and elaborated

75

further in the *Critique of Practical Reason* (1788). Human beings, according to Kant's formulation of what everyone ought to know in any case, immediately know how they should act: all actions should be undertaken out of respect for the law, which commands absolutely, without respect for persons, with no allowances for exceptional individuals or circumstances. What human beings cannot know, however, is the ground of the freedom by virtue of which they can honestly demand of themselves that they act on the basis of freedom, for this ground is "noumenal" and, as such, available only to a mode of intuition radically different from our own. And the consequences of this non-knowledge – which the critical enterprise as a whole endorses and which, as Kant famously writes in the Preface to the second edition of the first *Critique*, opens room for "faith" (B: xxx) – are considerable: no one can know whether or not an action is freely undertaken; no one can know whether or not an action is done out of duty or in view of certain consequences; and no one can therefore know whether or not the actions that one takes are indeed one's own *facta* – and not merely the result of a complex series of data. Making a moral judgment about anyone in particular, even about oneself, is sheer pretension. Judgments of individuals must be left either to the authorized judges of a particular legal order, who are in any case concerned solely with the legality of actions, or the God whom pure practical reason postulates for the sake of strengthening its self-consistency.

Restraining from moral judgment is therefore, a requirement of moral reflection. And despite its title, Kant exhibits this restraint in "On the Radical Evil in Human Nature." The essay does not presume to make distinction among human beings, judging this one good and that one bad; instead, the human being as a species is the object of its moral judgment, and the subsequent essays that make up *Religion* are simply concerned with the means by which the species can, without assistance from non-rational sources, make itself more pleasing to the God whose existence the personality of its members postulates. By making the species into the object of moral judgment, Kant turns "On the Radical Evil in Human Nature" into a counterpart to the "authentic theodicy" (8: 264) that he proposes in his previous essay: instead of interpreting nature from the perspective of its creator, so that all charges against the latter can be summarily dismissed, the essay interprets human nature from the perspective of its only "authentic" creator, namely the human being "itself," so that charges against the species can be, as it were, properly filed for each individual's evaluation. And this self-interpretation, as the untitled opening section vigorously argues, must be done a priori – but not entirely. The argument of the opening section is not only rigoristic, rejecting out of hand the possibility that a mixed moral judgment can be made, and it is not only dense, which is hardly surprising, since it unexpectedly introduces an entirely new term into Kant's moral terminology, namely *Willkür* (that dimension of the will in which something is chosen over something else); the argument is also uncharacteristically non-committal about its results. Experience, as the last sentence of this section notes, may still be of some value in making a moral judgment of the species, and it may – against everything previously argued – make a mixed verdict unavoidable:

> Because we cannot derive this disposition, or rather its highest ground, from some first time-act of the ability to choose [*ersten Zeit-Actus der Willkür*], we call it a characteristic of the ability to choose that belongs to it by nature (although the disposition is in fact grounded in freedom). However, that by the human being of whom we say that he is good or evil by nature we do not mean individuals (for otherwise one human being could be assumed to be good and another evil, by nature) but are authorized only to understand the whole species: this can only be demonstrated later on, if it happens that anthropological research [*anthropologischen Nachforschung*] shows that the grounds that justify us in attributing one of these two characters to a human being as innate are so constituted that there is no ground for exempting anyone from it and that the character is therefore valid for the species.
>
> (6: 25–26)

Anthropological research, in other words, may yet have the last word. A genuinely naïve group of human beings – or only a sole naïf, who would be as isolated as Job – may suddenly show up, in some distant part of the earth at some distant time, perhaps after another "natural revolution" (5: 419) about which the *Critique of Teleological Judgment* momentarily speaks. And everything said by philosophers who base themselves solely on a priori arguments would be rendered wrong. Precisely how and when anthropologists might come across such people Kant does not say; even more enigmatic would be the procedures for adjudicating their findings. Regardless of the difficulties to which it thereby falls prey, "On the Radical Evil in Human Nature" proposes anthropological research as a final court of appeal. Despite this higher court, the verdict at which the essay arrives must still be entirely certain; otherwise, its procedures for adjudication cannot be considered a priori. The peculiarity of this combination of preliminariness and certainty makes "On the Radical Evil in Human Nature" difficult to read, as though it were something of a compromise: Kant wants to proceed with the same degree of certainty as he had in the *Critiques*, and yet he also wants to preserve certain reservations, which would dangerously approach the practice of *reservatio mentalis* that he elsewhere condemns as "Jesuitical casuistry" (8: 344).

And there is good reason, as Kant himself indicates, for keeping the whole essay under wraps and making the thesis that it proposes – that human beings are evil by nature – a matter of secrecy. For the opposite thesis has the virtue of helping human beings become as good as it says they already are. Kant even speaks of the "heroic opinion [*heroische Meinung*]" (6: 19) that culminates in the revolutionary thought of Rousseau: despite all the evidence to the contrary, the counter-thesis proposes that human beings are good by nature and have lately been corrupted by, among other things, the great Leviathan, which encourages people to become cowards, conceal themselves, and so protect their lives at the expense of their souls. The moral heroes who proclaim such a thesis cannot fail to provoke the wrath of the state, for its guardians, as Kant repeatedly emphasizes, maintain that the people on the whole are no good, that they cannot be trusted either to think or act for themselves, and that they therefore need a strong master – in short, that they are evil at the root. The state can then justify itself in every circumstance by saying, in effect, that it serves the function of preventing natural evil from getting out of hand. By saying that human beings cannot change for the better, "political moralists" (8: 372), who are the trustees of the state, make human beings incapable of change.³ By saying the opposite and thus opposing the justification for the static character of the state, moral heroes set out to do the opposite: "it is presumably merely a well-meaning [*gutmütige*] presupposition of moralists from Seneca to Rousseau, adopted in order to press forward the indefatigable building-up [*unverdrossenen Anbau*] of that seed of goodness which perhaps lies in us, if one could only count on a natural ground for that [building-up] in the human being" (6: 20).

But this cannot be done. Such is Kant's thesis: one cannot "count on a natural ground" for the development of the dispositions toward the good in human beings. The question then arises: is Kant's thesis cowardly, with the proviso that anthropological research can dismiss his verdict one of these days – a proviso, however, that tends to make Kant look even more diffident, as if he were unable to formulate a thesis to which he can wholeheartedly commit himself? Instead of building up the seed, he lays bare its layers, and the reason for undertaking this process of dissection must lie in his *own* uprightness: he cannot honestly assume that the ground is secure enough for the cultivation of the seed of goodness. Experience weighs too heavily against this assumption. Uprightness is not heroic, and heroism is not upright: the parting of the ways of these two virtues expresses itself as the combination of certainty and preliminariness. The famous motto of enlightenment – "*Sapere aude!*" (8: 35) – means in this case: have the courage to propose a cowardly thesis.

Proof by virtue of its absence

The process of dissecting the seed of goodness into its component parts had been prepared by the three *Critiques*, and it results in the exhibition of three elements of goodness – or, more exactly, three elements of the "original predisposition toward goodness in human nature" (6: 26): the predisposition toward animality, humanity, and personality. Each of these "elements of the determination [*Bestimmung*] of the human being" (6:26) is good in itself; judgment concerns only the "form" in which each of these three elements are "combined" (6: 28). Whenever human beings subordinate the third element to either of the first two, they are evil, and the species as a whole is radically evil insofar as it makes this insubordination into the first and ultimate "maxim" under which it undertakes all of its acts and omissions. Insubordination, however, is limited, and this limitation means that human beings are only radically evil – not altogether evil, corrupt root and branch. For the superiority of personality over the other two elements is always recognized, even as these other elements – especially the second, the predisposition toward humanity, which calculates the ratios of happiness and misery – take precedence. What human beings cannot do, according to Kant, is make opposition to personality into a motive for action. In this case, the evil would not be radical but, rather, diabolical: "a *malevolent reason* [boshafte Vernunft], so to speak (an absolutely evil will), which exonerates [*freisprechende*] reason from the moral law, contains too much [ground for the imputation of moral evil], for opposition to the law would itself be thereby elevated to an incentive (for without an incentive the ability to choose cannot be determined), and so the subject would be made into a *devilish* being" (6: 35). Evil actions, in other words, always have ulterior motives: the promotion of happiness or the avoidance of misery. And since these ulterior motives are the first principles for the choice of an act or omission, human beings are corrupted at the root, regardless of how upstanding they may appear in the light of day.

With this thesis Kant prepares the way for the construction of an "invisible church" (6: 101) that will encourage the transformation of the form in which the elements of the predisposition to good are combined. The development of this "invisible church" is the occupation of the subsequent three essays that make up *Religion*. Before proceeding in this direction, however, Kant must secure the thesis, which he reiterates – and supports with a classical citation – in the title of the third subsection: "The Human Being is By Nature Evil, *vitiis nemo sine nascitur*, Horace" (6: 33). Not only must he secure it against the "heroic opinion" of Rousseau; he must also make sure that the species is only radically and not diabolically evil. And in this effort, his opponent is, so to speak, himself. For what else can the following quotation from the "Concluding Remark" of "On the Failure of All Philosophical Attempts at Theodicy" mean? Any evil done for its own sake, regardless of whether it produces any harm, is diabolical. Devils do not simply lie for the fun of it – which would at least give it a motive, namely the pleasure in dissembling themselves – but for the hell of it: that is, for no discernable reason, without an expectation that it will even yield pleasure. Such is the case with human beings, as every "contemplative misanthrope" discovers:

Only a contemplative misanthrope (who wishes evil to no one, but
is inclined to believe every evil) can be doubtful whether he should
find human beings *worthy of hate* or, rather, of *contempt*. The proper-
ties for which he would judge them qualified for the first finding
are those through which they intentionally inflict harm. That property, however, which seems to him to expose him to the second
judgment, can be none other than a penchant that is *in itself evil*,
even if it harms no one: a penchant for something that cannot be
used as a means for any purpose; something that is objectively good
for nothing. The first evil would be none other than the evil of
hostility (or, to put it mildly, of lack of love); the second can be none
other than *mendacity* (falsity, even without any intention to harm).

(8: 270)[4]

The thesis of radical evil retreats from the radicality of the misanthropy
that finds expression in the "Concluding Remark" of the previous essay.
But it does so only insofar as the thesis is *stated* – not insofar as it is proved,
if it can be properly proved at all. From two legitimate perspectives, then,
Kant's thesis can be challenged: from the perspective of moral heroism, which
opposes the guardians of the state, and from the perspective of contemplative misanthropy, which means no harm but cannot honestly exonerate
human beings from the charge that they regularly commit evil deeds without
any expectation of gain or fear of loss. The first perspective has a chance of
making human beings better, yet it is not sufficiently honest; the second
perspective, by contrast, may be honest, but it guarantees that human beings
will not improve. Between these two perspectives stands the thesis Kant
proposes, which has neither of their advantages and both of their disadvantages: it is not heroic, and it may not be altogether honest. The only reason
to adopt this thesis, in other words, is because it is *true* and can be *demonstrated* as such. No fact is adequate to this demonstration, however – not
even the "fact of reason" (5: 47),[5] since the latter is just another name for
personality. In a lengthy footnote to the section of the chapter on radical
evil entitled "The Human Being is Evil by Nature" Kant asserts that "the
proper proof [*der eigentliche Beweis*] of this sentence of condemnation
[*Verdammungsurteil*] by reason as it sits in moral judgment is to be found in
the preceding section rather than in this one, which contains only the con-
firmation of it by experience" (6: 39).[6] Yet, if readers take the time to reread
the preceding section, they will soon be disappointed: Kant claims that he
developed "the proper proof" when he has done no such thing. And this is
hardly surprising, since, as the same footnote proceeds to explain, nothing
in experience can "uncover" (*aufdecken*) the "intelligible act" that precedes all
experience. In the section to which his note refers Kant distinguishes three
modes of evil toward which human nature is prone, each of which corresponds to one of the dispositions, but nowhere in this analytic exercise does

he demonstrate the penchant itself: like the moral law, to borrow a striking image Kant deploys in his *Laying the Ground for the Metaphysics of Morals*, this *Hang*, as an "innate" penchant, hangs in the air without any means of support (4: 425–26). So, too, does the thesis of radical evil: it is as much a sheer thesis, a naked positing, as the altogether anterior, intelligible *Aktus* on which all subsequent ones depend. Kant may define the penchant for evil by means of certain critical distinctions, but he cannot justify the application of this term to anything in nature – or in human nature:

> The penchant toward evil is an act in the first sense (*peccatum originarium*), and at the same time the formal ground of all unlawful conduct in the second sense, which, considered materially, violates the law and is termed vice (*peccatum deriviatum*); and the first indebtedness remains, even though the second (from incentives that do not subsist in the law itself) may be repeatedly avoided. The former is an intelligible action, cognizable merely through reason, without any temporal condition [*bloß durch Vernunft ohne alle Zeitbedingung erkennbar*]; the latter is sensible action, empirical, given in time (*factum phaenomenon*).
>
> (6: 31)

Each of these sentences – and in particular the Latin phrases with which they are punctuated – deserves special attention; but it is immediately apparent that Kant does not demonstrate anything, least of all the thesis of radical evil, for in this passage he grants to the faculty of reason precisely that function from which, according to the *Critique of Pure Reason*, it is positively excluded, namely cognition. And according to the first *Critique* – but this amounts to the same – cognition cannot take place "without temporal conditions." The phrase *bloß durch Vernunft* (merely through reason) echoes the modest words of the title, *Religion innerhalb der Grenzen der bloßen Vernunft*, but it gestures in the very opposite direction: toward a mind that could cognize intelligible acts for the precise reason that it is able to recognize those "things" – or noumena – that are created in the act of intuiting them. Such a rational capacity would be in all senses *bloß*: it would be "mere" reason because it would not need the categorial accouterment of the understanding, and it would be an infinite rational capacity before which every finite being would stand naked. Kant would transcend the limits of mere reason were he to claim the capacity to know something *bloß durch Vernunft* – and he *must* do so: he *must* overstep these limits if he intends to make good on his promise and deliver a "proper proof" of the thesis of radical evil on the basis of which a purely rational religion is to be established. Without so much as saying so – and this silence, or this secrecy, is at the heart of this post-critical undertaking – Kant improperly "proves" the thesis of radical evil. He does not merely refer to an absent proof that he nowhere provides;

nor can it simply be said that Kant reveals the secret by concealing it. Nor can it simply be said that he is mendacious, although some notable readers of *Religion* have not refrained from this "sentence of condemnation by reason as it sits in moral judgment."[7] By declaring that the "proof proper" has been demonstrated in the previous section without having conducted anything but "improper" methods of proofs, Kant reveals the secret in secret, and thus does not properly reveal it but does not properly conceal it either.

The thesis of radical evil proves *itself* by virtue of the absence of any "proper proof" for its positing. Impropriety is another name for insubordination: human reason does not adopt the proper maxim for its actions, the one maxim that can be maximized to such an extent that it constitutes a universal law of action, yet only a maxim of this kind allows one to be properly oneself in practice. It is, of course, inappropriate to associate impropriety of proof with impropriety in practice, since the former is an entirely theoretical matter, whereas the latter concerns the principles of practical reason; but if the impropriety in proof touches on the foundation of practical reason, this objection is of little consequence. Only improper proofs of the thesis of primordial insubordination present themselves, and in the essay on radical evil these proofs traverse the distinction between theory and practice – so much so that this essay can justify the universalization of a maxim according to which the evil of the other is presupposed. That human beings are evil by nature, Kant writes, "means . . . that from what one knows of the human being through experience he cannot judge otherwise of him, or, that one can presuppose evil to be subjectively necessary in every human being, even the best" (6: 32). This "or" is far from being an innocent expansion: if one can presuppose evil in every human being, then one is justified in mistrusting everyone – even the best, even "I. Kant," who "spares" himself the trouble of a "formal proof" (6: 33) of the thesis, as he expends himself on a series of material ones.

The first of these improper proofs concerns the "state of nature." Kant disposes of those who "hope" to find natural goodness in this supposedly pristine state by referring them to various accounts of the "cruelties" distant, non-European peoples perpetuate upon one another. That Kant – without the slightest hesitation – trusts the books in which he found these accounts ought to be surprising, however, since mistrust is the first among the "litany of complaints" that alters the mood of those who are "disposed" (*gestimmt*) to grant a degree of firmly rooted goodness to those, like Kant and his travel writers, who are supposed to inhabit an "ethical condition" (*gesitteter Zustand*). Sanguine trust gives way to melancholic distrust whenever one reflects on "secret falsity even in the most intimate friendships, so that a moderation of trust in mutual disclosure even among the best friends is reckoned a universal maxim of prudence in intercourse [*Umgang*]" (6: 33). Everyone must presuppose so much bad will on the part of everyone else, that universal mistrust is the only reasonable maxim for social intercourse – even if this maxim cannot be universalized without contradicting itself and is, therefore, not only irrational but for the same reason evil as well. No wonder, as one of his friends remarks, Kant "adopted" the saying attributed to Aristotle: "My friends, there is no such thing as a friend."[8] The inconsistency of this saying accords with the self-contradiction into which the maxim of distrust issues upon its universalization. If the thesis of radical evil were only "subjectively necessary" to presuppose in practice and had no objective basis in the structure of human nature, it would be nothing more than an expression of the uncontested reign of the principle of prudence and would in this way confirm *itself*: it would be unimpeachable evidence of the evil about which this thesis speaks. And it would be evil in a quite precise sense, for the supposed "principle" of distrust could not be universalized without undermining the very communicative act in which it was expressed and thus could not be communicated – even articulated to oneself – without destroying the possibility of communication.

The blues

In the absence of proof that "human beings are evil by nature" (6: 32), Kant must assume that his readers will simply trust the author of the *Critiques* when he unexpectedly proposes this dismal thesis. But the very thesis with which he entrusts his readers is reason for universal distrust, including – or especially – distrust of anyone who makes universal mistrust appear reasonable. And, as Kant then proceeds to clarify the conditions under which he continues the meditations begun in the essay on radical evil, he makes apparent that there are good reasons to distrust him, even if the precise motives for his "secret falsity" toward his readership remain hidden. In the Preface to the second edition of *Religion*, dated 26 January 1794, Kant asserts that:

> to understand this book according to its essential content, only common morality is needed, without entering into the *Critique of Practical Reason*, still less with the theoretical *Critique*. When, for example, virtue as skill in *actions* conforming to duties (according to their legality) is called *virtus phaenomenon*, and the same virtue as enduring *disposition* towards such actions *from duty* (because of their morality) is called *virtus noumenon*, these expressions are used only because of the schools; the matter itself [*die Sache selbst*] is contained, though in other words, in the most popular children's instruction and sermons, and is easily understood.
>
> (6: 14)

Less than a year later, by contrast, Kant responds to a letter of stern reproof from Friedrich Wilhelm II in a different manner altogether: "I have," Kant reassures the king in the letter that he publishes after the latter's death in the Preface to *The Conflict of the Faculties* (1798), "done no harm to the public *religion of the country*." This last phrase is reason enough for distrust, for, as the *Religion* makes clear, religion – unlike "creeds" – cannot be localized. And Kant then proceeds to say: "this is already clear from the fact that the book in question [*Religion*] is not at all appropriate for the public: to them it is an incomprehensible and closed book" (7: 8).

The dedication of *Religion* could therefore read: "a book for everyone and no one." And if it is not quite this book, if it does not quite reach the aporia of address that marks Nietzsche's *Also sprach Zarathustra*, which is another great experiment in philosophical theology, its insufficiency in this regard cannot be explained away as a mere consequence of Kant's desire to assure certain members of his readership – "scholars of the faculty" (7: 8) – that his book was indeed meant for them. Nor can Kant's contradictory statements concerning the intelligibility of his book simply be ascribed to some private failure on his part to measure up to the principle of honesty that he passionately promotes. Nor can Kant's inconsistent accounts of his intended readership simply be attributed to the systematic dishonesty that prevails, according to Schopenhauer and Nietzsche, whenever philosophers, having turned into "scholars of the faculty," are at the disposal of the state.[9] When Kant writes at one time that the concepts in *Religion* are "easily understood" and soon thereafter declares that the book as a whole is "incomprehensible," he may be operating on the basis of a prudential maxim adopted in order to avoid royal displeasure; but this account of his motives – whether psychological or institutional – does not concede the possibility that his book may be "closed" from its inception: impossible to read, even for "scholars of the faculty." The act of understanding the thesis of radical evil, the act of opening up and comprehending this "incomprehensible and closed" book, demands that the "subjective necessity of evil" be recognized in absence of a proper proof of its objective foundation – and be recognized in terms of a "secret falsity" traversing all intercourse, including the discourse "before one's very eyes [*vor Augen*]" (6: 33). "On the Radical Evil in Human Nature" is placed before the eyes of its readers in a much more literal sense than "cruelties" of distant peoples about which Kant writes when he uses this well-worn expression, for these "cruelties" are accessible to the Königsberg-bound "scholar of the faculty" only through the medium of the travel-books. Distrusting "On the Radical Evil in Human Nature," in sum, is the condition of trusting its thesis – and vice versa.

Both trust and distrust presuppose a self that can trust itself when it assures itself that it is one. "On the Radical Evil in Human Nature" gives reason, however, to suspect that this presupposition is untrustworthy. In this sense, the essay is equal to its predecessor. Whereas the essay on the failure of philosophical attempts at theodicy speaks of the hidden sanctum "where the human being knows how to falsify even inner assertions before his own conscience" (8: 270), the essay on radical evil turns its attention to the experience of this falsification, namely good conscience. And whereas the former essay makes clear that only the conscientious are hounded by their own conscience, the latter indicates that those who enjoy peace of conscience are not innocent but, on the contrary, precisely the ones who falsify their inner assertions – who tell themselves, in the words of the *Doctrine of Virtue*, an "inner lie" (6: 430). Concealing from itself the source of its selfhood in the secret of freedom, the "I" hides from itself its responsibility for the actions it undertakes, and this hiding is itself an action for which it is responsible and from which it hides itself. Hiding this latter action from oneself does not mean that the self consists in the act of hiding from itself, although this conclusion has been independently reached and has given rise to various analyses of psychic "depth." Hiding from oneself the act of hiding from oneself leaves no room for the distinction between the hidden and the revealed, which is to say, no room for *anything* that can properly appear or properly remain clear of appearances. Kant has a name for the "subjective condition" in which all these critical distinctions evaporate: *Verstimmung*, "being out of tune," "distempered," "disposed." Having separated out and shown the "form of combination" of the three "elements of the determina-tion of the human being [*Bestimmung des Menschen*]" (6: 26), under the pressure of his own thesis Kant allows himself to be drawn toward a *Verstimmung* in which the *Bestimmung*, as "vocation," is revoked, and the *Bestimmung*, as "determination," is rendered indeterminate.[10]

Hiding the secret in which every action takes place means concealing from oneself the "fact" that every action is free and ought therefore to find its sole incentive in the law of freedom. Hiding the secret thus means concealing from oneself the difference between *virtus phaenomenon* and *virtus noumenon*, legality and morality, positive laws and the law that the "authentic self" (4: 457) posits. The Latin terms may be comprehensible only to "scholars of the faculty," but the concepts to which they refer are nevertheless "easily comprehensible," even to children. So says Kant. If, however, the distinction between *virtus phaenomenon* and *virtus noumenon* were to disappear in an act of supreme concealment, all subsequent actions would become "devilish." But the term *devilish* does not properly describe the disposition of those who have concealed from themselves the distinction between laws and the law, for the devil, as the "personification" of the evil principle, operates according to an underlying maxim in which opposition to the law – rather than any prospect of happiness – is a sufficient motive for action. By opposing the law for the sake of opposition, the devil recognizes it and thereby reveals, perhaps better than anyone else, the very distinction between *virtus phaenomenon* and *virtus noumenon*. Quite the contrary with those who enjoy "peace of conscience" (*Gewissensruhe*). Not to be troubled by the thesis that one's actions are rooted in evil is an act of evil in full bloom:

The *innate* guilt (*reatus*) [is] in the third [stage] . . . deliberate guilt (*dolus*), and is characterized by a certain *perfidy* [Tücke] of the human heart (*dolus malus*) in deceiving itself with respect to its own good or evil state of mind [*Gesinnung*] and, provided that its actions do not result in evil, which they could well do because of their maxims, in not troubling itself about its state of mind, but rather considering itself justified before the law [*vor dem Gesetze*]. From this originates the peace of conscience of so many human beings (conscientious in their own opinion) when, in the midst of undertaking actions in which the law was not consulted or at least did not count the most, they only escape evil consequences by luck, and even imagine themselves deserving, feeling themselves guilty of no such offenses as they see attached to others. . . . This dishonesty, through which one blows blue vapor in one's own face [*Diese Unredlichkeit, sich selbst blauen Dunst vorzumachen*] and which thwarts the grounding of an authentic moral state of mind in ourselves, then also extends itself outwardly to falsity and deception of others, which, if this is not to be termed malevolence [*Bosheit*], it is at least to be called worthlessness [*Nichtswürdigkeit*] and it lies in the radical evil of human nature, which (inasmuch as it puts out of tune [*verstimmt*] the moral capacity to judge [*moralische Urteilskraft*] in what regard one is to hold a human being [*man einen Menschen halten solle*] and makes accounting entirely uncertain, both internally and externally [*die Zurechnung innerlich und äußerlich ganz ungewiß*] constitutes the foul spot [*den faulen Fleck*] of our species, which, so long as we do not bring it out [*herausbringen*], hinders the germ of good from developing as it otherwise would.

(6: 38)

Since "peace of conscience" gives rise to the "hallucination of merit," it is not entirely at rest; on the contrary, it produces a strange element: "blue vapor" (*blauer Dunst*).[11] The origin of the expression "*sich selbst blauen Dunst vorzumachen*" (blows blue vapor in one's own face, hoodwink oneself, fool oneself) is appropriately obscure: alchemy, magicians' tricks, and tobacco are all possible sources. Many years earlier, while inquiring into the disastrous effects of the Lisbon earthquake of 1755, Kant had worried that "combustible and volatile vapor" might lower the temperature of the earth and thus produce a terrestrial "catastrophe" (1: 454). The "blue vapor" that makes its way into "On the Radical Evil in Human Nature" is even more volatile – and correspondingly more dangerous. Not only does it obscure the distinction between legality and morality; it likewise casts a shadow on the distinctions by which Kant seeks to capture the specificity of the human species. Only a few paragraphs earlier he had expressly denied that "malevolent reason (an absolutely evil will)" (6: 35) could be ascribed to human

86

reason and had, therefore, exonerated the species of the charge that they exonerate themselves from the moral law altogether. But the volatile blueness of the vapor in which the critical distinction between *virtus phaenomenon* and *virtus noumenon* evaporates sends *Bösartigkeit* in the direction of *Bosheit* and radical evil into the abyss of absolute evil – but *only* sends: *Bösartigkeit* never reach these nefarious destinations, because, in order for them to do so, *virtus noumenon* would have to be recognized as such and made into something like a counter-element to which all the elements of the "disposition to the good" would be henceforth subordinated and in which they would be, in combination, destroyed. The haze in which all moral judgment becomes clouded by clear conscience allows for no such recognition. According to one of the doctrines that emerges from Kant's reassessment of subjective powers and principles he undertakes in the course of his *Critique of Judgment*, every judgment presupposes an appropriate *Stimmung* (mood), and the very ability to judge, *Urteilskraft*, consists in a prior "attunement" or "harmonization" of the relevant mental faculties.[12] Nowhere in his discussion of the "pure practical power of judgment" (5: 68) in the *Critique of Practical Reason* does Kant entertain the possibility of a *Verstimmung* that would disable the moral power of judgment altogether. Whereas the power of judgment allows pure practical reason to establish a "typic" of nature in which duty appoints everything its place, the disabling of this power in *Verstimmung* allows judge and judged alike to slip away into a vaporous medium. If, therefore, moral judgment – which consists in the ability to separate out the moral from the non-moral, the law from mere legality, *virtus noumenon* from *virtus phaenomenon* – does not rest on, and emerge from, a proper *Stimmung*; if it is *verstimmt* from the start, then the power of judgment on which the very inquiry Kant pursues – "is the human being evil from the outset?" – is permanently distempered.

"Peace of conscience" and conscientiousness are mutually exclusive. Not only does Kant indicate that he is untrustworthy when he supposedly proves that human beings are radically evil and cannot therefore be trusted; he makes the confession of untrustworthiness mandatory for all those who want to exonerate themselves of the accusation that they are untrustworthy. The denial of the thesis that Kant supposedly proves – the proposition, namely, that one must presuppose everyone, including oneself, to be fundamentally insubordinate – amounts to the counter-thesis that at least one human being deserves to enjoy a placid conscience. And who better to exempt from the thesis of radical evil than oneself, for the placidity of one's own conscience could serve as incorrigible proof of the counter-thesis? All projections of placidity onto others, by contrast, would remain precisely that: mere projections, indemonstrable conjectures. And any demonstration based on such a projection or conjecture would remain an informal, improper, or – in the most precise sense of the term *uneigentlich* – proof. As Kant vigorously argues in the opening section of *Religion*, moreover, in matters of morality, *tertium non datur*: there is no "third" alternative between or beyond the determination that the human being is either good or evil.[13] The very demands of proof, therefore, cast anyone who disagrees with Kant – or, to translate a standard German expression into colloquial English, anyone who is "not in tune" (*stimmt nicht*) with him – into the diffuse atmosphere of "out-of-tuneness" (*Verstimmung*) that is itself proof of the thesis. Denying the thesis of radical evil, in short, proves it *e contrario*. This proof cannot quite work, however, since the only *proper* evidence that the counter-thesis can claim – a calm conscience – distempers "the power of moral judgment" to such an extent that it allows a human subject to slip away from the sentences pronounced by its own conscience.

As if to indicate this out-of-tuneness *properly*, as if to make the *Verstimmung* reverberate in his *own* vicinity, Kant adds an apparently redundant footnote only a few sentences after he parenthetically mentions the possibility of "the moral power of judgment" being "put out of tune": "the proper proof of this condemning judgment [*Verdammungsurteil*] of reason as it passes moral sentences is to be found in the preceding section rather than in this one." And he thus *lies* – or lies to himself. Or hides. Or hides from himself the absence of any "formal," "proper," "literal," or "authentic" proof of the judgment that separates out the human species, condemns it, and damns it, not to hell, but to hope. And in place of proper proof, Kant identifies "a foul spot" (*ein fauler Fleck*),[14] which distinguishes the human species from other possible specifications of the human genus. Only this "foul spot," whose devilish provenance is undeniable, remains intact after all critical distinctions have evaporated into thin air – or "blue vapor."

If the distinction between *virtus noumenon* and *virtus phaenomenon* disappears, so, too, do the distinctions on which all talk of "accounting" and "accountability" (*Zurechnungsfähigkeit*) depend. Whatever else "blue vapor" may do, it wipes the slate clean: it amounts to a feigned naïveté. The atmosphere in which the "blue vapor" appears is, however, precisely the opposite of the one that fosters the naïf. Whereas the latter knows nothing of accounts and accounting, the former announces itself during those periods and in those places where the techniques of accounting have risen to such a high degree of prominence that the only viable distinctions are those of price:

A member of the English Parliament exclaimed in the heat of debate: "Everyone has his price, for which he sells himself." If this is true (which everyone can decide for himself), if nowhere is there virtue for which a level of temptation cannot be found that is capable of undermining it, if whether the good or evil spirit wins us over only depends on which offers the most and affords the promptest pay-off, then what the apostle says may well [*möchte wohl*] be universally true of the human being: "There is no distinction here, they are all

under sin – there is none who does good (according to the spirit of
the law), not even one."

(6: 38–39)

"*May well* be universally true": this startling declaration, which follows on
the equally surprising announcement that "everyone can decide for himself,"
makes the thesis that Kant is in the process of proving, uncertain. And this
happens at the very moment when "blue vapor" renders all accounts uncertain. If an account is uncertain, however, it is not an account in the proper
sense of the term. Few passages in Kant's corpus are as unexpected as this
note of hesitation: at the point where he is prepared to conclude the argument for his thesis, he wavers, placing the entire passage in the conditional,
and asking his readers to decide for themselves, as though the essay were a
waste of time, perhaps even a postponement of the solemn decision that each
subject of the moral law must make for itself. For all its rhetoric of proof,
in other words, the essay has only demonstrated that one can be "entirely
uncertain [*ganz ungewiß*]" (6: 38) about the state of one's "conscience"
(*Gewissen*) – which is equivalent to saying: one can clear away the appeal of
conscience by cheerfully coloring oneself blue.

"A multicolored, diverse self"

Accountability and conscience are two dimensions of personality. The self
evades accountability by making all accounts of itself uncertain – and thus
clears its conscience. Only those who act out of respect for the law deserve
a clear conscience, however; those who follow the law to the letter, by
contrast, seek to keep their conscience at rest by making it unclear – even
to themselves – whether or not they act out of respect for the law. The ability
to count oneself as one is at the root of all counting, accounting, and accountability. The self that obscures itself in its own self-produced "blue vapor"
can no longer be counted – or count itself – as one. Which is to say: the self
is no longer a self, properly speaking. It is no longer aware of the "authentic
self" (4: 457). From the perspective of practical reason, such a self falls short
of "personality" and approaches the limit of evil, even though it always acts
in accordance with the law. Theoretical reason has no place for a self that is
not one. But such a self is not, therefore, altogether unimaginable. And Kant,
for his part, momentarily imagines such a self in the second edition of the
Critique of Pure Reason: "only because I comprehend their manifold in a
consciousness do I call them all together *my* representations; for otherwise I
would have as multicolored, diverse a self as I have representations of which
I am conscious [*nenne ich dieselbe insgesammt* meine *Vorstellungen; denn sonst
würde ich ein so vielfärbiges, verschiedenes Selbst haben, als ich Vorstellungen habe,
deren ich mir bewußt bin*]" (B: 134).

89

Taken to its limit – and no longer taken for the basis of an "invisible church" (6: 101) – the thesis of radical evil moves in the direction of this "multicolored, diverse self." The "blue vapor" into which the self disappears is the mark of this movement. So, too, is the constitutive inconsistency of the statement toward which the thesis of radical evil tends: no human being can say in all honesty "all human beings are liars." Insofar as the thesis posits only a propensity to "inner" falsehood, it cannot be accused of paradoxical inconsistency. And insofar as the vapor of self-obfuscation is *only* blue, the self that hides from itself retains sufficient consistency to be counted as one. The diversity of the self is, in this case, limited according to an identifiable strategy: the self, which wants to make itself appear pure, discolors itself and therefore diversifies itself into an apparently guiltless subject of positive law and a patently guilty subject who malevolently avoids its own conscience. By making the self certain about its guilt, religion within the limits of bare reason, as the subsequent essays of the volume make clear, performs a double function: it unifies the self and, as a result, founds an "invisible church" that lends a degree of strength to its members' resolutions to do better. If, however, the blueness of the vapor in which the self disappears is only one shade of a "multicolored, diverse self," then the inconsistency of the self is constitutive of its problematic existence: it cannot be counted as one, still less as an evil one. The "multicolored, diverse self" that Kant lets himself imagine for a moment thus escapes counting, accounting, accountability – and therefore all calculation of prices. For the same reason, moreover, this self, which cannot be one, exists only as a constitutively inconsistent plurality.

Kant is, of course, well acquainted with one collection of this paradoxical kind, namely "the world," which, understood as the complex of all things-in-themselves, cannot be given, cannot be cognized, and cannot therefore even be said to exist – or not. Any attempt to grasp the world as a whole generates an antinomy that, according to Kant, "awakens" (4: 338) the mind to the task of critical self-reflection. The constitutively inconsistent plurality that momentarily announces itself in the image of a "multicolored, diverse self" is a parody of the world that metaphysicians dream of grasping. Or, in reverse, the world about which metaphysicians dream is a parody of the plurality toward which the image of a "multicolored, diverse self" momentarily gestures. In either case, the "critical enterprise" wants nothing to do with it: the dreams of metaphysics disappear in the light of critical self-reflection, and the image of the "multicolored, diverse self" appears only for the sake of its repudiation. An unmistakable trace of the former can be saved, however, for the thought of a "kingdom of ends." And a reflection of this kingdom takes shape in the "invisible church" for which Kant argues in the subsequent essays of *Religion*. Those who belong to this church – which cannot be identified as one from any terrestrial perspective and indeed may appear as many – recognize their personality, acknowledge their guilty conscience, accept the vicarious sacrifice performed by the moral ideal, and resolve to make themselves better despite all. By contrast, the only remaining trace of the "multicolored, diverse self" appears in the blueness of the vapor into which the self evaporates whenever it obfuscates its own guilty conscience.

Throughout the 1770s and 1780s Kant had strenuously argued for skin color as the principal criterion for distinguishing among the races, and a faint trace of this argumentation appears in his identification of the "foul spot" that distinguishes the human species from other possible kinds of humanity.[15] But nowhere outside of the reference to "blue vapor" does the self, as distinguished from its body, appear colored in the Kantian corpus. Since, however, the coloration of the self that evaporates into a less-than-lovely blueness is limited, so, too, is the corresponding self-diversification: the self can recognize itself as a case of moral failure, after all. Such is the point of the essay on radical evil. In other words, there is still hope. This is not true of the "multicolored, diverse self." It is hopeless – and free: free of all accounts, accounting, and calculation, including the calculation of guilt or debt; free, therefore, of every association with prices, including the price at which everyone, according to Kant's rendition of Walpole's famous remark, would exchange him- or herself; free, finally, of the sacrificial economy with reference to which Kant, for one, manages to salvage a trace of Christian doctrine within the limits of bare reason. Once the "invisible church" makes good on its invisibility, it, too, disappears from view: it cannot be recognized as one church among others, as one community among others, or even as a self-consistent multiplicity of moral selves. All talk of an "invisible church" may then become something of a joke, since it has the potential to raise a tense expectation that suddenly turns into nothing. But in the evanescent community of this laughter something like a "multicolored, diverse self" may suddenly appear – out of the blue.

5

UNDER THE SIGN OF
FAILURE

Toward Eternal Peace

Projectiles of peace

Toward Eternal Peace is written under the sign of failure.

The slogan "eternal peace" can be announced only under the sign of failure because the term *eternity* does not belong either to the vocabulary of politics or to the lexicon of the "critical enterprise" (5: 170). Speaking of anything as "eternal," including peace, demands that the speaker take leave of both politics and critical self-reflection, both of which take their point of departure from an abandonment of eternity in favor of time, timing, temporality, and temporizing – so much so that the "critical enterprise" presents time as the single, absolutely universal condition of human experience. No use of the term *eternity* henceforth goes without saying, and as long as the success of words is measured by their ability to express univocal concepts, the phrase "eternal peace," if not eternal peace itself, is doomed to failure. One of the expressions of this failure is the customary translation of *ewig* by "perpetual," but this – almost inevitable – failure of translation is already prepared in the German word *ewig*, for, as Kant writes in the opening article of the treatise, the qualification of the term "peace" by this adjective is "suspicious" (8: 345).[1] Those who qualify the term *peace* arouse the suspicion that they speak of peace only in order to prepare for war. The word *eternal* cannot say what it means, and neither can the announcement of "eternal peace."

Toward Eternal Peace is, for these reasons – and more to come – written under the sign of its own failure. Images gather around the word *eternal* because it cannot be properly grasped, and the specific image by which Kant first illuminates the title of his little treatise – that of a graveyard – is an emblem of human fallibility. But Kant goes even further in the direction of failure: not only does he place an insignia of lost life at the beginning of his treatise, he also sets a condition on the interpretation of his "philosophical project" that guarantees its failure. *Toward Eternal Peace*, in other words, is written not only under the sign of failure but under the *protection* of failure as well. Such is the double function of the *Schild* (sign, shield) with which

Kant begins the only one of his texts that he describes in its title as *philo-sophical*. By professing to fail, the treatise guards itself against those in power who might fear its success. As long as the project Kant proposes in *Toward Eternal Peace* is understood as nothing more than a "sweet dream,"[2] as long as it is understood as a failure from the start, there can be no reasonable objection to its publication. According to the interpretative premises of those who review the publication of philosophical treatises, *Toward Eternal Peace* does not apply to "the real world." There is, for this reason, only one condition imposed on its readers: they must understand that the treatise only *appears* to be a treaty and that it, therefore, cannot be taken seriously.

At the inception, therefore, Kant must lay down an interpretative condition. To the extent that the prologue sets out the terms by which the text can be read as it is intended, it cannot be read in the same way as the rest of the treatise: it must remain silent about its own intentions. Whereas the body of the treatise is directed toward the conditions under which eternal peace can be achieved, the prologue directs its attention toward this "toward."[3] Far from granting access to "eternal peace," however, the opening words articulate the impasse on the way toward this long-sought destination, and it does so by showing the difficulty of reading the sign of failure after which the treatise is named:

Toward Eternal Peace

Whether this satirical superscript on that Dutch innkeeper's sign [*Schild*] upon which a graveyard was painted is valid [*gelte*] for human beings in general, or especially for heads of state, who can never get enough of war, or perhaps only for philosophers who dream that sweet dream, may be set aside. But the author of the present [treatise] conditions himself in this way: since the practical politician places the theoretical one at his feet, looking down with great self-satisfaction and regarding him as an academic, who, with his ideas devoid of reality, brings no danger to the State (which must proceed from principles of experience), and whom one can always allow to fire his eleven projectiles all at once without the world-wise statesman having to turn around; in case of a conflict with the theoretical politician, the practical one must proceed in a consistent manner and not suspect a danger to the state behind the opinions that the latter openly expresses and ventures in the hope that they would meet with good luck. – By this *clausula salvatoria*, the author will herewith know himself expressly guarded in the best form against all malicious interpretation.

(8: 343)

Only because the innkeeper brings the phrase "toward eternal peace" into relation with an emblem does there arise a question concerning its validity.

The emblem alone may give rise to questions of accuracy, even truth, but not of validity; and the prepositional phrase cannot by itself be considered either valid or invalid. The emblem of the graveyard does not so much turn the prepositional phrase into a definite judgment – which in this case would be a last judgment – as give some directions for the interpretation of "toward," and by doing so, it poses the question "to whom do these directions apply?" Those to whom they apply are the ones for whom they are "valid." The directions could then be interpreted in the following ways: if the sign applies to human beings in general, they should seek peace in the grave, "for the dead do not fight any longer" (Leibniz); if it applies to heads of state, they should see the grave as the outcome of their insatiable desire for war; if it applies to philosophers, they should rouse themselves from their dreams and awaken to the sober reality of inter-state conflict. By superimposing directions over an emblem, the innkeeper produces something like a signpost for those who seek the road to peace; but insofar as this sign says to those for whom it is valid that there is no peace in this life – or on this road – it is a self-negating sign. If, however, a sign does not give directions, then it is not simply a sign but the replacement for an absent sign and, in the case of the sign posted by the innkeeper, the absence of a directional sign presents itself in an image of irreparable loss: the gravestones through which a graveyard is recognizable are themselves signs by which the end of life's road is marked and shields in which the loss of life is protected in perpetuity. The innkeeper's sign thus indicates that the "toward" of "toward eternal peace" is uninterpretable. By showing sign-posts of a passage for which we have no valid concepts and about which we can therefore make no valid judgment – the passage "from time into eternity"[4] – the sign says "no passage," or in Greek, *aporia*: there is no path to peace; this, the gravestone, marks the end of the road.[5]

If there is no path to peace, there can be no method by which this goal can be secured, and if it is understood in advance that no method is valid, then no proposal for peace poses any danger: each one is null and void from the start. Kant may therefore put aside the question concerning the validity of the sign posted by the innkeeper by answering this question in advance: the sign is a sign of the absence of any sign giving directions to the place called "Eternal Peace." Once *Toward Eternal Peace* has been placed under this sign, Kant can raise a general question of validity: under what conditions does any genuine peace treaty apply? And this is precisely the question to which he responds in the first article of the treatise: "1. 'No conclusion of peace [*Friedensschluß*] shall be valid [*gelten*] if it is made with a secret reservation of the material for a future war'" (8: 343). A question concerning the validity of a local sign gives way to a question concerning the validity of peace treaties in general; but this question itself is a generalization of the aporia to which the local sign points, and this aporia is inscribed in the very term for

94

peace: *Friedensschluß*, "conclusion of peace." Kant doubtless means by this word a treaty by which war comes to a conclusion, but it could also mean the exact opposite: peace's conclusion, an end to peace and, thus, the inception of war. The decision to use this duplicitous word is, moreover, anything but arbitrary, for, as Kant indicates in the second "definitive article," seemingly more exact terms like "peace contract" or "peace treaty" (*Friedensvertrag*) are even more inadequate: "without a contract [*Vertrag*] among peoples under itself [the throne of reason], peace cannot be founded or secured. There must therefore be a league [*Bund*] of a peculiar kind, which one could call a league of peace (*foedus pacificum*) and which would be distinguished from a peace contract [*Friedensvertrag*] (*pactum pacis*), since the latter seeks to end *one* war, whereas the former seeks to end *all* wars forever" (8: 356). A "conclusion of peace" would be the name for this non-contractual contract: a "contract among peoples" that does without contractual obligations; a contract without contract. No wonder the term *Friedensschluß* succumbs to ambiguity. Yet, even if another word were chosen to replace it, the aporia would not be avoided, for the article in question would still say: peace is concluded only among those for whom war has come to a conclusion – which is tautological and, for this reason, less a preliminary article than the articulation of the impasse.

Just as Kant is allowed to leave aside the question for whom the superscript is valid, the "practical politician" is under an obligation to grant Kant's treatise a certain leeway: the "pins" or "projectiles" (*Kegel*) of this "project" are "Ideas" which, according to the self-defining policy of the "practical politician," are "devoid of reality" (*sachleer*). The treatise entitled *Toward Eternal Peace* occupies precisely the position with respect to anonymous "practical politicians" that the sign entitled "toward eternal peace" occupies with respect to Kant, the "theoretical politician." Since Kant will conclude the "definite articles" for eternal peace by proposing a certain right to "hospitality [*Wirtbarkeit*]" (8: 358), he associates himself even more closely with the *Gastwirt* (innkeeper) under whose sign he presents his treatise. Just as the innkeeper poses no threat to his guests – or else he would not be a *Gastwirt* – Kant's treatise poses no danger to the state. Only an innkeeper who is known to be harmless could place the emblem of a graveyard at his door; otherwise, as a sign of a more permanent inn, it would be a threat, and the Dutchman would have to be associated not with Kant but with those Barbary pirates and European states – especially the Dutch one[6] – that violate the international right to hospitality. The same can be said of Kant's treatise, for it, too, having been immediately translated into French,[7] relies on the hospitality of an international readership. *Toward Eternal Peace* may leave the innkeeper's sign aside, but it never departs from the *place* of this sign. Within the economy of the treatise as a whole, the place occupied by this sign is the polemical site of "satire."

Satire

In the last – and oddly unnumbered – "Remark" of the Critique of Aesthetic Judgment, Kant seeks to understand the "affect" of laughter by proposing that it "arises when a tense expectation is suddenly transformed into nothing" (5: 332). The wit of the Dutch innkeeper can be explained accordingly: wayward travelers expect to receive directions to a hoped-for place called "Eternal Peace" but are, instead, directed nowhere – or better yet, directed downward. The innkeeper's sign can thus be considered a joke to the second power. Not only does it transform a tense expectation into nothing, it does so by way of a reference to nothingness. If, as Kant suggests in the same "Remark," bursts of laughter are monuments to cognitive failure, then the painted gravestones can even be read as the illustration of their origin in a radical failure of our cognitive capacities: their inability to grasp the sudden transformation of life into death. And this lamentable transformation is never far from the jokes Kant tells for the purpose of illustration:

> [I]f the heir of a rich relative wants to arrange a solemn funeral for him but laments that he cannot quite succeed in doing so, because (he says), "The more money I give to the mourners to look sorrowful [*betrübt*], the happier they look," then we laugh out loud, and the reason is that an expectation is suddenly transformed into nothing. One should note that it must not be transformed into the positive opposite of an expected object – for that is always something and can often cause sorrow [*betrüben*] – but into nothing. For if in telling us a story someone arouses a great expectation, and at its conclusion we immediately see its untruth, that displeases us, as in, for example, the story of people whose hair is supposed to have turned gray in a single night because of a great grief. By contrast, if in response to such a story another jokester [*Schalk*] tells in a very round-about manner a story of the grief that a merchant who, while returning from India to Europe with all his fortune in merchandise, was forced to throw everything overboard in a terrible storm, and was so upset that on that very night his *wig* turned white, then we laugh, and it gives us satisfaction, because, for a time, we throw back and forth like a ball our failure to grasp [*Mißgriff*] some object that is otherwise indifferent to us, or rather the idea we have been pursuing, while we merely intended to grab it and hold onto it. It is not the dismissal of someone as a liar or an idiot that awakens our satisfaction here, for the latter story, even by itself, told with the appearance of seriousness, would make a group of people laugh heartily, whereas the former story would not even be worthy of attention.
>
> (5: 333–34)

The author of *Toward Eternal Peace* occupies the same position as the jokester who makes fun of a failed colonialist enterprise – only inverted: whereas the latter assumes a serious demeanor in order to keep his listeners interested in his long-winded story, the former begins by declaring that his short treatise is nothing more than a game. The ball that eludes our grasp in the joke about the white wig turns into the projectiles Kant tosses out in his "game of ideas [*Spiel der Ideen*]" (23: 155). That Kant erases the phrase "game of ideas" in the published version of the Preface indicates that he does not want to give away the whole thing by simply saying "this is a joke," but the effect of the published preface is precisely the same: even without saying "don't take me seriously," it makes sure that those who play serious roles in the regime of Friedrich Wilhelm II will know that the objects with which he plays are only parts of an elaborate game. The treatise, there-fore, has little chance of eliciting laughter: there is no tense expectation that anything will come of it, least of all "eternal peace." When Kant takes over the story of the Dutch innkeeper, however, he adds one telling detail: the inscription "toward eternal peace" is described as "satirical." The same can be said, up to a point, of the like-named treatise as well. The point where its satirical intention fails is at the beginning, for – unlike, say, Swift's *Tale of the Tub*, which Kant must have re-read shortly before writing *Toward Eternal Peace*[8] – it undermines its comic potential by declaring its status as a game.

Toward Eternal Peace can, however, retain the satirical character of the innkeeper's sign on the condition that its eleven projectiles hit a target – only not the target toward which they, in unison, are said to aim, namely "eternal peace." Satire is successful only if it strikes something, and it must strike its target with enough force to deflate its pretensions. Taking the air out of those who give themselves airs is the principal aim of satire. In the case of *A Tale of the Tub*, priests who claim divine afflatus are under attack; and Kant's only attempt at Swift-like satire, *Dreams of a Spirit Seer* (1766), takes aim at a mining engineer who extensively records his visits to other worlds. At the end of a section entitled "Anti-Kabbalah" Kant even borrows Swift's preferred explanation for the puffed-up character of enthusiastic priests: "whenever a hypochondriacal wind blows in the guts, it is a question of which direction it takes: if it goes downwards, it comes out a f—; but if it goes upwards, it is an apparition or sacred inspiration" (2: 348).[9] By saying that claims to divine afflatus are the result of flatulence, the satirist promptly deflates those who mistake their gassiness for greatness. A line from *A Tale of the Tub* that makes its way into *Toward Eternal Peace* captures satire *in nuce*: what Swift says of wisdom in general – "'tis a *Nut*, which unless you chuse with Judgment, may cost you a Tooth, and pay you with nothing but a *Worm*"[10] – Kant applies to Jacques Mallet du Pan's counter-revolutionary wisdom, which is supposedly drawn from long years of political experience: "'What forms of government let fools contest;/Whate're is best administered

97

is best.' [Pope] If that means the best administered government is the best administered, then he has, in Swift's expression, 'cracked a nut and been rewarded with a worm'" (8: 353). Those who are proud of their ability to crack nuts discover to their dismay that they are no better off than anyone else. Kant's claim that the success of a joke does not depend on its capacity to dismiss its subject as a "liar or idiot" is dubious in its own right and untenable with respect to satire, which aims to show that its targets are either liars, idiots, or a combination of the two: idiots who lie to themselves in order to make themselves seem wiser, grander, or closer to God.

Toward Eternal Peace may not be as intricately structured as *A Tale of the Tub* — few texts are — but Swift can be taken for its guiding spirit. In the coda to "On the Common Saying: That May Work in Theory But Not in Practice" (1793) Kant explicitly discusses the threat of ridicule to which the opening of *Toward Eternal Peace* responds:

> [A]n enduring universal peace brought about by the so-called *balance of powers in Europe* is a mere figment of the imagination, like *Swift's house*, whose architect built it so perfectly in accordance with the laws of equilibrium that as soon as a sparrow lit on it, it collapsed. — "But that states," one will say, "will never subject themselves to coercive laws, and the proposal for a cosmopolitan nation, to whose power all individual states should voluntarily accustom themselves in order to obey its laws, may sound ever so nice in the theory of an Abbé St Pierre or of a Rousseau, yet it does not work in practice. For this proposal has at all times been ridiculed [*jederzeit verlachen*] by great statesmen and even more by heads of state as a pedantic-childish idea that comes out of the academy."
>
> (8: 312–13)

And one can say the same about Dutch innkeepers: statesmen, heads of state, and innkeepers all laugh at immodest philosophers making great plans for "an enduring universal peace," which, regardless of their dazzling complexity, are in effect nothing. To this laughter Kant responds by way of Swift — first in the final paragraphs of "On the Common Saying" and then more extensively in *Toward Eternal Peace*. First, he answers the accusation of ineffectualness by acknowledging its truth: he will not puff himself up. Kant's apologetic response to Mendelssohn, who apparently complained about the satirical character of *Dreams of a Spirit Seer*, is valid for *Toward Eternal Peace* as well: "It seemed to me wisest to forestall other people's mockery by first of all mocking myself" (11: 70). Indemnified in this way, Kant then reverses the direction of the accusation and throws out a series of projectiles against "practical politicians" who seek to secure an enduring peace by balancing power. Far from being wise architects, they are liars and idiots, for they forget to include the nuts and bolts that bind the parts of their intricately designed construction together – without informing anyone who has to inhabit their house of its structural failure.

Toward Eternal Peace goes even further, moreover, in the direction of satire. Not only are the rare politicians who devise plans for enduring peace consigned to the category of stupidity, so, too, are the statesmen and heads of state who are as scornful of such plans as they are contemptuous of philosophical projects. Putting on airs is, of course, an integral feature of both statesmen and heads of state. Without distinguishing themselves from those over whom they rule, they could not maintain their positions. One can always say, as Kant does in his response to Hobbes's assertion that the head of state can never be in the wrong, that rulers have not been "blessed with divine inspiration and elevated above the rest of humanity" (8: 304); but this is not satire – and it is not particularly effective critique either. Few, if any, statesmen or heads of state are vulnerable to the accusation that they, like Swedenborg, think that they can communicate with another world; on the contrary, a resolute this-worldliness is a badge of honor. What they believe about themselves is not that they are recipients of divine afflatus, even if they claim for themselves "divine right." Rather, they are convinced that they are fundamentally different from those over whom they rule. The more powerful they are, the more exalted they believe themselves to be. And of all those who are subject to the whims of European princes and privy consuls, none are in a weaker position than the so-called "savages" who live on territories that they seek to make into their own. Their claim to these places rests, in part, on this belief in the superiority of their supposedly civilized condition. Even if they do not present themselves as the leaders of the "civilized world," they regard themselves as eminent representations of a higher degree of humanity. *Toward Eternal Peace* takes aim at this pretension. Swift, once again, can be seen as the guiding spirit. Whereas "A Modest Proposal" casts the rulers of England as cannibals, who are prepared to eat Irish children, if only the price is low enough, Kant's treatise calls the rulers of European states something even worse: "The difference between European and American savages consists precisely in this, that while many of the latter tribes have been entirely eaten by their enemies, the former know how to make better use of those they have conquered than to consume them and would rather increase the number of their subjects and thus also the quantity of instruments they have to wage even more extensive wars" (8: 354–55).

European rulers may present themselves as the representatives of civilization, but they are more "savage" than those whom they treat as such. With only a slight alteration in tone – which would bring it in the vicinity of satire, properly speaking – *Toward Eternal Peace* could present itself as another "modest proposal": that the rulers of Europe put an end to the haphazard method in which their subjects are born by establishing breeding facilities for the production of good physical specimens of the human species, so that they can conduct even more entertaining spectacles of warfare. And as Kant knows well, having duly weighed – and ultimately rejected – Maupertius's proposal for the establishment of state-controlled, human breeding farms (2: 241), such proposals are not limited to philosophers inspired by Plato's *Republic*.[11] The modesty of Maupertius's proposal stands in stark contrast to the immodesty of the various proposals for perpetual peace that philosophers like Abbé St Pierre and Rousseau have drawn up. The slight trace of another "modest proposal" may even be perceptible in one of the opening words of *Toward Eternal Peace*: the statesman can find no reason to disallow Kant from firing "his eleven projectiles [*elf Kegel*]" (8: 343), which is to say, the treatise as a whole, with its six "preliminary articles," three "definitive articles," and two appendices. *Kegel* not only means "pins" in particular and "projectiles" in general; it also means "bones," especially those of human beings. The new game of throwing out projectiles of peace, in other words, is reminiscent of the apparently long-forgotten practice of casting human bones for the sake of fateful gods and cannibalistic kings.[12]

All of these "modest proposals" have one thing in common: the satirist presents himself as a remnant from the state of nature – not, however, a state of nature that is imagined to be paradisal or innocent. Whereas the naïf, according to the same unnumbered "Remark" of the third *Critique* that contains Kant's explanation of laughter, inadvertently reminds the members of civilized society that they have regrettably distanced themselves from "the simplicity of nature" (5: 335), the satirist willfully makes the same audience aware of the fact that they only *pretend* to have departed from the state of nature, that they have puffed themselves up into thinking that they are superior to those who live far from the *civitas*.[13] The premise of satire is that natural life is not only *not* paradisal; it is – to use the term Kant invokes in "On the Radical Evil in Human Nature" – fundamentally "perverse" (6: 30). The naïf only needs to learn the principal lesson of Kant's recent contributions to the *Berlinische Monatsschrift* to turn into a satirist. And nothing shows this transformation better than *Toward Eternal Peace*: from the perspective of statesmen, heads of state, and Dutch innkeepers, Kant would be judged utterly naïve, since he shows no evidence of having engaged with the real world; knowing that human beings are by nature perverse, however, his naïveté presents itself as the "modest proposal" that he simply be allowed to throw out a few *Kegel* – which, as insiders would know, both commemorate and prognosticate cannibalistic festivals.

Natural life is mired in evil – not because those who are "uncivilized" necessarily want to harm anyone else but, rather, because they think nothing of using others of their kind as means toward their own particular ends. Satire is oriented toward the meanness of human beings. According to the etymology of the term, satirists are "saturated" (*satur*). The word does not indicate what satisfies the satirist, however. Walter Benjamin proposes an answer: "The satirist is the figure in which the cannibal was received by civilization."[14] Cannibalism, however, is only one form of satisfaction – and not even the most extreme. Creating breeding farms for human beings holds out the prospects of even greater satisfaction. Just as the naïf innocently discloses the "jokester in ourselves" (5: 335), the satirist does the same – but with a perverse twist: the inner jokester, who, upon encountering a naïf, regrets having fallen away from "the simplicity of nature," learns that he has only fooled himself into believing that he has distanced himself from his original condition. With the emergence of the satirist, not only is the joke on the jokester – this is already true with the appearance of the naïf – but the jokester can no longer pass off the joke by laughing at someone else. Kant's dubious conclusion to his abbreviated analytic of wit does not there-fore apply to satire: "It is not the dismissal [*Abfertigung*] of someone as a liar or an idiot that awakens our satisfaction here" (5: 334). On the contrary, the aggressive character of satire, which wants to "finish off" (*ab-fertigen*) its targets, confirms its premise: that human beings are evil by nature; that creaturely life is perverse; that, from the perspective of a civilized race, the human species looks like a bunch of Yahoos. Satire is palpable only because its targets do not recognize themselves as such. No one is clearer about the irony of satire – it succeeds only by failing – than Swift himself: "Satyr is a sort of Glass, wherein Beholders do generally discover every bodys' Face but their Own."[15]

Erasing *race*

There is, however, an utterly obvious way to put an end to warfare among sovereign states: grant one of these states dominion over the entire surface of the earth. This is not a far-fetched plan, reserved for medieval treatises like Dante's *De Monarchia*. According to Kant, every ruler of Europe wants to fulfill Dante's end by machiavellian means. Nature, however, thwarts this desire and thus condemns European rulers to continual failure. Frustration is a constitutive feature of sovereignty – so much so that an alternative title for *Toward Eternal Peace* could be *On the Failure of All Political Attempts at Global Domination*: "the desire of every state (or its ruler) is to establish an enduring peace, hoping, if possible to dominate the entire world. But nature *wills otherwise*. It uses two means to prevent peoples from inter-mingling and to separate them: the difference of *languages* and of *religions*" (8: 367). After the word *religions* Kant immediately adds a footnote that contradicts the body of the text: "*Differences in religion*: a wonderful expres-sion! Precisely as if one spoke of different *moralities*. No doubt there can be different kinds of historical *faiths*. . . . But there is only a single religion, valid for all men in all times" (8: 367). This inconsistency is remarkable. At no other place does Kant write a word only to undermine its value in an accompanying footnote: it is a technique more appropriate to the author of *Gulliver's Travels* or *Tristram Shandy* than the philosopher who wrote the *Critique of Practical Reason*. An earlier draft of *Toward Eternal Peace* gives an indication of what might have contributed to this strange inconsistency, for Kant had originally identified three differences among peoples – "races, languages, and religions" (23: 170). In the final version he erases *races* in fact and *religions* in effect. The retraction of the latter term by means of a sarcastic footnote can even be read as the last trace of the technical term *race* not only in this passage from *Toward Eternal Peace* but in all of Kant's publications of the 1790s. Even in the *Anthropology*, which, given the series of lectures from which it is largely drawn, should devote a major section to the "character of the races" (7: 182), Kant cuts short his discussion and simply refers interested readers to J. C. Girtanner's work.[16] With very few exceptions – almost all of which will be examined in subsequent chapters of this study – the word never appears again in late Kant.[17]

No one can know why Kant decided to do away with *race* from *Toward Eternal Peace*; Kant himself may not have known. Perhaps he did not want to enter again into the controversies around the term that had been spawned by his three essays on race: "On the Different Human Races" (1775), "The Determination of the Concept of Race" (1785), and "On the Use of Teleological Principles in Philosophy" (1788). Perhaps, for the same reason, he did not want to add yet another footnote to a battle of the books that, in his estimation, he had already won. Yet, this reluctance to enter into a new debate or add another footnote would be surprising, since the treatise nowhere else spurns controversies and welcomes digressive footnotes, including a long digression on the non-European etymology of the word *pax* (8: 359–60). And in any case, if only Kant had erased the term *religions* and replaced it by "historical creeds," he could have saved himself the trouble of adding a footnote in which he makes fun of his own terminology. More importantly, however, race, for Kant, is a thoroughly natural phenomenon, unlike religion and even language, which is supposed to be a vehicle of reason.[18] Discussion of racial differences, for Kant, may only be appropriate for "natural history," in contrast to "natural description" (2: 443; 8: 100; 8: 161), since the validity of racial categories is based on teleological judgment; nevertheless, these categories, unlike those of religion and language, can be considered entirely natural.[19] To say that nature, by establishing racial differences, thwarts the ultimate intention of European rulers would not only be completely unobjectionable from the perspective of Kant's theory of race; it might even disclose a daring new dimension. The erasure of *race* is therefore a puzzling act. The oddity of Kant's giddy self-sarcasm – "*Differences of religion*: a wonderful expression!" – is compounded by the fact that, less than a decade earlier, he had strenuously argued for a concept of natural differences among members of the species that, in his opinion, could be of inestimable value for future anthropological research.[20]

The erasure of the term *race* is as enigmatic as any of Kant's self-corrections. Just as the retention of *religions* in the plural can be understood in two divergent ways, so, too, can the erasure of *race* in the singular. *On the one hand*, the statement that nature does not wish that human beings speak only one language and profess only one religion means that French will never be the world tongue, regardless of how well post-Revolutionary France may fare, and that Christianity will never be the world religion, regardless of what priests, missionaries, enthusiasts, and Friedrich Wilhelm II may dream. That the multiplicity of races cannot be reduced to one means, in turn, that all non-white races will not, as he claims in a notorious note, be wiped away.[21] In other words, Kant may have struck out the word *race* because he still holds the conviction in 1795 that the white race is destined, after all, to dominate the planet, as the other races succumb to their supposedly "inferior" nature. *On the other hand*, saying something to this effect would destroy the very basis on which he launches his "philosophical project," for even a slight suggestion that the race of Europeans is destined to dominate the earth immediately plays into the hands of the European rulers from whom he sharply distinguishes himself. Their inhospitality may be morally unjustifiable; but it would still be justified from the perspective of nature. A kind of "natural right" would support their claims to every part of the globe. And Kant, who in the *Anthropology* refuses to count the Germans among the "civilized nations of the earth" (7: 312) for fear that readers might judge him arrogant, would be saying, in effect, "I am superior to those who inhabit the other continents – not because of anything I have accomplished, still less because of my moral comportment, but because of the race to which I belong." These two divergent explanations for the erasure of *race* from *Toward Eternal Peace* reinforce each other, moreover. Kant may still believe that all non-European races are destined to extinction, but he has good reason to keep this opinion to himself. In the second edition of *Toward Eternal Peace* Kant adds a "Secret Article" in which it is tacitly agreed that philosophers should have the right to make public their views. An even more secret article might also be at work – an article that forbids European philosophers from publishing their views on race.

The silence of the late Kant in matters of race cannot simply be attributed to his preoccupation with other issues. He fails to make good his promise in the Preface to the last *Critique* to proceed "without fail" (5: 170) to the "doctrinal" dimension of the critical system and, instead, concentrates on a variety of miscellany, including some reflections on the influence of the moon on the weather, an analysis of a minor conflict in mathematics, and an extended debate with the likes of Johann Schlosser and Count Leopold zu Stolberg. By contrast, during his so-called "silent decade" of the 1770s, when he was working assiduously on the *Critique of Pure Reason*, he had enough time to write and significantly revise "On the Different Human Races." With respect to race, the 1770s is no decade of "silence." And during the 1780s, when all of the *Critiques* were written – and much more besides – Kant found enough time to write two substantial essays that clarify and defend his concept of race. That he should allow a concept of such potential magnitude for the "human sciences" to disappear entirely from his public persona is of some significance, especially since it could be considered among Kant's most influential contribution to the natural sciences of the next century. The *Universal Natural History*, after all, was unknown to Laplace who, in any case, proposed a much more rigorous version of the same general conception of solar evolution. When Eric Voegelin defends the Critique of Teleological Judgment as the most viable account of the systematic organization of nature in his *Idea of Race*, he does not bother to ask himself why Kant decided to drop his defense of the concept of race by the time he writes the third *Critique* – and thereafter as well.[22]

One more element of this question makes it even more puzzling and the late Kant's erasure of race from his writing even more enigmatic: the thesis of radical evil could be understood to make the use of racial categories all the more appealing – and for reasons other than those of natural-scientific systematicity. That human beings have a "perverse" character means that they have no character, which is to say: none of their words can be trusted, not even the words they speak to themselves in the privacy of their hearts. As Kant notes in the "Concluding Remark" to "On the Failure of All Philosophical Attempts at Theodicy," "the human being knows how to falsify even inner assertions before his own conscience" (8: 270). From a "pragmatic point of view," it is therefore necessary to divine their intentions by non-linguistic means. And here the concept of race would be of some help: racial characteristics can reveal what people without character cannot – the desires and aversions that they hide even from themselves. Because the natural marks of race are not subject to the faculty of choice, they cannot be corrupted. These marks, so the argument runs, betray the intentions and motivations of those who are naturally corrupt better than their words. In this respect, the thesis of radical evil supports the kind of racialism that would rapidly develop in nineteenth-century Germany: since it is impossible for anyone to trust what anyone says, social distinctions require a system of characterological signs.

The radicality of the thesis of radical evil, however, thwarts this program from the start – and sends it into a different direction altogether: toward the thought of another possible kind of human being whom future anthropologists may eventually encounter. In the meantime, the words of Paul are valid: "'There is no distinction here'" (6: 38–39). Regardless of the linguistic, religious and "racial" distinctions among peoples, every member of the human species subordinates the absolute commands of practical reason to the pragmatic calculations of potential gains and losses. All human beings can thus be seen to belong to a single race, whose specifying feature consists in a "foul spot," as Kant emphasizes in the concluding paragraph of the "Announcement of the Near Conclusion of a Treaty for Eternal Peace in Philosophy" (1797):

Lying ("from the father of lies, through which all evil has come into the world") is the actual foul spot on human nature, however much the tone of *truthfulness* (according to the example of many Chinese grocers, who place above their shops an inscription in golden letters that reads "here one is never deceived") is the usual tone, above all, in matters that concern the supersensible. – The command *you ought not lie* (even if it were done with the most pious intentions), inwardly incorporated as a principle into philosophy conceived as a doctrine of wisdom, would alone be able not only to bring about eternal peace in philosophy but also to secure it for all time to come.
   Königsberg   I. Kant

                  (8: 422)

Unless the "foul spot" is eradicated, the treaty for eternal peace in philosophy can always only be announced as near, for, even if peace were announced, the announcement could not be believed – and would not therefore be an announcement of peace but only a vociferous prolongation of war. But no announcement to the effect that the "foul spot" has been eradicated can be believed until it has indeed been eradicated. Chinese merchants thus occupy the same position as European philosophers: all place themselves under shields that affirm their truthfulness, but since their signs are credible only insofar as they are indeed truthful, these signs say, in effect, nothing. And the same is true of all "natural" characteristics: none can be believed, not even the characterological system of tones, since the "foul spot" marks "human nature." Drawing attention to the differences among human races is therefore a distraction – or worse: it plays into the hands of European statesmen who mendaciously present themselves as superior to those over whom they exercise arbitrary power.

"The Antichrist"

From the perspective of "The End of All Things" (1794), which Kant had published shortly before *Toward Eternal Peace*, the retention of *religions* is as curious as the erasure of *race*. For, according to the last sentence of this essay in rational eschatology, Christianity is destined to become the world religion:

> Should it ever come about that Christianity ceases to be worthy of love (which could certainly happen if, instead of its gentle spirit, it were armed with dictatorial authority), then disinclination toward, and resistance against it would have to become the dominant mode of thought for human beings, because in matters of morality there is no neutrality (nor even a coalition of opposing principles); and the *Antichrist*, who is taken as the harbinger of the last day, would begin his doubtless short regime (presumably based on fear

and self-interest); then, however, because Christianity would indeed be *destined* [bestimmt] to be a universal world religion but would not be *favored* by fate [*vom Schicksal* begünstigt] to become so, *the* (perverted) *end of all things*, with respect to morality, would make its entrance.

Königsberg   I. Kant

(8: 339)

By the time Kant publishes *Toward Eternal Peace* a few months after this sentence appears in print, fate must have intervened, for the treatise unambiguously asserts that no religion is destined to become a "universal world religion." Nature not only does not favor any religion; it is positively disinclined toward all of their global aspirations. And a fateful event did occur on October 1, 1794: King Friedrich Wilhelm II of Prussia, while exercising his magisterial right to issue "sovereign sentences" (*Machtsprüche*), reprimands Kant for his "abstinence" and therefore commands that his subject conform to "our sovereign will" (11: 525). Recognizing that Christianity had finally become unworthy of love, Kant responds, as predicted, with resistance – not open revolt, to be sure, but subtle sabotage. Solemnly promising the king that he would cease altogether from lecturing or publishing anything "touching on religion [*die Religion betreffend*]" (11: 530), he contradicts his own conviction that there is only one religion, properly speaking, and publishes a sentence touching on *religions*. By retaining and yet instantaneously repudiating this inconsistent pluralization of *religion*, he keeps his word, while at the same time breaking its spirit. However nonsensical *religions* may be, it says something very specific in its context: there will never be a "universal world religion." Which is to say: "the Antichrist" has arrived in the person of Friedrich Wilhelm II. As a result, *"the* (perverse) *end of the world"* has begun to make its entrance. Given the last sentence of "The End of All Things" and the subversive use of the term *religions* in Kant's next publication, there can be no other reasonable conclusion.[23] Christianity, for Kant, is destined to leave its destiny unfulfilled. "With respect to morality" – and without any angelic fanfare – all things are approaching their end.

Chance

By retaining the inconsistent plural of *religion* Kant subtly rebels against a king whom he obviously despised. In this regard, the word *race* would have led in the wrong direction entirely: toward a consideration of natural differences among races rather than the political equality of all those who are subject to arbitrary executive decrees. The structural position of an "academic" like Kant and that of the "savage" is the same. Both are subordinate to those whose feeling of superiority expresses itself in extra-legal actions: "one part of the world that feels itself to be superior [*überlegen fühlt*] to another, which does not even stand in its way, will not fail to exercise the means of increasing its power by plundering or even conquering this other part of the world" (8: 371). Even if rulers need no rationale for this feeling of superiority – for they are, after all, in positions of unchallenged power – the same cannot be said of their apologists, against whose opinions *Toward Eternal Peace* is principally aimed. The rationale of these "practical politicians" is succinctly formulated in the Preface to the treatise: "practical politicians" are intimately familiar with the ways of the world, and their familiarity makes them into masters of chance. Counting on this rationale, Kant emphasizes that the statesmen who censor philosophical manuscripts cannot deny his treatise its chance for success, for, as they must admit for the sake of consistency, the chance that the "eleven projectiles" of the project will eventually hit something is zero: success, in other words, is "impossible" (23: 155). *Toward Eternal Peace* must therefore be allowed to "venture" out into the world. If, however, the venture fails to fail as expected, this impossibility cannot be attributed to anyone's intention – not even to that of the author, who, after all, is only playing a game that he concedes in advance. The only agent that can be held accountable for such impossible success is, therefore, "luck" (*Glück*). In other words, nothing is accountable for this event, should it ever, *per impossibile*, come to pass. Kant therefore places the sole valid clause of the counterfeit treaty he publishes under the title *Toward Eternal Peace* at the end of the Preface – a clause that absolves him of any responsibility for the consequences of his pin toss. This "little saving clause" responds in advance to the possibility that, by publishing his reflections on another dimension of practical philosophy, Kant will, once again, be censured by the king for failing to bend his public opinions to "our sovereign will": "the practical [politician] must proceed in a consistent manner and not suspect a danger to the state behind the opinions that the latter openly expresses and ventures in the hope that they would meet with good luck [*gut Glück*]. – By this *clausula salvatoria*, the author will herewith know himself expressly guarded in the best form against all malicious interpretation."

The *clausula salvatoria* saves the author from accusations that his treatise intends any heresy, which, in his case, is heresy with regard to the doctrine of unchallenged sovereign power. The term *clausula salvatoria* does not belong to the terminology of classical Roman law.[24] As one might expect, the concept of a "saving clause" gains currency only when "salvation" from the law is of the utmost concern, on the one hand, and beliefs are legal matters, on the other. From a certain perspective, Pauline doctrine in its entirety can be comprehended as a "small saving clause": outside the letter of the law a clause – or a closing word – abrogates the law in favor of grace. Whenever this happens, someone is "saved." If the luck to which Kant appeals can be distinguished from grace – and it is the point of a lengthy footnote in the section on the "Guarantee of Eternal Peace" to lay out the terms for this distinction (8: 361–62) – the clause by which the opening of the treatise closes should be understood less as a "saving provision" than as an *exit sign*, for it provides a way out of the impasse expressed in the Dutch innkeeper's sign. According to the *clausula salvatoria*, the author cannot be held responsible for the effects of his treatise, since the "practical politician" admits that it can have none; its effectiveness can therefore be ascribed to "good luck" alone. If, however, its effectiveness can be ascribed *only* to luck – and not to agents who carefully devise stratagems through which they can increase the likelihood of successfully accomplishing their ends – it outdoes "practical politicians" at their own game. And if *something* or *some word* escapes the calculations of those who seek to master chance, then statesmen can never secure for themselves the final say: it will always have been possible that certain words they deem "impractical" – philosophical projects, dreams, even jokes – will have been effective, "real," and therefore, in their terms, "practical" after all.

Kant thus abandons *Toward Eternal Peace* to the domain in which practical politicians operate. Outside of a few remarks in the *Critique of Pure Reason* – which drew Goethe's attention[25] – Kant says little about chance within the parameters of the "critical enterprise": it belongs to the domain of "pragmatics" rather than "practice" in the rigorous sense. And the "pragmatism" of "practical politicians" consists in their ability to gain control over circumstances, while making the most of every opportunity. Outdoing politicians at their own game, Kant makes his treatise into a sheer "venture." The treatise is so completely abandoned to chance that it cannot be brought under the control of a pragmatic rule derived from observation of political expedience. If, however, chance cannot be mastered, then there may also be a chance for something other than chance. And this aporetic chance is not only what Kant contemplates in those sections of *Toward Eternal Peace* where he investigates the possibility of founding a world-federation of republican states; the treatise is *itself* a chance of this kind. If it is lucky, the world of political reality will no longer be based on luck. But this does not mean that politicians, having perfected the state to the point where it operates either as a frictionless machine or a well-formed organism, will have finally mastered chance; on the contrary, the world of political bodies, like Epicurus' cosmos,[26] will have been paradoxically "founded" on chance – "paradoxical" because the chance on which it will have been founded is groundless; it is only a chance for something other than chance, a chance that cannot be seized as such.

Only the chance for something other than chance – not the chance statesmen wish to master or the goddess Fortuna whom princes woo – points a way out of the exigent contingencies to which these politicians appeal whenever they justify otherwise unjustifiable measures, clauses, or decrees. "Something other than chance" can, of course, be described in eminently critical terms: it is the non-contingent principle of right. But the very immunity of what Kant calls "practical principles" from contingency means that the long-promised but long-delayed *Doctrine of Right* cannot account for the chance on which *Toward Eternal Peace* stakes its venture. Not only does this chance escape political mastery, it escapes a properly criticized philosophical vocabulary. Yet this chance cannot simply go without a name, for, as a "contract of peoples," it is, in every sense of the word, a "public" matter. There is no chance for this impossible chance unless it is named, and so Kant goes in search of one in the first appendix to the treatise, "On the Guarantee of Eternal Peace." To speak of a guarantee is to acknowledge certain risks; but the point of a guarantee is, of course, to reduce these risks by devising some form of compensation for any failure that might perchance occur. Kant has no trouble naming the guarantor of eternal peace. Taking his vocabulary from Lucretius, from whom he had early learned how to write a *Universal Natural History*, he calls it "the great artist nature (*natura daedala rerum*)." Speaking of Daedalus in this context is a mark of modesty; an immodest proposal, by contrast, would use the term *providence* and be exposed, in turn, to the unhappy fate of the artisan's son:

> When, as here, it is a matter merely of theory (not of religion), the use of the word "nature" is more appropriate for the limits of human reason . . . and more *modest* than an expression for a providence of which can have no cognitive knowledge, and on which we, in a fit of hubris [*vermessenerweise*], take flight as on Icarus's wings in order more closely to approach the secrets of some unfathomable intention.
>
> (8: 362)[27]

Like Daedalus, however, *natura daedala rerum* guarantees its artifacts only up to a point. For Daedalus, the guarantee extends to the edge of the lower atmosphere; for Kant, to the lineaments of the heart: wherever there are secrets, the guarantee is invalidated. And when Kant discusses a "people of devils" who "possess understanding" (8: 366), the limits of the Daedalean guarantee come to light. Just as the term *nature* comes to Kant's aid in the appendix to the treatise, *natura daedala rerum* "comes to the aid" of that which "practical politicians" know to be wholly impractical: "the honored but practically impotent general will, grounded in reason" (8: 366). As a result of nature's assistance, an otherwise intractable problem becomes "solvable":

> So order and establish a constitution for a group of rational beings who require universal laws for their preservation, although each is secretly [*insgeheim*] inclined to exempt himself from such laws, that, while their private attitudes conflict, these nonetheless so cancel one another that their public comportment succeeds in the same way as if they had no evil attitudes.
>
> (8: 366)

Since a solution to this problem can be calculated, it is *only* a problem, not an aporia, and the calculability of the problem is precisely what the artisan of nature guarantees. *Natura daedala rerum* has only a single complex function here: to make up for the tendency of human beings to exempt themselves in secret from the principle they publicly profess. This is, as it were, the "secret" intention of *natura daedala rerum*: to replace trust, which cannot in principle be guaranteed, by calculation, which can. As long as secret intentions are calculable – everyone can be expected to want what makes himself or herself happy – the problem remains solvable. But as the first "preliminary article" makes clear and the rest of the treatise corroborates, secrecy is anything but unproblematic when it comes to a proposal for *eternal* peace.[28] The problem posed by a treaty of this sort – which is less a closed contract than an open forum – is unsolvable; but its very insolvability is paradoxically its salvation: it escapes the "principles of experience" on the basis of which statesmen, heads of state, and "practical politicians" stake their claim to superiority.

The remnant race

A peace treaty can be guaranteed but not its eternality. Unless a peace treaty is "eternal," however, it not only does not establish peace; on the contrary, it prolongs the war. Eternity cannot be guaranteed. And the same is true of the term *eternity*: there is no guarantee that it even makes sense. As Kant notes at the beginning of "The End of All Things," *eternity* would "say nothing" (*nichts sagen*) if it is supposed to designate an "infinite passage of time" (8: 327) – and what else is it supposed to designate in a treatise entitled *Toward Eternal Peace?* For the term to say something, however, the time of "eternal peace" either must be limited or must be something other than time, properly speaking: in Kant's terms, *duratio noumenon*.[29] This time for something other than time can present itself "in" time only as an interruption of the temporal continuum. *Toward Eternal Peace* turns toward an interruption of time that shows the limit of "eternal peace": it lasts only as long as the human species exercises dominion over the surface of the earth. The contrast to the proposal for "eternal peace" is, then, the program for *eternalization*: "the moralizing politicians, who, on the pretext that human nature is not capable of the good in accordance with the Idea as reason prescribes it, gloss over the principles of the state contrary to right, make improvement *impossible* and eternalize [*verewigen*] the violation of right" (8: 373).

By saying that their subjects are incapable of acting in accordance with the Idea of goodness and cannot therefore regard this Idea as anything but ineffective and unreal, "moralizing politicians" incapacitate the subjects of whom they speak, including themselves. As long as human beings are incapacitated, they cannot do anything about the conditions that occasion their impotence, and these conditions are thereby "eternalized." Nothing could be more sharply distinguished from this program of eternalization than the project with which it might be confused: that of projecting eternal peace. Because the program and the project are so different from each other, however, they are easily confused: the project of eternal peace appears to be a program of eternalization, and the program of eternalization can be seen from a certain perspective to be a project of eternal pacification. The projectiles launched by each side thus threaten those who launched them. Practical politicians prove their power to the degree that they are able to make their word come true by saying it: more exactly, by saying that human beings cannot improve themselves and must therefore be suppressed, they make human beings incapable of improvement and in need of constant suppression.[30] The impotence of those who speak for "eternal peace" reveals itself in the same way: they are unable – and, according to Kant, should not try[31] – to make their word come true merely by saying it. The words of "theoretical politicians" do not make anything happen, which means, in sum, that they appear impotent dreamers and are forever exposed to uncontrolled chances.

Toward Eternal Peace can thus be read, in reverse, as *Away from Eternalization*. But the way out of eternalization cannot itself be eternalized: it, too, must be exposed to chance, and the only chance that constantly opens up a way is the inconsistent chance for something other than chance. One name for this chance is already inscribed in the title of Kant's treatise: *eternity*. For this term designates a time for something other than that of the temporal continuum. If, however, the chance for something other than chance is eternal, it could take place at *any* time – which means that every "philosophy of history," like every philosophical attempt at theodicy, is condemned to failure. Nowhere is this failure more apparent in *Toward Eternal Peace* than in the sole passage of the treatise in which Kant dons Icarus's wings and approaches the atmosphere of providence:

> When someone transgresses his duties toward another who is just as lawlessly disposed toward him, then whatever *happens* [geschieht] to them as they wipe each other out is entirely right; enough of their race [*Race*] will always remain so that this game [*dieses Spiel*] will not cease, even in the remotest times, and late descendants [*späte Nachkommenschaft*] can thereby take them as a warning example [*ein warnendes Beispiel*]. In this manner, the course of world events justifies providence.
>
> (8: 380)

Only here does Kant use the term *race* in *Toward Eternal Peace*, and it is one of the few occurrences of the term in his late writings. The race appears to be the human race in general – but not quite. "Late descendants" of the race must outlive its own self-destruction, and these latecomers must be divided from the race of which they are members. This self-division, which corresponds to self-destruction, depends, however, on a stringent condition: the latecomers must interpret the catastrophic event of self-destruction as a "warning example," which says, in effect: "do not take your race as an example." In other words – those of the Hebrew prophets, whom Kant often vilifies, particularly in his late writings, including in a footnote to *Toward Eternal Peace*[32] – the race turns into a "remnant."[33] The remnant "race" exists only as long as it interprets itself as different from its own race. It must be constitutively inconsistent: part of the race and apart from the race at the same – always later – time. And, of course, there have been enough examples of mutually lawless members of the human race for this remnant of the race to arrive at any time. At the end of the *Anthropology from a Pragmatic Point of View* (1798) Kant provides a perspective from which to grasp the un-expected appearance of the term *race* in a treatise that elsewhere avoids it: "If one now asks: whether the human species [*Menschengattung*] (which, if one considers it as a species [*Spezies*] of rational *earthlings* in comparison with rational beings on other planets, as a set of creatures originating from a single demiurge, can also be called a *race* [Rasse]) – whether, I say, it should be seen as good or an evil race, I must admit that there's not much to brag about" (7: 331–32).[34] The remnant "race" does not inhabit another planet but, instead, indicates that the character of this one has changed. After all, the angel whom Kant quotes near the beginning of "The End of All Things" – in a gesture worthy of Swift's "excremental vision"[35] – points to this out-of-the-way planet when he is asked for directions to "the toilet for the whole universe" (7: 331). The Dutch innkeeper who begins *Toward Eternal Peace* points in the same direction.

The dismal prospect that the solemn "play of mourning" (*Trauerspiel*) called "history" will be seen as an unendurable "farce" (*Possenspiel*) as soon as its spectators finally realize that "the never ending play is eternally the same [*ein ewiges Einerlei*]" (8: 308) cannot be foreclosed, as Schiller proposes in a con-temporaneous series of Open Letters, by the establishment of an "aesthetic state" that gives free reign to the "play drive" (*Spieltrieb*).[36] Rather, for Kant, the thought of the eternal return of the same generates both a dream and a nightmare: the dream of a duly constituted federation of independent states, all of which have bid adieu to their former condition of "savage (lawless) free-dom" (8: 357); and the nightmare of massive mutual-annihilation. The dream has, of course, generated the greatest interest among Kant's readers, then and now, doubtless because it can be transformed into a program for international politics. The nightmare, by contrast, has gone largely unnoticed. But the dream may only be a screen for the nightmare, which, as Kant dares to say, alone justifies providence.

The way out of the "game" (*Spiel*) lies in "a warning example" (*ein warnendes Beispiel*). The catastrophic interruption of the *Spiel* appears as a commem-orative *Beispiel* that forever warns a late-coming "race" of the catastrophe in

112

store for anyone who resumes the *Trauerspiel*. Such is Kant's "play of ideas [*Spiel der Ideen*]" (23: 155).[37] By playing out this innocent game to its catastrophic end, Kant enters into close proximity with Hölderlin, who, in an interrupted poem about the conditions of peace, asks of the poet that his own transgression be made into a "warning example":

das warnende Lied den Gelehrigen singe
[sing the warning song to those able to learn][38]

6

IN THE NAME OF
FRIENDSHIP; OR THE CASE
FOR INCONSISTENCY

Hypocrisy and hypercritique

In the fall of 1797 Kant asks a favor of Johann Heinrich Tieftrunk. Several years earlier Tieftrunk had sought guidance from the aging philosopher for his defense of the *Critique of Pure Reason* against those who, as he writes, seek "to provide it with a foundation or even to abandon it in favor of new principles that they attempt to discover and establish" (12: 172). More recently, Tieftrunk had asked Kant to give him some guidance for his edition of, and commentary on, excerpts from the *Critiques*. Kant accepts the latter proposal and then makes a request in return: "This is an opportunity for me to ask that you remember my hypercritical friends [*hyperkritischen Freunde*] Fichte and Rheinhold with the circumspection that their service to science fully deserves" (12: 207). Kant asks this of Tieftrunk, whom he addresses as "treasured friend" (12: 222), because he no longer feels capable of summoning the mental discipline required to develop the requisite critiques of the post-critical enterprises of his "hypercritical friends." In the fall of 1797 he admits as much to Fichte himself, whom he likewise addresses as "treasured friend":

> I could scarcely think ill of you if you were to consider my nine months' delay in answering your letter a lack of friendship and courtesy. But you would certainly forgive my behavior if you knew the state of my health and the weakness of old age, which have forced me to give up all lecturing, and not for the sake of my comfort. I now and then give evidence of my existence through the channel of the *Berlinische Monatsschrift* and also recently through the *Berliner Blätter*, which I do as a means of maintaining myself by way of agitating my meager vital forces; in these writings, however, I find that I throw myself almost entirely into the practical field, gladly leaving to others the subtlety of theoretical speculation, especially when it concerns its more recent, most extreme tips of the apexes [*neuern äußerst zugespitzen Apices*].

You and my other philosophizing friend will understand that I choose no other journal than the *Berliner Blätter* for what I have recently completed only because I am an invalid. This is the cause: because in this way I see my completed work finished and judged in the fastest possible manner, since it, like a political newspaper, satisfied the expectation only as quickly as the daily mail; but I do not know how long it will last that I can work at all. . . .

With complete respect and friendship I am at all times, etc.

I. Kant

(12: 219–20)

It is unlikely that any of Kant's "philosophizing friends" would interpret this letter as anything other than what it appears to be: an unambiguous expression of long-standing friendship. Even those among his friends who knew that, despite his protestations to the contrary, he had indeed undertaken new investigations into theoretical topics as recently as 1796 and that his letter to Fichte is therefore not entirely honest would not have suspected that his vow of friendship could not be taken at face value.[1] And even if a reader takes into account the mere formality of the final lines, with which Kant often ended his letters, particularly in his later years, the words themselves still amount to something of a promise, which says: "I will be true to you." Yet, less than two years later Kant publishes an acerbic Open Letter in which he denounces the hypocritical character of his "hypercritical friends." Casting himself in the role of Caesar and Fichte in that of Brutus, whose pretence of friendship is an indispensable element of a murderous conspiracy, Kant declares that he has always said exactly what he means, regardless of what he has actually said. Discovering the spirit of his letter is thus a pointless exercise – or worse: an attack on his person, tantamount to a *crimen laesae maiestatis*. Kant then proclaims a sovereign sentence, which consists in dismissing further discussion of what the *Critiques* are supposed to mean. They mean what they say. So says their author, who, by saying as much, interprets his own writings authentically:

Since, finally, the reviewer [of Johann Gottlieb Buhle's *Entwurf der Transcendental-Philosophie* in the *Allgemeine Litteratur-Zeitung*] maintains that the *Critique* [*of Pure Reason*] is not to be taken *literally* with respect to what it teaches about sensibility and that, instead, anyone who wants to understand the *Critique* must first master the requisite (Beckian or Fichtean) *standpoint*, because the *Kantian* letter, just like the Aristotelian one, will kill the spirit, I therefore again hereby declare that the *Critique* is to be understood according to the letter and is to be considered merely from the standpoint of common understanding, insofar as it has been sufficiently cultivated to such abstract investigations.

115

There is an Italian proverb: "May God protect us only from our friends, we'll keep watch over our enemies ourselves." There are indeed well-meaning friends who are well disposed toward us but get everything reversed (clumsy) in the choice of the means that favor our ends; but there are also deceptive, cunning so-called friends who aim for our ruin and yet use the language of well-wishing (*aliud lingua promptum, aliud pectore inclusum genere* [who say one thing and have in their hearts another]). Before these so-called friends and their carefully laid traps one cannot be too well guarded.

(12: 397)

Keeping a vigilant watch over false friends is as much a part of the post-critical predicament as discovering a means to fill in the holes that prevent the "entire critical enterprise" (5: 170) from being entirely finished. In a private letter to Christian Garve, whom Kant calls "dearest friend," he acknowledges a "gap [*Lücke*]" (12: 257) – only to deny the same in his public denunciation of Fichte a few months later.[2] Both the Italian and the Latin proverbs he quotes in his Open Letter apply especially well to himself, as Garve, a student of Cicero, would doubtless have recognized. So, too, would have all the "hypercritical friends" whom Kant variously addresses in private as "dear," "dearest," and "treasured" friend. In a curious section of the *Anthropology from a Pragmatic Point of View* entitled "On Permissible Moral Semblance [*Schein*]" Kant authorizes the use of the term *friend* without corresponding feelings of friendship: "*Shows of deference* (compliments), the whole of *courtly* gallantry, and the warmest verbal assurances of friendship are not always the truth ('My dear friends: there is no such thing as a friend.' Aristotle)" (7: 152). Yet Kant includes a caveat here: such pronouncements are permissible not only because no one believes them in any case but "above all, because these signs of benevolence and respect, which are empty at first, by and by lead to real attitudes of this kind" (7: 152). If, however, the empty signs do not find fulfillment, the semblance of friendship is indistinguishable from duplicity. According to Kant, his "hypercritical friends" are hypocrites, professing friendship while seeking his destruction. And, in reverse, Kant can scarcely be defended against the same charge, privately presenting himself as a trustworthy friend in the fall of 1797 and publicly denouncing Fichte as a pernicious enemy in the summer of 1799. It is little wonder, then, that in his Open Letter Kant places himself in the company of Aristotle, whose apothegm on the non-existence of friendship interrupts his justification for using the term *friend* when, by all rights, *enemy* should be invoked instead. Nowhere is this apothegm more applicable than in the "apexes" of hypocritical hypercritique – at the summit points of theoretical speculation, which do not lend themselves to mutual accommodation and general "understanding," for they are as exacting as the end-points of daggers.[3]

The friend vanishes

Many of the circumstances that led Kant publicly to denounce Fichte – at the worst possible time, when he was exposed to a more intense version of official censure than Kant himself had experienced – remain rather murky.[4] One aspect of this controversy can, however, be determined with a reasonable degree of accuracy: the text to which Kant refers in his letter to Fichte must be "On a Supposed Right to Lie out of Philanthropy" (1797), for it is the only essay he published in the *Berliner Blätter*. Kant's Open Letter against Schlettwein appeared in the *Berliner Blätter*, and it, like its successor, demands that *Critiques* be read *"according to the letter*, not according to a purported spirit that lies therein (since one can then import into them whatever one finds pleasing)" (12: 393–94). But the declaration against Schlettwein was originally published in the *Allgemeine Litteratur-Zeitung* and can scarcely be understood as a contribution to practical philosophy – except perhaps as a warning to Fichte. By writing and publishing "On a Supposed Right," as Kant tells his "treasured friend," he accomplishes two goals: he finds a channel by means of which he can make his existence known, and he finds a means of agitating his vital forces during a period of their apparent paralysis. The two goals are intimately related: by enlivening himself, Kant demonstrates he is alive; affecting himself, he affects others. And the effect of "On the Supposed Right" is unambiguous: it solidifies the image of the aging philosopher as a cold-hearted moralist who is so rigorous in his line of argument and so inflexible in his application of principles that he would, without the slightest hesitation, sacrifice the life of a friend for the sake of an abstract principle.

Forcefully – even violently – reacting against Benjamin Constant's *Des réactions politiques* (On Political Reactions, 1796), Kant says nothing about a friend. But this refusal is by no means innocent, for Constant most definitely does. Arguing that we have a right to mislead murderers who demand to know whether or not we are harboring our friend whom they intend to kill, the French *philosophe* seeks to show the absurdity of denying this right by reproducing a scenario proposed by an unnamed German philosopher. Kant responds by denying both the legality and general legitimacy of the right to lie – and by erasing the term *friend* altogether. More than simply a dispute over a narrow legal issue, the debate between Constant and Kant, which they both present as a dispute between representatives of two contrasting national characters, takes its point of departure from the image of a friend in danger and poses a basic social, legal, and political question: in whose name should one act? For Kant, only a single name responds to this question: "the great, sublime name" of *duty* (5: 86). Since, however, *duty* is not, properly speaking, a name but rather a common noun, whose commonness runs counter to its supposed sublimity, it cannot fail to come into conflict with certain proper names, among which are those of our friends.

The conflict between the improper name of duty, which demands absolute propriety, and the proper names of friends, who are generally willing to forgive a degree of impropriety, plays itself out in the debate between the old German philosopher and the young French *philosophe*.

Kant opens his essay by citing Constant's single sentence story about friendship, murder, lying, criminality, legality, the possibility of society, and a certain German philosopher who says dangerous things and seems to be none other than Immanuel Kant. The Open Letter he publishes against his false friend Fichte in a similarly transient venue may have nothing in common with "On a Supposed Right" – one concerns the foundations of knowledge, the other the foundations of the legal order – but the two are identical in terms of the perceived threat of a murderous conspiracy:

> In the journal *Frankreich im Jahr 1797*, Part VI, No. 1, "On Political Reaction" by Benjamin Constant contains the following (p. 123).
> "The moral principle 'it is a duty to tell the truth' would, if taken unconditionally and singly, make any society impossible. We have proof of this in the very direct consequences drawn from this principle by a German philosopher, who goes so far as to maintain that it would be a crime to lie to a murderer who asked us whether a friend of ours whom he is pursuing has taken refuge in our house."[5]

In a footnote to his translation of Constant's tract, K. F. Cramer informs his readers that the *philosophe* had told him that he was referring to Kant, and in a footnote to this footnote Kant concedes the point: "I hereby grant that I actually said this somewhere or other, although I cannot recall where" (8: 425) – and for good reason: no such place has ever been found in his previous writings. Yet there is something even stranger about Kant's admission than the fact that he cannot recall having invented a story in which a friend is pursued by a murderer and indeed never published anything of the kind. When he retells the story Constant imagines he has taken over from his own work, he drops the word *friend* and replaces it with *enemy*. Whereas Constant tells the story of someone acting in the name of friendship, Kant concerns himself with a scene of enmity:

> It is indeed possible that, after you have honestly answered "yes" to the murderer's question as to whether his enemy is at home, the latter has gone out unobserved, so that he would not meet up with the murderer and the deed would not be done; but if you had lied and said that he is not at home, and he has actually (although unbeknownst to you) gone out, with the result that, by so doing, he has been met by the murderer and thus the deed has been done, then you may by right be accused of being the author of his death. For if you had told the truth to the best of your knowledge, then

neighbors might have come and apprehended the murderer while searching the house for his enemy, and the deed would have been prevented.

(8: 426–27)

Whatever else may be said about the strange twists Kant gives to the story he admits to having invented, this much is clear: the friend has not simply gone into hiding but has vanished altogether; the relation between "you" and the one in danger has been effectively neutralized. Kant may have forgotten the story he cites at the beginning of his short essay. After all, he admits that his memory is faulty. Or he may have wished silently to alter the terms of debate, to make them less emotional, and more appropriate for inclusion in a legal dispute. Or he may have had entirely different reasons for changing a story of friendship into one of enmity – reasons that only his most treasured friends would have been able to detect, and even they would have only understood up to a point. One such reason concerns his mother, about whom he tells the following story to various friends – perhaps in order to elicit sympathy, perhaps in order to warn them of the dangers of friendship, perhaps only in order to let them know the circumstances of her untimely death:

Kant's mother had a friend whom she tenderly loved. She was engaged to a man to whom she had given her whole heart, without violating innocence and virtue. Disregarding his promise to marry her, he faithlessly took the hand of another. As a result of the pain and suffering, the deceived woman fell victim to a fatally high fever. She refused to take the medicine prescribed for her. Kant's mother, who attended her on her deathbed, tried to give her a full spoon of the medicine, but her sick friend refused it, claiming that it was disgusting. Kant's mother believed that the best way to convince her of the opposite would be to take a spoonful herself. She did, then became aware that her sick friend had already used the very spoon. At the very moment she did this, nausea and a cold shudder overtook her. Her imagination increased and heightened both. When she discovered blotches on the body of her friend, which she recognized as spots [*Petechien*, indicative of smallpox], she declared immediately "this would occasion her death," then laid down that very day and died soon afterwards as a sacrifice to friendship [*Opfer der Freundschaft*].[6]

Acting in the name of her friend, without regard to her duties – as a mother, for instance – Anna Regina Kant impetuously becomes a "victim" (*Opfer*) of friendship. The dangers friendship poses from the perspective of duty are as effectively demonstrated in this story of sacrifice as in the scenario

119

that Constant recounts: the dying friend turns into a deadly enemy. Perhaps Kant so readily confesses to having said what Constant attributes to him because he remembers that his mother sacrificed herself in the name of friendship – or remembers telling stories to this effect. How better for Kant to "agitate" his "vital forces" than to recall, even against his own will, the scene of his mother's death? Without so much as hinting at the reason, Kant allows the term *friend* to disappear from his contribution to the *Berliner Blätter*, and the title of his essay indicates the mist into which the term disappears: "philanthropy" (*Menschenliebe*). Precisely what this word means in the context of the essay is difficult to say; Kant uncharacteristically leaves it undefined, and since, as he indicates in the *Doctrine of Virtue*, which he will soon publish, the "love" in *Menschenliebe* can be understood in two ways – either as a "practical love" or "the love that delights in [human beings]" (6: 450) – the ambiguity of the term is irreducible.[7] This ambiguity has a positive function: it indicates that agents who act out of *Menschenliebe* do not know why they act. And the same is true of those who discover a supposed right to act on its basis: they are hiding from themselves. Constant, according to Kant, cannot possibly be himself – he cannot be *constant* – when he proposes that one has a right to act in the name of friendship.[8] Kant, by contrast, is constant in opposing Constant. And, for whatever reason, the term *friend* vanishes from his demonstration of Constant's inconsistency.

The disappearance of the friend in Kant's scenario is doubtless a minor matter, especially since Constant never explains the significance of making a *friend* – not a neighbor, stranger, or family member – into the one in whose name we are authorized to act in emergency circumstances. In the section of *Des réactions politiques* to which Kant responds, Constant directs his arguments against "reactionary" ideas like those of Burke, which favor the arbitrariness of prejudice over the stability of principles, and like Kant, he insists on the absolute necessity of fully articulated principles for the security and soundness of any political institution; but Constant also concedes that certain "intermediate principles" are sometimes required for the application of abstract principles to particular instances.[9] He therefore seeks to discover a "mean of applications" for resolving political and legal dilemmas. Yet, Constant never concerns himself with the middle term around which the story of persecution ultimately revolves – namely, secrecy – and he never considers the place of friendship in relation to the two basic categories around which his argument is structured. Friendship, however, may be the very relation in which the arbitrariness of prejudice and the constancy of principle are "mediated." Constant thus fails to pursue the more far-reaching lines of thought suggested by the story he tells: that the possibility of something like society depends on an always local – never universal or universalizable – "right" to keep one's friends to oneself; that friendships, which depend on a certain degree of openness and are themselves open-ended, make possible other forms of openness or "publicity"; that friends, in short, make claims out of which social or political spheres arise but which, for this reason, cannot be integrated into an abstract set of universal rights, laws, and principles – but cannot be reduced to effects of "prejudice" either. Constant says nothing of the kind, for he had already neutralized the relations between the friends about whom he writes even before Kant found himself named in the pages of *Frankreich*.[10] And yet Kant's alteration of the friend into an enemy, even if it is inconsequential, is nevertheless instructive: it indicates that the name of the friend finds no place – not even the reassuring space of explicit exclusion – in his recently published *Doctrine of Right*.

Keeping track of one's friends

Critiques of, and outright rebellions against, the neutralization of relations among legal personae and political agents are attracted to figures of the friend, members of the family, and loved ones in general. It is even possible to formulate a law of this attraction: the more thoroughly these relations are neutralized, the greater attraction these figures exert. They serve as reminders that relations cannot, or should not, be neutralized, that certain forces of attraction – and not simply the explicit words of a contract – structure the spheres in which individuals find room for action. It is not difficult, moreover, to specify one of the primary places from which the specific figure of the friend returns: from the classical world; more exactly, from famous Greek and Roman figurations of friendships, mythical as well as historical, and from certain classical accounts of friendship, especially Aristotle's *Nicomachean Ethics* and Cicero's *Laelius de amicitia*.[11] And here again Kant proves instructive, for his work also witnesses the return of the friend – not in the *Doctrine of Right*, to be sure, but in the concluding section of its companion volume, the *Doctrine of Virtue*.[12] Between the publication of these two complementary volumes as the comprehensive *Metaphysics of Morals*, appears "On the Supposed Right," which can be understood as its ephemeral fulcrum.

After defining perfect friendship as "the union of two persons through equal mutual love and respect" (6: 469) and presenting this union in terms of the two opposing forces – "love can be regarded as attraction and respect as repulsion" (6: 470) – Kant returns to classical examples and accounts of friendship. But this return is far from simple, for, according to Kant, modern writers of *Romane* (novels, romances) are the ones who feel themselves most strongly inclined to represent pure and complete friendships, whereas *the* classical authority, namely Aristotle, inconsistently denies the very existence of the friend. The contemporaneous cult of friendship, which finds its most apt expression in J. W. L. Gleim's striking reformulation of a popular saying, "*vox amici, vox dei*,"[13] is a corollary of what Kant elsewhere calls "moral enthusiasm" and which he similarly associates with the process of "novelization": an ideal – be it perfect friendship or moral perfection (5: 86)[14] – is represented as something that can be realized "in time." The account of the temporal realization of the ideal can then take an endless variety of narrative forms, including ones that are centered around the murder of mothers: "Friendship thought as attainable in its purity and completion (between Orestes and Pylades, Theseus and Pirithous) is the hobby-horse of novelists [*Romanenschreiber*]. On the other hand Aristotle says: My dear friends, there is no such thing as a friend! The following remarks draw attention to the difficulties in a perfect friendship" (6: 470).[15]

Of all these difficulties none is more perilous to friendship than the duty of friends to identify each others' fault, for this duty, grounded in the kind of love that seeks to help others perfect themselves, places every friend "in constant danger of losing something of his friend's respect, since he is observed and secretly criticized by him; and even the fact that he is observed and mastered will seem in itself offensive" (6: 470). Kant, like his predecessors and his contemporaries, then proceeds to distinguish betweeen different kinds and degrees of friendship; but these strange words of warning – "even the fact that he is observed and mastered [*beobachtet und gemeistert*]" – suggest that friendship founders on a disturbing equation: observation is equivalent to mastery; being seen by a friend means being in his or her power. This equation becomes even more disturbing in light of the Latin word with which Kant had translated the decisive term of his moral psychology, if not of his entire practical philosophy – *Achtung* (respect, attention) – in the previous section of the treatise: *observantia*.[16] To respect one's friends is to watch over them as a night watchman might survey the inhabitants of his town; but only one who is – or has been delegated by – a master can fulfill this policing function. Even if friends do not reveal much of themselves to each other and thus fall short of perfect friendship, they still vie for a position of mastery or, perhaps more disturbingly, are pressed into a secret policing function. Every opportunity for friends to see each other is also a chance for each to get the better of the other.

Editors and translators of Kant have been so disturbed by the implications of this equation of observation with mastery that they have proposed the reasonable suggestion that Kant meant something else: the friend is not *gemeistert* (mastered) but, rather, *gemustert* (tested).[17] There can be no testing, however, without a certain mastery of the subject under scrutiny, so the equation remains unaltered: to be under observation may not amount to mere passivity, but it is equivalent to being in the observer's power. The desire to make Kant say something other than *gemeistert* is understandable, for he seems little disturbed by this anthropological observation. Of far greater importance to him are the more obvious disadvantages that befall friends who *actively* reveal too much of themselves. It is possible, according to Kant, for self-revelation to have no purpose outside of itself, and the need to open oneself up to another can indeed be cultivated to the point where it is an end in itself; but such self-revelation can still serve the ends of the one to whom it is made, and these ends may be devious ones. It is therefore always safer to keep oneself hidden. Revealing oneself to another, by contrast, is fraught with danger. Every story of friendship may not revolve around the threat of murder, as Constant's does, but no account of friendship would be adequate unless it comes to terms with the atmosphere of violence in which they are formed:

> The human being is a being meant for society (though he is also an unsociable one), and in the culture of the social condition he feels strongly the need *to open* himself to others (even with no ulterior purpose). But on the other hand, hemmed in and cautioned by fear of the misuse others may make of his disclosing his thoughts, he finds himself constrained *to close up* inside himself a good part of his judgments (especially those about other people). He would like to discuss with someone what he thinks about his associates, the government, religion and so forth, but he cannot risk it: partly because the other person, while prudently keeping back his own judgments, might use this to harm him, and partly because, as regards disclosing his faults, the other person may conceal his own, so that he would lose something of the other's respect by presenting himself quite candidly to him.
>
> (6: 471–72)

And partly – readers might add, even if Kant prudently keeps silent on this matter, for he cannot count all his readers among his friends – because certain forms of governance make it dangerous for friends to open themselves to one another. At the conclusion of his *Doctrine of Virtue*, however, Kant returns to the certain considerations that would be more appropriate in his *Doctrine of Right*. Without straying far from the text, moreover, it is possible to identify one form of government that makes it less likely for friendships to be formed: one that, like the Prussian monarchy under Friedrich Wilhelm II,[18] uses its power to enforce theological doctrines. A certain politics of friendship can thus be adduced from these lines: it is a duty, according to Kant, to enter into friendships; whatever unnecessarily hinders the execution of this duty is illegitimate; any form of government that makes it more dangerous and thus less likely for friendships to be formed ought therefore to be transformed. Regimes can even be judged according to the degree to which they make friendships more likely: the less dangerous it is to open oneself to another, the better the chances for forming friendships, the better the regime.

But this conclusion leaves out of account the more disturbing dimension of Kant's exposition of friendship: the equation of observation with mastery. This equation goes to the heart of friendship, for it runs counter to the condition in which friendship alone is possible – that of equality: "in his relation to his neighbor how can a human being ascertain whether one of the elements requisite to this duty (e.g. benevolence toward each other) is *equal* in the disposition of each of the friends?" (6: 469). To this question Kant suggests an answer: friends cannot be *certain* that their disposition toward each other is equal; indeed, they can scarcely be sure of their own disposition, for "the depths of the human heart are unfathomable" (6: 447). But it is, nevertheless, possible for friends to *present* themselves to each other *as* equals. Finding a perspective from which equality can be presented is therefore of considerable importance. Such a perspective can disengage observation from mastery by mastering the act of observation in advance of everything observed. In the last paragraph of Kant's excursus on friendship, almost as an afterthought, he finds an appealing perspective in the figure of the brother:

> A friend of human beings [*Menschenfreund*] as such (i.e. of the whole species) is one who takes an aesthetic [*ästhetisch*] interest in the well being of all human beings (rejoices with them) and will never disturb it without inner regret. Yet the expression "a *friend* of human beings" is somewhat narrower in its meaning than "one who merely loves human beings" (a philanthropist). For the former also includes the representation and the taking to heart [*Vorstellung und Beherzigung*] of *equality* among them, and hence the idea that in putting others under obligation by his beneficence he is himself under obligation; as, so to speak [*gleichsam*], brothers under a universal father who wills the happiness of all.
>
> (6: 472–73)

Fraternity

Nothing is less surprising in this context than the appearance of the friend in the guise of the brother. By presenting friends from the equalizing perspective of brotherhood, Kant, who elsewhere calls the founder of Christianity a "friend of humanity [*Menschenfreund*]" (8: 338), can even disguise himself in Christian garb: "one is your master, but you are all brothers" (Matthew 23: 8).[19] Once the equality of all human beings is "taken to heart," it is no longer adequate to *profess* universal love; it must be felt – and indeed felt so strongly that the feeling cannot be expressed without recourse to a figural expression: "as, so to speak, brothers under a universal father." Fraternity, which Kant, perhaps for prudential reasons, does not name as such, can then become the figuration of limitless friendship, and this lack of limitation finds expression in two dimensions: in a small society of brethren who grow ever closer together, on the one hand, and in a community of brothers that promises to extend itself beyond every established border, on the other. These two dimensions are themselves united, for Kant, in a specific event: not, of course, in any supposed renewal of Christian brotherhood at the turn of a momentous century but, rather, in the experience of distant observers of the French

Revolution, all of whom, according to a text Kant will publish soon after the appearance of the *Doctrine of Virtue*, undergo a feeling that "borders closely on enthusiasm" (7: 85). The source of this affect lies in their ability to transcend in their imagination the borders of their own states and regard the "event" (*Eräugnis*) of a revolution founded on purely legal principles.[20] Although absent from the event itself, these observers endanger themselves when they reveal their "sympathetic participation" in the action, for the governing authorities under whose watchful eye they live are by no means enthusiastic about the prospect of states founded on the idea of universal rights. Because they endanger themselves for no self-serving reason, the feeling of the spectators can be interpreted as "an historical sign" (7: 84) – a sign that history continually progresses toward greater and greater degrees of legality. All men will be, then, brothers under the single master named "duty." Suspicious of the highly charged term *fraternity* for numerous reasons, including its enormous appeal to German pietistic preachers – whose ranks include his only brother, with whom he had cordial relations at best[21] – Kant makes no mention of it in the course of interpreting the "historical sign," but everything he says about the spectators of the French Revolution indicates that, although their feeling may only "border" on enthusiasm, they fit squarely in the circle of fraternity: *almost* everyone can be included.

Fraternity cannot encompass everyone for one simple reason: it makes no sense to speak of brotherhood unless this term is distinguished from others. In Kant's account, it is the "universal father" who cannot belong to the fraternity he establishes but who, as a father – and not, say, a mother – cannot simply be excluded either. Fatherhood, however, is only one of the many familial relations in contrast to which brotherhood is defined; so, too, are sisterhood, motherhood, the absence of siblings, and all familiar relations that cannot be captured according to the alternative between male and female. And it is not only in contrast to other familial relations that brotherhood is comprehensible; it is also in contradistinction to other manners of household management, other laws of the family residence or, in other words, other "economies." According to the *Doctrine of Right*, the friend of the human being, unlike the philanthropist, gives only to those whom he owes; more exactly, he gives only to those whom he feels "in his heart" that he owes, although no explicit contract, agreement, or promise stipulates that he owes anything. Only a community whose members acknowledge a mutual and yet entirely implicit debt to one another is fraternal: a debt that amounts to a universally shared secret. Because the depth of this debt is limitless the friend can represent his fraternity as extending *ad infinitum*. The sister, the mother, and even perhaps the lone father – to name only these three – would presumably be figures for other economies.

Only when friendship expands beyond the perfect friendship of the very few – or only two – does the friend, for Kant, begin to represent himself as a brother. The renewal of interest in the theory, representation, practice, and history of friendship over the last few decades can be understood accordingly, for this interest is largely motivated by one or both of the following demands: that friendship be disengaged from its subordination to ethical and legal principles that, stemming from and developing out of Christian ideas of an unconditional love for all neighbors, regardless of their goodness or merit, disallow and de-legitimate the partiality and selectivity without which there can be no friendship; and that friendship be freed from its fraternal figurations. "One is master, but you are all brothers": this saying brings friendship into the orbit of fraternity and demands that every relation of friend to friend be mediated by a master – or his representatives. Even if the relation between master and disciples can still be called friendship, the former is a friend of an entirely different order precisely because he cannot be *simply* another brother, and the same is true of those who represent him.[22] As Kant echoes the saying "all ye are brethren," he allows the relation of friend to friend once again to vanish – this time into a "friend of the human being" who figures himself as, and feels himself to be, a brother among equals.

Friendship thus forms a decisive point from which it is possible to contest two imposing positions: that of legal, ethical, and political universalism and that of phallo- or phratro-centrism. Recent explorations of the phenomenon of friendship, particularly ones conducted by feminist philosophers and writers, have taken aim at both positions at once.[23] Other inquiries into friendship, many of which concentrate on classical discussions of the theme, concern themselves with the problem of justifying – or demonstrating the unjustifiability of – the partiality and selectivity of every friendship. Still other investigations into the literary, cultural, and social history of friendship have sought to free it from fraternity by focusing on the specific forms, practices, figures, and configurations of female friendship. Whenever friendship is represented in terms of fraternity and brothers are implicitly or explicitly understood to be prohibited from relating to one another in a sexual manner – regardless of how sexuality may itself be understood – friendship is effectively removed from the sphere of sexuality. Dissociating friendship from fraternity tends in the opposite direction – toward explorations of the sexual practices through which different kinds of friendships are defined, even if by way of prohibition.[24] In one of his last interviews Michel Foucault draws attention to the complex relation between sexuality and friendship, and he notes that under certain historical conditions this relation is one of mutual exclusion: "I think now, after studying the history of sex, we should try to understand the history of friendship, or friendships. That history is very, very important."[25]

Derrida with Kant

There can be no history of friendship, however, unless there is such a thing as a friend. About this matter, there have been some doubts. Kant, for one, denies that there is such a thing – not only in late publications such as the *Doctrine of Virtue* and the *Anthropology* but also in private, as one of the men whom he befriended late in his life reports: "Kant adopted Aristotle's blinding paradox: My dear friends, there is no such thing as a friend."[26] This "blinding paradox" serves as the focal point for Derrida's *Politiques de l'amitié* (hereafter PA). No insight can be gained into the history and structure of friendship, unless both its history and structure include a radically an-historical and de-structuring moment of inconsistency, in which the friend is not one – and is not, then, converted into an enemy. By reflecting on the dictum attributed to Aristotle from a variety of perspectives, including that of the *Doctrine of Virtue*, Derrida seeks to discover a point from which friendship can be dissociated not only from fraternity but also from every representation of the relation of friend to friend in terms of ego and alter ego and, even more generally, in terms of a symmetrical affinity of like to like. An incalculable non-relation traverses every relation of friend to friend. As Derrida indicates in the Preface to *Politiques de l'amitié*, the analyses of certain canonical expositions of friendship that he proposes, however exacting, make only two demands – imagine a friendship beyond fraternity and ask what the politics of a non-fraternal friendship might entail:

> Why would the friend be *like* a brother? Let us dream of a friend-ship that goes beyond this proximity of the cogeneric double, beyond parenthood, the most as well as the least natural of parenthoods, when it leaves its signature, from the outset, on the name as on a double mirror of such a couple. Let us ask ourselves what would then be the politics of such a "beyond the principle of fraternity."
>
> (PA: 12)

Dissociating friendship not only from all vestiges of fraternity but also from every interpretation of the relation of friend to friend as a relation of like to like, ego to alter ego, does not mean, however, that, for Derrida, friendship should henceforth be understood simply in terms of its opposite – as an asymmetrical and non-reciprocal relation between non-equals, which, *a limine*, could be conceived only as an infinite relation to the absolutely other. The dream of freeing friendship from fraternity does not therefore consist in sacralizing friendship, which would doubtless result in a familiar configuration – that of each "brother" to one "master" or, to cite once again a secularization of this sacralization, "*vox amici, vox dei.*" In the course of Derrida's analyses of various discussions of friendship from Aristotle, Cicero, and Montaigne to Kant, Nietzsche, and Carl Schmitt, the idea of friendship begins to encompass both of these interpretations at once *and* to reject each of them in turn: the relation of friend to friend is both a reciprocal relation of equals and a non-reciprocal, asymmetrical relation of each one to an absolutely other – *and* also, as a paradoxical addition, a non-relation or a "relation without relation [*rapport sans rapport*]" (PA: 331).[27] Such is the constitutive inconsistency of the pronouncement attributed to the inventor of logic as a formal science: "*o philoi, oudēs philos.*"[28] For Derrida, these words pose the problem of a "democracy to come":

> Having made a *problematic* scansion appear in a sort of history of friendship, a scansion which would have introduced dissymmetry, separation and infinite distance in a Greek *philia* which did not tolerate them *but nevertheless called for them*, it would now be a matter of suggesting that a democracy to come – still not given, not thought; indeed, put down or repressed – not only would not contradict this dissymmetrical curving and this infinite heterogeneity, but would in truth be demanded by them.
>
> (PA: 259)

In an effort to measure the space of this "democracy to come" *Politiques de l'amitié* turns toward the section of Kant's *Doctrine of Virtue* devoted to friendship, for, according to Derrida, this short discussion offers something of note, perhaps even something entirely new. Although Kant may introduce friendship under the sign of intimacy, his proposal to distinguish friendship from love by defining the former in terms of repulsion emphasizes the distance that friends must take with respect to one other. What Greek *philia* "did not tolerate but nevertheless called for" is thus accomplished in Kant *up to a point*: Derrida underlines this phrase throughout *Politiques de l'amitié* but never so emphatically as in his analysis of the fraternal figure with which Kant concludes his considerations of friendship. Up to a point, Kant's effort to conceive of acts done in the name of friendship from the infinitely distant perspective of the "great, sublime name" of duty gives him a chance to encompass two contradictory demands: that the relation of friend to friend be one of equals, on the one hand, and that it be a non-hierarchical relation of asymmetrical and non-reciprocal non-equals, on the other. Friendship, for Kant, stops being a matter of distance and returns to the spirit of proximity only at the point where the friend no longer can name his friends, having become a "friend of humanity."[29] At this point, instead of returning to – and disclosing the political dimensions of – the paradoxical saying he had adopted, "O my friends, there is no such thing as a friend," Kant retreats to a figure of fraternal affiliation. In this way, he forges a link among all those "friends of human beings" who would otherwise become what they already are – distant, discrete, and defined less by their relation to one another than by the common interruption of their "relative" status:

> At the center of this familial schema, at the center of what can again be called *oikeiotēs*, the brother occupies the unique place, the place of the irreplaceable. . . . Is it not from the place of this very place

that we gaze over the *horizon*. . . .? A place can never be situated anywhere but under a horizon, from out of this limit that opens up and closes off at one and the same time. Is it not from off this bank and under this horizon that a political phallogocentrism has, *up to a point*, determined *its* cosmopolitan democracy, *a* democracy, qua cosmo-phratrocentrism?

(PA: 294)

As long as the figure of the brother is at the center of friendship, it skews the space of the "democracy to come" in whose name Derrida writes *Politiques de l'amitié*, for this space tolerates everything but this: a central figure in and through which the schemata, images, and ideas of friendship are to be defined. The qualification on this assertion – "as long as" – is important: Derrida issues a "warning" at the end of *Politiques de l'amitié* in which he states that "despite the appearances that this book has multiplied, nothing in it says anything *against* the brother or against fraternity. . . . I have never stopped asking myself, I request that it be asked, what is meant when one says 'brother,' when someone is called 'brother' . . . *Up until now*. I am wondering, that's all, and request that it be asked, what the implicit politics of this language is" (PA: 338–39). This final warning comes as a response to a letter of Blanchot that Derrida cites with little commentary: "it was obviously the Nazi persecution. . . . which made us feel that the Jews were our brothers."[30] Derrida's reticence to make any remarks about this letter is, as he concedes, "the disquiet that incites the book" (PA: 338). The disquiet generates afterthoughts in two senses of the word: thoughts after the fact, in this case that of the catastrophe of the Nazi regime; and thoughts that pertain to missed chances, in this case those that seek to resolve "the Jewish question" in a friendly manner. One of those chances is of particular significance for the public world in which Kant placed also hopes for the enlightenment of the human race as a whole: the friendship between Gotthold Ephraim Lessing and Moses Mendelssohn.

Arendt with Lessing

The friendship between Mendelssohn and Lessing spans all but the last years of Kant's public life. The famous friendship between these two representatives of the *Aufklärung* made its entrance into "the world of reading" (8: 37) under almost the same circumstances as the entrance of the only other *Aufklärer* whose achievements and failures could be seen to surpass their own. The Académie Royal des Sciences et Belles-Lettres in Berlin proposed the following theme for its prize contest of 1755: "examine the system of Pope, contained in the proposition: All is good." To this prize contest Mendelssohn and Lessing respond with bursts of laughter: *Pope a Metaphysician!*[31] Kant, by contrast, makes some sketches for the contest; instead of developing them into a prize essay, he concentrates on a non-metaphysical treatise entitled *Universal Natural History and Theory of the Heavens* (1755), which, however, includes copious quotations from Pope's *Essay on Man* (1: 242, 259, 318, 349, 360, 365). And the end of the friendship between Mendelssohn and Lessing is even more intimately tied to Kant's entrance into the world of publication, for, as is well known, the friendship did not come to an end so much with Lessing's death in 1781 as with F. H. Jacobi's presumptuous publication of the great ironist's dying confession that he had always been a Spinozist – a confession that, if true, meant that his friendship with Mendelssohn had always been something of a joke. The post-critical predicament is more thoroughly stamped by the resulting "pantheism controversy" than by any other events in the "world of reading." And yet, despite the fact that Kant reluctantly accepts the challenge of responding to the controversy in "What Does It Mean: To Orient Oneself in Thinking?" (1786) and despite his decision to take Mendelssohn to task for rejecting Lessing's idea of historical progress in the last section of "On the Common Saying: That May Work in Theory but not in Practice" (1793), he never once considers the specific status of their friendship – not even in passing. The later essay describes Lessing as Mendelssohn's "friend" (8: 307) and the earlier one concludes with an appeal to "Friends of the human species and what is holiest to it" (8: 146), but this very appeal to nameless friends indicates the degree to which Kant misses an opportunity to reflect on the nature of their singular friendship.

The missed chances of this friendship are the motivating force of Arendt's "On Humanity in Dark Times: Address on Lessing."[32] That Arendt knows for sure that chances have been missed distinguishes her time from that of Kant, and this knowledge permeates her inquiry into Lessing's remarkable capacity for friendship and his equally remarkable aversion to fraternity. One sentence of her address is sufficient to indicate the point of departure for her afterthoughts: "in the case of a friendship between a German and a Jew under the conditions of the Third Reich it would scarcely have been a sign of humanness for the friends to have said: Are we not both human beings?" (*Von der Menschlichkeit in finsteren Zeiten* (hereafter VM): 38; *Men in Dark Times* (hereafter MDT): 23). In contrast to the particularly "dark" time to which she refers, the "dark" time of Lessing, Mendelssohn, and Kant could at least make the question "are we not both human beings?" into a starting point for a discussion of what it means to be human – or for *any* discussion. And every discussion brings the things under discussion into the hands of a humanity capable of asking itself what it means to be human. Arendt's address takes its point of departure from the imperative that this – or any other – discussion must begin. Such an imperative cannot, however, express itself in the inquisitive or inquisitorial order "talk!" Nor can it find expression in Friedrich II's reformulation of this command: " 'argue as much as you want and about what you want, but obey!' " (8: 41). Her talk to the "Free

City" of Hamburg therefore goes in search of a formulation of this imperative that does not presuppose the existence of an exalted position beyond
discussion – whether in the form of an inviolate truth, an incontrovertible
principle, or a violent prince.

The search for a formulation of this imperative brings Arendt to Lessing's
Nathan der Weise (Nathan the Wise, 1779), whose eponymous hero is modeled on Mendelssohn and which, she emphasizes, treats the appeal to friendship as an imperative in its own right. Arendt's address takes its direction
from two short sentences from Lessing's play, for these sentences give expression to the imperative of discourse that does not ground itself in any doctrine, any claim to power, or any supposedly self-legislating subject: "Be my
friend"[33] and, even more dramatically, "We must, must be friends."[34] This
double "must" in the context of a play that famously declares in one of its
opening scenes that "no human being must have to [*Kein Mensch muß
müssen*]"[35] is no small matter. The declaration that "no human being must
have to" is tantamount to the assertion of transcendental freedom: human
beings stand outside the sphere of natural necessitation. Kant, who owned a
copy of *Nathan der Weise*,[36] develops at least two arguments for this assertion:
human beings must presuppose transcendental freedom in their capacity as
agents; and the "sole fact of pure reason" (5: 31), which consists in moral self-
consciousness, serves as a sufficient basis for the conclusion that we are free
after all. In either case, however, human beings "must have to": they must
subordinate their inclinations to an absolutely universal law. The "must,
must" of "We must, must be friends" is different. Doubling the "must" makes
good on the assertion that no one "must have to," for the second *must* does
not propel the agent into another sphere of necessitation; semantically super-
fluous, it gestures toward a zone in which the word *must* is meaningless. And
one name of this zone is "friendship."

Freedom from necessity makes friendship eminently historical – under the
condition, of course, that history, too, is removed from the sphere of necessity. If, as Hölderlin wrote, "in good times there are seldom enthusiasts,"[37]
Arendt could say with respect to Lessing and Mendelssohn: in bright times
there is no need for friendship. The imperative "Be my friend!" is a response
to an obscured world, a call for orientation in thinking that has little to do
with the appeals of Mendelssohn and Kant, since the point of orientation is
not the "*need* of reason" (8: 139) but, rather, the need of friends to call themselves "friends" while conceding that there is no such thing:

> In history there are times in which the space of publicness [*Raum
> des Öffentlichen*] darkens and the substance of the world [*Bestand der
> Welt*] becomes so questionable that human beings demand nothing
> more of politics than that it show due consideration for their indi-
> vidual interests and private freedom. Those who have lived in such
> times and been formed by them have probably always been inclined

131

to have little respect for the world and its publicness, to ignore them as far as possible, or even to overleap them and, as it were, reach behind them . . . in order to come to an understanding with one another without regard for the world that lies between them. In such times, if things go well, a peculiar kind of humanity develops.

(VM: 19; MDT: 11–12, translation modified)

This kind of humanity, which cannot be "produced" and whose development depends on chance, is not only compassionate but understands the distinguishing trait of the human being to lie in "an inner repugnance, as he [Rousseau] put it, to see a fellow human being suffer" (VM: 20; MDT: 12). But – and this is the critical point – such compassion goes in two directions: it issues into fraternity or friendship, and never the two at once. Whereas the former is uncritical – every example of a given kind, good or evil, can be enlisted into the brotherhood – the latter cannot do without certain criteria of selection, even if they remain always obscure. The imperative "Be my friend!" not only responds to the obscurity of the world; it also *articulates* this response and thus interrupts the mute feelings of both compassion and revulsion, which, each in its own way, reflect and intensify the obscurity of the world.[38] Lessing, who, unlike Rousseau, chooses the selectivity of friendship over the apparent inclusiveness of fraternity, therefore had to present himself as a particularly acrimonious polemicist.

But Arendt, like Kant and Derrida, is not against fraternity; on the contrary, she insists that it has its place – not among or between human beings, to be sure, but in the restricted spaces of the displaced, oppressed, and persecuted. Fraternity is non-selective because persecution consists at best in being deprived of choice, at worst in being captured and selected: "This kind of humanity actually becomes inevitable when the times become so extremely dark for certain groups of people that it is no longer up to them, their insight or choice, to withdraw from the world. Humanity in the form of fraternity invariably appears among historically persecuted peoples and enslaved groups" (VM: 21; MDT: 13). Drawn together in the absence of the "interspace" (*Zwischenraum*) that constitutes, for Arendt, the world, these peoples and groups generate warmth, and "the warmth of persecuted peoples is a great thing" (VM: 22; MDT: 13). But this warmth is similarly limited; it cannot communicate itself beyond the collapsed spaces to which the persecuted are confined. Without communicating, however, it can appear to illuminate. And yet, whenever the times are "dark," according to Arendt, the warmth of fraternity attracts those who are still able to move about at will,[39] and it even gives the appearance of being able to give direction to free movement – or movements consecrated to freedom:

[I]n "dark times" the warmth which is the pariahs' substitute for light exerts a fascination upon all those who are so ashamed of the

world as it is that they would like to take refuge in invisibility
. . . The rationalism and sentimentalism of the eighteenth century
are only two aspects of the same thing; both could lead equally to
that enthusiastic excess [*schwärmerische Überschwang*] in which individuals feel ties of brotherhood to all human beings.

(VM: 26–27; MDT: 16)

To this warmth – and the movements it generates – Lessing says "no."
And this renunciation, for Arendt, makes *his* call for friendship altogether
critical: it neither exalts nor belittles; rather, it separates and distinguishes.
The "must, must" of friendship that, as Arendt notes, run like a "*leitmotif*"
through *Nathan der Weise* are as far removed from proclamations of "*vox
amici, vox dei*" as his polemics are from invective. The grounds on which
Lessing stakes his critique of fraternity and decides on the criteria for the
selection of his friends can be found in neither reason nor sentiment, neither
principle nor prejudice; and if these criteria are indeed those of friendship –
and not features through which members of a fraternity are identified and
are able to identify themselves – they can never be justified in advance
of the discussion they nevertheless make possible. Friendship, in sum, is
necessarily selective; but it is impossible to justify the criteria of selection,
and so the imperative "Be my friend!" is, in its own way, non-selective: not
based on an idea or sentiment and yet not based on nothing – a whim,
velleity, or phantasm – either. It is precisely this lack of foundations
and "irrational" non-foundations that accounts for the quality of Lessing's
mind that Arendt finds most astonishing: his "objectivity." And this double
lack – no solid foundations, no yawning abysses – guarantees that the non-
formal and non-transcendental "logic" of friendship will be constitutively
inconsistent.

Arendt emphasizes from the beginning the paradoxical character of
Lessing's "logic" of friendship: "we are astonished that Lessing's partisanship
for the world could go so far that he could even sacrifice to it the axiom of
non-contradiction, the claim to self-consistency, which we assume to be
mandatory for all who write and speak" (VM: 13; MDT: 8). Lessing, in other
words, is inconsistent. And his inconsistency is itself inconsistent; it obeys
no recognizable law, least of all the law of sacrifice whereby one gives up
something in order to receive something else in return. The constitutive
inconsistency of Lessing's logic demands that the imperative "Be my friend!"
be combined with the assertion: "and there is no such thing" – as yet.
Whereas fraternity designates a consistent class, friendship cannot. The
command "Be my friend" demands that the one who issues this command
welcome a certain inconsistency and thereby "sacrifice" the chance of attaining the truth. In this respect, according to Arendt, Lessing's thought is drawn
into the vicinity of – and yet sharply diverges from – that of Kant. Although
she devotes only a single paragraph to the "critical enterprise," it is in this

paragraph that she is able to determine the inconsistent "logic" of friend-ship. The debate between Constant and Kant over the politics of friendship comes to life again in Arendt's address – but with one major difference: Lessing, who is an incomparably greater antagonist than Constant, gleefully accepts inconsistency in accordance with the ungrounded and yet non-abyssal, unprincipled and yet unprejudiced, non-Aristotelian and yet non-Kantian "logic" of friendship.

Both Kant and Lessing, according to Arendt, "would certainly have been prepared to sacrifice truth," but Kant would do so only for the sake of the freedom to which this sacrifice testifies – freedom, which, because of its absoluteness, takes over the systematic function of the truth it replaces. Such is the import of categorical commands, which can be interpreted as though they were divine prescriptions – this is the content of religion – but cannot, for the same reason, be debated. The immediacy of the command leaves no room for anything other than obedience: "[Kant] would scarcely have agreed with Lessing that the truth, if it did exist, could be unhesitatingly sacrificed to humanity, to the possibility of friendship and of discussion among human beings" (VM: 44; MDT: 26–27, translation modified). Lessing would do precisely that: without hesitation he would sacrifice truth for the sake of a possible friendship, a friendship to come, and thus a friendship that "exists" nowhere outside of the imperative – which is neither hypothetical nor categorical – "Be my friend!" This sacrifice of truth is not, however, a sanc-tion for lying.[40] Nor is it a reason to propose once again "a right to lie." Friends, *as friends and only as friends*, without a trace of fraternity, tell one another what they *deem* to be true – or, to use Kant's terms, which, for Arendt, miss the chance of thinking through their own political potential,[41] they *judge* to be beautiful.

On this point Arendt closes her essay: it is the last word of worldly wisdom because in making a display of this "deeming," which does not amount to claiming ignorance, a character like Nathan takes leave of both science and sentiment. Friends must tell one another the truth, regardless of the danger they thus run; but they must tell one another what they deem to be true not for the sake of the truth but for the sake of the friendship that the un-necessary "must, must" makes possible. Friends must say what they deem to be true – without reserve and without bounds. Least of all can the range of such truthfulness be restricted to a closed circle of friends, each of whom has implicitly or explicitly sworn an oath of loyalty to all the others. Friends, as friends, owe one another what they deem to be true because they have sacrificed *the* truth, which has no need of friendly intercourse, for the sake of *possible* friendships or, in other words, friendships to come – not for the sake of certain friendships they are confident they have secured. As a friend, therefore, one must absolutely say what one deems to be true, whoever may hear or overhear; but insofar as *the* truth has been sacrificed for the sake of friendship and not for sake of something like intellectual honesty or scientific

134

probity, the *must* in "friends must say what they deem to be true" cannot be grounded and cannot, as a result, carry any weight. If, however, the atmosphere in which things are said is permeated by persecution – murderers knock on the door, demand to know the whereabouts of their enemies, and paralyze those at the threshold – then it is only possible to tell the truth for one's own sake, for the sake of certain fraternal feelings, or for the sake of the truth itself. In all of these cases, one thing is clear: allies may abound; but the possibility of friendship has vanished, and as this possibility vanishes, appeals to necessity become all the more urgent – and all the less credible.

7

REVOLUTION IN THE AIR; OR THE END OF THE HUMAN REGIME ON EARTH

The death of cats in Copenhagen

In the last years of the eighteenth century, revolution was in the air. Kant often spoke about it – so much so that some of his friends began to fear for his health and safety. The revolution about which Kant spoke most often was not, however, the one that began in Paris. The aging philosopher paid attention to the events surrounding the French Revolution, of course; indeed, he went so far as to declare in the central part of *The Conflict of the Faculties* (1798) that the German spectators of the revolution, who courageously express their near enthusiasm for one party in the conflict, constitute an "*historical sign* (signum rememorativum, demonstrativum, prognosticon)" (7: 84). By reading this sign, without reliance on any supernatural insight, an earth-bound philosopher can confidently propose a "Soothsaying [*wahr-sagende*] History of Humanity" (7: 87) that affirms the constant progress of the human species toward the better. This is not to say that individuals are somehow becoming more honest; the truth- or sooth-saying history does not say anything about the history of sooth- or truth-telling. The universal enthusiasm of the spectators indicates, rather, a receptivity to the Idea of right, which is, in itself, sufficient grounds for the prediction that the species will organize itself in progressively more "republican" forms. Friedrich Theodor Rink paints a vivid picture of Kant's own enthusiasm for the spread of revolutionary forces into other European lands:

One can easily imagine that Kant, like all thinking and non-thinking men, warmly took part in the French revolution. It constituted one of the essential subjects of daily conversation, and his judgments concerning particular events of the revolution, like the reasons for his expectations and hopes, were incisive and consistent. Of course, in the meantime, many things ended up differently than he had thought, and then it was very difficult for him to exchange his presuppositions for historical facts. Egypt, for example, was already for a long time in the hands of the French before he could be convinced that Bonaparte had not sailed toward Portugal for the purpose of conquering this kingdom, as he had expected.[1]

Immediately after these remarks – which indicate both the depth of Kant's aversion to the European-wide *ancien régime* and the degree to which he was unprepared for the development of new forms of imperialism with its demise – Rink recounts another, rarely discussed revolution in which the philosopher takes an even greater interest. It is a revolution in the air. Its signs are, on the one hand, the death of unusually large numbers of cats in Copenhagen and, on the other, the ill health from which Kant himself suffered. The revolution in France and the revolution in the air began at approximately the same time:

> The most common topic of conversation by far was the origin and nature of an electric property of the air, which, according to his own admission, he did not comprehend. In one of the first years of the 1790s, if I am not mistaken, reports appeared in various European countries, especially in newspapers, that the death of huge numbers of cats had been perceived. Something similar had been noticed here and there with respect to birds. The reviewer of a natural-historical work in the Jena *Allgemeine Litteratur Zeitung* around this time had surmised that a peculiar electrical disposition of the air could be the cause of this mortality among animals. Kant took up this idea, and since the beginning of his own feelings of ill health dated from this time, he soon came to the supposition that the same electric property of the air was at fault. . . . He expected his convalescence only after a change of this condition.[2]

That Kant would also describe this sudden alteration in the disposition of the air as a "revolution" cannot be doubted. Immediately before he reports a scene in which Kant insists that the Hebrew name *Immanuel* be spelled out as a commemoration of what would prove to be his last birthday, Johann Gottfried Hasse records the following remarks: "I have never once in my entire life been sick; I have never needed a doctor and hope never to need one. – That I have been so powerless stems from a revolution in the air [*Revolution in den Luft-Straten*], which has been in place for several years;* and when it changes and everything comes back in line, I can again get well."[3] Hasse's annotation reads: "He dated this revolution from the time of the death of cats in Copenhagen, about which there was, a few years ago, much to read in the newspapers. Often and in great detail he spoke about the air, but left the whole matter in a certain chiaroscuro."[4] A note in one of the later convolutes of the *Opus postumum* confirms Hasse's report: "The electricity in the air throws off my nervous system entirely; yet I hope [for a] *contra revolution* against the two-year (*Erlanger Zeitung*) [duration] of the death of cats" (21: 89–90).[5]

No one seems to have been more disturbed by Kant's persistent talk of a revolution in the air than Ehregott Andreas Christoph Wasianski, who interprets his insistence on attributing his powerlessness to atmospheric conditions as an unmistakable sign that the old man has finally lost his wits:

> Every one of the objections to his theory he sought to avoid. His conviction of its certainty would only be increased thereby, so that his friends, out of consideration and tact, did not contradict him. ... Who of his sympathetic friends would have obscured the prospect of light for this suffering man by introducing unnecessary doubts? Who would have robbed him of the last hope of improvement by contradicting him? His daily assertion, which he repeated on any given day more than once, that nothing but electricity is the cause of his illness, removed from his friends any doubt that nature had claimed its rights over him and that he began to sink under the burden of the years. Kant, the great thinker, now stopped thinking.[6]

To this day, biographers of Kant repeat this remark, sometimes without indicating its specific context.[7] Kant, who had included his essay "On the Power of the Mind to Master its Feelings of Sickness by Sheer Resolution" in *The Conflict of the Faculties*, must have been out of his mind, for, if he were not sick in the head, he would have been able to master his feelings of powerlessness by sheer resolution.[8] Or, failing that, he could have simply admitted that his friends were right and he was wrong: his situation is hopeless. Old age is responsible for the woes that he suffers. And who knows what is responsible for the death of cats in Copenhagen?

A friendly joke

Suppose, however, that Wasianski's interpretation is in error. There is certainly no harm in entertaining this possibility for a moment. Wasianski himself gives good reason for doing so, moreover. Without being aware of the inconsistency, he shows that in another circumstance, Kant is reluctantly willing to concede that his friends are right and he wrong. Such is the case with the question of friendship:

> Kant adopted Aristotle's blinding paradox: My dear friends, there is no such thing as a friend. He did not seem to attribute the usual sense to the word *friend*; rather, to him, it was taken as something like the word *servant* in the concluding line of a letter or in the common greeting. On this point I was not of the same opinion as him. I have a friend in the full sense of the word, whose value makes

it impossible for me to agree with Kant's opinion. Until now [the end of the 1790s] Kant had been sufficient unto himself, and since suffering was something he knew only by name, he needed no friends. Now oppressed by weakness to the point of almost collapsing, he looked around for support, without being able to hold himself upright any longer. I had a chance to express my disbelief in relation to that paradox during one of the times in which he urgently assured me of his friendship, and he was open-hearted enough to admit that he now agreed with my opinion and no longer considered friendship to be a mere chimera.[9]

To this scene, which gives a concentrated image of the last years of Immanuel Kant, one could add the stage direction "bursts of laughter." It is clearly Wasianski who, here, confuses *friend* with *servant*. Kant no longer has friends to whom he can fully open himself but, rather, servants – or comforters – who support him when he is on the verge of collapsing. Much of Wasianski's *Immanuel Kant in the Last Years of his Life* gives this impression; all of Hasse's *Remarkable Utterances* does. Aristotle's paradox is therefore even more blinding than Wasianski is able to see: he proves that his friend is right by making him admit that he is wrong. It would have been both impolite and dangerous for Kant to have laughed at this moment, but the scene is, for all its pathos, unmistakably comical. And Kant's adoption of the atmospheric theory of illness may not be so different from his adoption of Aristotle's paradox. In the latter case, his friends are not supposed to believe him, and the same may be true in the former: he may have no intention of persuading his friends to share his opinion that the wide-scale death of cats in European cities has something to do with his own suffering, for, like his suffering, the opinion is *his* – perhaps even his alone. He has more in common with dying cats than with healthy friends. What sort of friend could believe this? Wasianski may have confused an elaborate joke, which, according to Kant, aims to produce a momentary cognitive collapse, with the breakdown of the jokester's own mind.

Electrifying events

Suppose, however, that Kant's persistent talk of revolution in the air is neither the sign of senility nor an elaborate joke but is, instead, a reasonably respectable response to a potentially alarming situation about which he may have had little evidence beyond a few reports in various journals but which still warrants some scrutiny. Kant was by no means unfamiliar with meteorological speculation. For much of his academic life he gave lectures on "physical geography," which included copious reflections on the "walnut" in which the "kernel" of the earth is "wrapped up."[10] And even before he began his career as a teacher with the delivery of his Master's thesis *On Fire* (1755), he showed a keen interest in the electrical qualities of the atmosphere, hailing Benjamin Franklin as the "Prometheus of modern times" (1: 472) for having robbed thunder of its weapon. A similar Prometheanism expresses itself in the command with which he commences his *Universal Natural History*: "Give me only matter, and I will build a world out of it for you" (1: 229). And something of this Promethean spirit gives direction to his series of articles on the famous Lisbon earthquake of 1755. Of course, Kant has no intention of robbing earthquakes of their weapons; but he wants them to be understood from a global perspective, which, moreover, precludes any presumption that the earth was created solely for the purpose of its human inhabitants: "The human subject is so taken with itself [*so von sich selbst eingenommen*] that it sees itself as the sole aim of the institutions of God, as though there were no other surveying mark for the establishment of standards for the governance of the world" (1: 460). In this respect, Kant's reports on the Lisbon earthquake are comparable to Voltaire's travesty of theodicical reasoning; but one of the distinctive qualities of these reports removes them from the general debates around the validity of optimism: their strong sense of foreboding. The earthquake of 1755 may only be the beginning of a terrestrial "catastrophe" (1: 459). Far from being local events, which cause devastating yet only momentary tremors, earthquakes are of global proportions, producing – among other things – large quantities of "combustible and volatile vapor" that can make verdant regions into stormy deserts. Being so close to the arctic zone, Königsberg is especially vulnerable, since volatile vapor generally lowers surface temperatures and "lets us feel something of the winter at the North Pole" (1: 454).

In one of his reports on the terrestrial disturbances of 1755 Kant notes that the earthquake seems to have made magnets go awry, but he refrains from offering an explanation, since "we know too little about the hidden nature of magnets to be able to give a reason for this phenomenon" (1: 455). Under the influence of Sebastiano Canterzani, whose geological speculations began to appear in German translation in the early 1780s, Kant became convinced that earthquakes are principally electric events. Thunder storms and earthquakes are, in a sense, reciprocal phenomena: "Electrical material condenses for a while in the clouds and discharges itself on the earth; this is a storm. Or it condenses for a while in the earth and discharges itself in the clouds. This is an earthquake. Wherever there are old volcanoes, there is much electrical material and therefore many earthquakes."[11] For similar reasons, as he notes in a lecture on physical geography in 1793, earthquakes generally occur near coastlines, where "electricity is felt most strongly."[12] And Wilhelm August Lampadius's *Versuche und Beobachtungen über die Elektrizität und Wärme der Atmosphäre* (Experiments on, and observations of, the electricity and warmth of the atmosphere, 1793), which includes an appendix on Jean André de Luc's theory of atmospheric electricity, gave

Kant a solid point of support for his conviction that diffuse electricity played a decisive role in all meteorological phenomena: the more electricity in the air, the greater its elasticity, the lower the atmospheric pressure.[13] Violent hail storms are particularly powerful manifestations of atmospheric electricity.[14] Yet, for the most part, as Kant regularly emphasizes, the circulation of "electrical material" tends toward a generally beneficent equilibrium. The third volume of the Vollmer edition of the *Physical Geography* includes a description of a daily cycle of electrical discharge, which rivals in prose some of the poetic depictions of terrestrial equilibrium that Kant would have found while perusing Ludwig Brockes' *Irdisches Vergnügen in Gott* (Earthly satisfaction in God): "Electricity increases during the morning when vapors ascend, until the heat of the sun dries the air, halting the circulation of electrical material, which then gathers in the upper regions of the atmosphere, only to die away to such an extent that the vapor and dew make the air once again into a conductor at night."[15]

Thunder storms and earthquakes are not the only phenomena that register disturbances in the otherwise harmonious cycle of atmospheric electricity; the same is true of both "optical meteors" such as the aurora borealis and corporeal meteors. The upper atmosphere is awash in "igneous meteors," which exchange positive and negative electricity.[16] Franklin and Volta had shown, according to Kant, that the atmosphere is always at risk of becoming suddenly overloaded.[17] And the consequences of elevated levels of atmospheric electricity are far from negligible: storms disrupt the local environment; earthquakes disturb the globe; and meteors shower down on the earth.[18] No wonder Kant began to worry as he read reports about a revolution in the air: storms might develop, which, could, in turn, give rise to earthquakes, and the upper atmosphere, with its abundant amounts of igneous meteors, might then attract greater numbers of celestial meteors. And this is not even the last of the fatal consequences of elevated levels of atmospheric electricity. Near the conclusion of "Something on the Influence of the Moon on the Wind and the Weather" (1794) Kant briefly discusses the "community" (*Gemeinschaft*) of "the air of higher (*jovial*) regions, lying beyond the region of lightning, with the subterranean (*volcanic*) air, which lies deep under the mountains and clearly manifests itself in many meteors" and then immediately adds: "Perhaps to this [community] belongs also the make-up of the air that renders some illnesses in certain countries at a certain time *epidemic* (actually, ravaging) and that shows its influence [*Einfluß*] not merely on a *people* [Volk] of human beings but also on a people of certain species of animals or plants" (8: 323). The neutral term "influence," which is the subject of the essay as a whole, suddenly assumes the sinister sense of *influenza*. A revolution in the air, in sum, could mark the beginning of a terrestrial catastrophe of unprecedented proportions: not only would the earth be altered from its depths to its uppermost regions; "peoples" of the human, animal, and plant kingdoms would also succumb to raging illnesses. With a catastrophe of this magnitude in mind, Napoleon's adventures seem paltry in comparison.

Around the same time as Kant turned his attention to the seemingly minor question whether the moon exerts any influence on atmospheric conditions, he drew up a detailed plan for the construction of a device that would measure the elasticity of the air. Wasianski, who recounts this request in detail "so that one of Kant's ideas, which he perhaps communicated to me alone, would not be entirely lost,"[19] was apparently under the impression that Kant sought to measure the electrical levels of the air and therefore called the device an "electrometer."[20] Since Wasianksi misconstrued what Kant wished to construct, mistaking an elaterometer for an electrometer, it is not surprising that he failed to take his friend's efforts seriously. Yet he was probably not entirely wrong in thinking that Kant wished to discover a way to measure the level of atmospheric electricity. Given the premises of Kant's meteorological speculations, an accurate measurement of the elasticity of the air would indicate the degree of diffuse electricity in the upper atmosphere. On the basis of this knowledge, moreover, a variety of electrical events – from thunder storms and earthquakes to the aurora borealis and even massive meteors – could be monitored and perhaps even predicted. Wasianski reports that Kant was elated when he believed that the elaterometer worked properly and correspondingly depressed when he later discovered that his device was a failure.[21] Apparently without telling anyone, including his friends, Kant persisted in his efforts, since a sketch of a device similar to the one Wasianski describes appears in a draft of the *Opus postumum* (22: 250–51) that Adickes dates around 1798.[22]

Regardless of the many questions surrounding Kant's attempt to construct an elaterometer in the 1790s, this much is certain: he became increasingly concerned with major alterations in atmospheric conditions in the last decade of the eighteenth century. And it is equally certain that during the same period he returned to one of his earliest preoccupations: reflecting on the possibility of terrestrial "catastrophe." Beginning with a brief reference in the second part of the third *Critique* to an archaic "revolution" (5: 419) that set the stage for the "regime" (*Reich*) of plants and animals, which, in turn, gave way to human domination of the planet, Kant began to entertain the thought that another revolution might lie in store for the earth – a revolution that would run counter to the intentions and purposes of its human inhabitants.[23] If Franklin can legitimately be called the Prometheus of modernity, Kant might have been its Cassandra. Instead of foretelling the overthrow of the human regime on the basis of reports that atmospheric conditions had suffered a revolution, however, he publicly announces that the human species as a whole is constantly progressing toward the better and privately tells acquaintances that he himself is in danger – along with cats in "Basel, Vienna, Copenhagen, and other places."

"The end of all things"

"Something Concerning the Influence of the Moon on the Wind and Weather" is not among Kant's major essays of the 1790s; but it shows the degree to which his meteorological reflections are bound up with weightier matters. Taking up a problem posed by Georg Lichtenberg – "The moon should have no influence on the wind and the weather, yet it does have an influence on them" (8: 317) – Kant concludes that the moon cannot directly affect atmospheric conditions but may exert an "indirect influence" on the wind and weather under the assumption that there is "*imponderable* matter (or matters) [*Materie (oder Materien)*] extending itself far above the height of the ponderable air (and for this reason more exposed to alteration by a stronger attraction of the moon), covering the atmosphere" (8: 322).[24] Kant does not, however, end his essay with this tentative proposal, which, as some of his friends would have known, is reminiscent of the basic tenets of "animal magnetism."[25] After indicating that "imponderable matter" may have something to do with the "constitution of the air" that gives rise to raging epidemics among human, animal, and vegetable "peoples," he reflects on the "something" (*Etwas*) of his title and shows the affinity between meteorological beliefs and religious convictions: as we get older, we come to understand in both cases how little we understand what we once thought we understood well. And in both cases the lack of understanding cannot be remedied by further education. Everyone talks about "the heavens" – the sky, the dwelling place of God – but no one understands anything about this place. And we are all, therefore, condemned to another, indefinitely long childhood:

> This "something" is therefore only small and indeed little more than the admission of ignorance: which, however, since a [Jean André] de Luc has shown to us that we by no means understand what a cloud is and how it is possible (something that was child's play twenty years ago), can no longer be particularly striking or estranging. Yet this is precisely what happens, just as with the cate-chism, which we learned by heart as children and believed we understood but which, as we become older and more reflective, the less we understand and therefore deserve to be sent back to school once again – if only we could find someone (other than ourselves) who understood it better.
>
> (8: 323)

In the letter that accompanies the submission of "Something Concerning the Influence" to J. E. Biester, editor of the *Berlinische Monatsschrift*, Kant compares his little essay to Swift's *Tale of the Tub*: both works provide "a momentary diversion from the constant noise about the same thing"

(11: 495), which in Kant's case is, of course, the Revolution of 1789 and the newly arisen Reign of Terror. Chatting about the weather under tense political circumstances can be taken for a strategy of avoidance – under the condition, of course, that the weather is not equally threatening. The end of "Something Concerning the Influence" indicates, however, that the weather may indeed be a threat, especially if the "community" of imponderable matter adversely alters the "constitution of the air." The next essay Kant publishes in the *Berlinische Monatsschrift*, ominously entitled "The End of All Things" (1794), goes one step further in this direction: "Some see [the omens of the last days] in increasing injustice . . .; or in bloody wars igniting all over the earth. . . . Others, by contrast, [see these omens] in unusual alterations in nature, in earthquakes, storms and floods, or comets and atmospheric signs" (8: 332). And "The End of All Things" takes the concluding remarks of "Something Concerning the Influence" one step further in another direction: instead of simply saying that we do not understand the religious instruction that we once thought we understood perfectly well, the later essay investigates the modes of understanding what cannot be understood in its own terms. In this respect, "The End of All Things" is an amplification of the conclusion to "Something Concerning the Influence" – and in one further respect as well: both are concerned with the possibility of "indirect influence": the moon on the earth in the first case, the philosopher on the state in the second.

At the end of the letter he sends to Biester accompanying "Something Concerning the Influence," Kant promises to deliver "The End of All Things" as soon as possible – and then adds, again alluding to *A Tale of the Tub*, that the new essay "will be partly doleful, partly funny to read [*teils kläglich teils lustig zu lesen*]" (11: 497). Not only are some parts of the essay funny – such as the passage in which Kant dryly notes of an angel mentioned in the Apocalypse of John, "If one does not assume that this angel 'with his voice of seven thunder' (v. 3) wanted to shout nonsense . . ." (8: 333) – and some parts clearly doleful; the funny parts are sad and the sad parts funny. For the thought of the end of all things is doleful, and reflecting on this thought, which yields no knowledge, tends to arrest the cognitive powers and thereby induces laughter. Whereas Kant can rely on the theory of laughter he offered in an unnumbered "Remark" in the Critique of Aesthetic Judgment, he has no readily available explanation for the doleful character of thoughts about the end of all things. Immediately before he interrupts his own thought by injecting an untitled "Remark," Kant therefore goes in search of such an explanation: "why do human beings expect *an end* of the world *at all*? And if this is conceded to them, why precisely an end with terror (for the greatest part of the human species)? . . ." (8: 330).

The ellipsis after the two questions is Kant's own. Something is excised from his discussion: it may be a series of similarly oriented questions; it may be an answer he does not wish to make public. Or it may be that the questions momentarily halt cognitive functions and leave, in turn, a sign of this caesura. Whatever the answer to *this* question may be – why doesn't Kant bring his questions about the end of the world to an end? – he does provide individual answers to the two questions he explicitly poses. The first makes reference to an essential feature of rational beings in general and, the second, to a specific feature of human beings in particular: "The basis of the *first* seems to lie in the fact that reason says to them that the duration of the world has value only insofar as the rational beings in it are in conformity with the final end of their existence; if, however, this is not supposed to be achieved, then creation appears purposeless to them, like a play [*Schauspiel*] that has no outcome and makes known no rational aim" (8: 330–31). The play, in short, should have a well-devised outcome; or, failing that, it should promptly come to a halt. In either case – good play or bad – an end is required. Ends are as essential to the structure of rational spectatorship as beginnings are to that of free agency. Agents experience the world as though it were at its beginning; spectators in preparation for its end. And for human beings, in particular, this end is a doleful prospect, since, in their capacity as agents, according to Kant, they more or less vaguely recognize that they are responsible for the failure of the rational beings in the world to act in conformity with the final end of the world: "the *second* is based on the opinion that the make-up [*Beschaffenheit*] of the human species is so greatly corrupt as to be hopeless; to put an end to them, and indeed a terrible one (for the greatest part of humanity) is the only measure [*Maßregel*] in accord with the decency of the highest wisdom and justice" (8: 331).

Something of what Kant elides can be discerned from these remarks. An expectation of a catastrophic end of *all* things follows from two implicit premises: that the world exists for the sake of its rational inhabitants; and that the human species is both exceptional from the perspective of theoretical cognition and corrupt from the perspective of moral judgment. Since human beings are cognizant of no other rational species, they consider themselves exceptions to the general order of creature and thus, out of ignorance, ennoble themselves into a cosmic – admittedly corrupt – aristocracy. Common law does not therefore apply to them; only special "measures" can be taken as a result of their criminality. And this is precisely what is expected: that the highest wisdom and justice will take a "measure" – and not apply a legal standard – against the human species in light of its general corruption. A sovereign sentence (*Machtspruch*), which overrides every legally valid decision (*Rechtspruch*), brings an end to the lawful processes that govern the world. Just as the world is said to begin with a divine sovereign sentence – "let there be light" – so, too, it is expected to end with one: an executive order that makes all things pay for the corruption of the human species. Whereas the citation of the original sovereign sentence is harmful only to reason in its theoretical capacity, entangling it in an irresolvable antinomy, the expectation of the final sovereign sentence is an expression of the very corruption that the judge of the world is expected to punish. Hence, the source of sadness: the expectation of punishment, which under other conditions would be the mark of conscientiousness, is punishable, for in this case it is evidence of its lack. And hence the source of laughter: the expectation of punishment ironically brings about the very punishment that is expected.

The doleful-comic character of "The End of All Things" is concentrated into a single word: *Maßregel*, a "measure" (*Maßnahme*) that takes the form of a "rule" (*Regel*), which, however, applies only to a single case. Human beings expect that they will be condemned. If they expected that the condemnation would take the form of a universal law that they themselves legislated, they would be saved; since, however, they expect that this condemnation will take the form of a sovereign "measure," which treats them as though they were exceptions to the law, they are victims of their own expectations. Not long after Kant publishes "The End of All Things" he involves himself in a philosophical debate with Johann Schlosser and Count Leopold zu Stolberg concerning the validity of intellectual intuition – this at a time when he shies away from engaging with the thought of his "hypercritical friends" (12: 207). Instead of debating Fichte and Schelling, or even only Beck and Rheinhold, in other words, he takes on philosophers of the stature of Schlosser and Stolberg. But there is good reason for doing so. As the title of the essay in which Kant launches this debate indicates, "On a Newly Arisen Superior [*vornehmen*] Tone in Philosophy" (1796), the primary target of his polemic is the nobility – or more exactly, the attempt to pass off philosophy as a noble activity. Something similar can be said of "The End of All Things": it, too, takes aim at those who pass off the human species as the corrupt nobility of creation. There are certain differences, however, between the targets of these contributions to the *Berlinische Monatsschrift*: whereas the superior tone that has been adopted in philosophy is recent, the sense of human exceptionality is ancient; whereas the ennobling of philosophy is conceived as its reward for intellectual intuition, the ennobling of the human species is expressed by the expectation that only a "measure" can be taken against it; and whereas the later essay mocks those who champion gracious silence over the labor of speech, the earlier essay is an extended exercise in ellipsis.

"The End of All Things" is structured around silence. The inclusion of ellipses is only an explicit manifestation of this principle. Soon after Kant provides reasons for the expectation of a catastrophic end of all things, he interrupts his discussion with a "Remark." Anyone familiar with the structure of the *Critiques* would expect from such a "Remark" a digression. The unnumbered "Remark" in the Critique of Aesthetic Judgment, for example, concerns a variety of topics from laughter to the naïf; the numbered "Remark" in the Critique of Teleological Judgment concerns intellectual intuition and the intuitive intellect. The "Remark" that interrupts "The End of All Things," by contrast, lays out the structure of the essay as a whole. Far from

146

being a digression, it is a methodological guide to the exposition of "The End of All Things." The essay, from this perspective, is closer in structure to *A Tale of the Tub* than to the *Critique of Judgment*. And the proximity to the structure of Swift's satire is intensified by the fact that the "Remark" retrospectively justifies the opening part of the text and at the same time does without the very analysis that this justification seems to justify:

> *Remark*: Because here we merely have to do (or thereby to play) with ideas that reason itself creates, the objects of which (if they have any) lie wholly beyond our circle of vision, which are in this way, although excessive for speculative cognition, not for this reason to be considered entirely empty but are, instead, handed over to us by lawgiving reason itself — not in order to ruminate [*nachgrübeln*] on what they are in themselves and according to their nature [*ihrer Natur nach*] but, rather, as we have to think of them on behalf of moral principles, directed toward the final purpose of things (whereby those things that would otherwise be entirely empty receive an object of practical reality): because of all this, we have a *free field* in front of us, this product of our own reason, the universal concept of an end of all things, to divide and classify what stands under it according to the relation that it has to our cognitive faculties.
>
> The whole will accordingly be divided into, and represented as three parts: 1) the *natural** end of all things, according to the order of moral ends of divine wisdom, which we (with a practical intention) can *well understand*; 2) the *mystical* (supernatural) end of all things, in the order of efficient causes, about which we *understand nothing*; 3) in the *counternatural* (perverse) end of all things, which we ourselves brought about by *misunderstanding* the final purpose. The first of these has already been treated, and the two remaining follow.
>
> (8: 332–33)

Understanding well, not understanding, and misunderstanding: these are the three basic modes of understanding, as they are themselves understood by the faculty of reason in accordance with the "typic of the pure practical power of judgment" (5: 67). The faculty of reason and the power of judgment allow a "free field" to be understood in terms of the three modes of understanding without any help from "the understanding" (*der Verstand*). The understanding, which constitutes the world that we are able to experience, has no business with a field that lies beyond all possible experience. Understanding, in this case, replaces the faculty of the understanding, and a transcendental hermeneutics takes charge of, divides, and frolics in a transcendent field. The function of such hermeneutics does not, however, go without saying, especially since the term that designates whatever is well understood, not understood, and misunderstood – namely *nature* – must be itself understood before anything under its rubric can be understood. And *nature* is well understood only under the condition that it not be understood as it is commonly understood. Whereas it is generally understood in contrast to *thesis*, *technē*, or "culture" – all of which are understood as products of human ingenuity – it should be understood as opposed to whatever is un- or counter-lawful: "*Natural* (*formaliter*) means what follows necessarily according to laws of a certain order, whatever it may be, hence also the moral order (therefore not also the physical one). Opposed to it is the *non-natural*, which can be either supernatural or *contranatural*. What is necessary from natural causes is also represented as *materialiter*-natural (physically necessary)." Nature, in other words, is a legal process; its opposite is whatever interrupts and impedes this process. Nature can be well understood, since its laws are our own doing; a sovereign sentence, by contrast, cannot: the latter takes the form of a "measure" that arrests a legally valid process and thereby interrupts everything "natural (*formaliter*)."

This interruption is the sad-comic moment from which "The End of All Things" issues and toward which it heads: members of the human species expect a cosmic catastrophe, which would be all well and good, except that this expectation expresses a conviction that they are exceptional. If evil consists at bottom in exempting oneself from the law, the corruption of the species lies in an intensification of this exceptionalism: they expect that this corruption will be punished by a non-legal "measure." Only one thing can save members of the species from this vicious cycle of expectation and punishment. Kant hesitates to speak about it. Perhaps in the ellipsis after the two questions concerning the dread human beings feel when thinking about the end of all things he gestures toward it. In the long footnote that interrupts the sentence in which he provides an answer to the second of these questions, he is slightly more explicit. At stake, once again, is exceptionalism – not however, in the sense that human beings, for all their corruption, are raised above the other things of which they are aware but, rather, in the sense that the human species is an exception within the order of rational world-beings. The most striking version of this exceptionalism derives from a "Persian wit" who represents the earth as a "*cloaca*, where all the excrement of other worlds has been banished" (8: 331). Kant will not go so far – at least explicitly: he distinguishes himself from those who represent "our earth world, the place of sojourn for human beings [*unsre Erdenwelt, den Aufenthalt für Menschen*]" (8: 331) as contemptible by maintaining that they pay too little attention to the disposition to the good in human nature. But for Kant the long footnote has another function as well: it distinguishes the "earth-world" from "other worlds," both of which are distinct from "the world." In one and the same stroke, it allows for a subtle distinction between the "earth-world" and "the place of sojourn for human beings," since the earth could have been – or could become – "a place of sojourn" for some other species of rational beings. By the contingent fact that human beings are the only rational being of which they are aware, they grant themselves a patent of nobility and, cognizant of their corruption as well, place the whole world under the same condemnation that they dimly understand that they deserve. Hybris and humility are combined to the point of near identity. The announcement that there are other kinds of rational world-beings would eliminate the exceptionalism that is not only corrupt but expects all things to pay for this corruption.

Kant makes no such announcement, for, if he were to do so, he would doubtless be considered a *Schwärmer*, who, by "swarming" in the air, has lost touch with terrestrial reality. Instead of announcing that other species of rational beings give reason for the continued existence of the cosmos in the absence of a reason based on human conduct, he all but declares in the concluding sentence of "The End of All Things" that the "Antichrist," as harbinger of the end of the world, may have finally made his entrance:

> Should it ever come about that Christianity ceases to be worthy of love (which could certainly happen if, instead of its gentle spirit, it were armed with dictatorial authority), then disinclination toward, and resistance against it would have to become the dominant mode of thought for human beings, because in matters of morality there is no neutrality (nor even a coalition of opposing principles); and the *Antichrist*, who is taken as the harbinger of the last day, would begin his doubtless short regime (presumably based on fear and self-interest); then, however, because Christianity would indeed be *destined* to be a universal world religion but would not be *favored* by fate to become so, *the* (perverted) *end of all things*, with respect to morality, would make its entrance.
>
> Königsberg   I. Kant
>
>   (8: 339)

Kant keeps silent about the name of the Antichrist, whose short reign may have just begun. "The End of All Things" takes its point of departure from this suppression of its end. Who can doubt, however, that the name of the potential Antichrist is the self-styled Christian prince himself, that is, Friedrich Wilhelm II, whose proposals for "reformation" of Christianity Kant had, only sentences before, called foolishness? Soon after making this near declaration – which, had it been announced in so many words, would have made Kant into an outlaw – two things happen: the king addresses a letter to Kant in which he expresses his great displeasure with his subject's treatment of religion, and Kant makes extensive plans to build an elaterometer. Whereas a successful elaterometer would allow human beings to prepare themselves in some measure for the terrestrial alterations to which they are mercilessly exposed, nothing in principle can prepare a subject – still less a

149

subject who describes himself as "most loyal" (7: 10) – for the unambiguous expression of royal contempt. Receiving such censure is perhaps comparable to being struck by lightning. In any case, the letter from the king must have come as quite a jolt. To be sure, it did not come out of the blue; but the preparations Kant made for its eventual arrival could only have clarified the countervailing traits of the shock experience: paralyzing and enervating in the very same stroke.

Arrested thought

In one respect at least, Kant's prognostic powers are impressive: the reign of the Antichrist – otherwise known as Friedrich Wilhelm II – was quite short; it lasted only three more years. The brevity of the Prussian king's earthly reign is due in no small measure to electrical influences – or, more exactly, to certain theories of electrical influence. Around the time he publicly reproached Kant, the king began to suffer from an enigmatic illness, and as was well known at the time, he wholeheartedly committed himself to magnetic and electrical forms of treatment:

> When the condition of the king rapidly declined in the middle years of the 1790s, those who were peripheral to the medical establishment congregated around him. The French playwright M. de Beaunoir gave the prescriptions to [the king's mistress] Countess Lichtenau in which, among other remedies, the following was ordered: the king must take an electrical bath twice a day, and during the bath a magnetized hand must be placed on his lower body – either that of the countess, Count Brühl, or Beaunoir himself; "one could also invite the famous Puysegur from Paris." The king died on the 16th of November, 1797.[26]

Around the time of the king's death, his "most loyal subject" begins to finally publish the metaphysical treatises he had promised in the Preface to the *Critique of Judgment*. And he also began to suffer from an enigmatic illness that he would, in reverse, attribute to electrical influences – as if the king's fanciful cure were Kant's phantasmagoric curse. In any case, it is tempting to understand Kant's complaints as a displacement of the threat under which he lived during the last years of Friedrich Wilhelm II's reign: the king orders him to think differently; he cannot make himself do so, and yet he cannot simply disobey the order either. Some of his friends – Johann Benjamin Erhard, for example, who published *Über das Recht des Volkes zur Revolution* (On the right of the people to a revolution) in 1795 – would advocate disobedience to tyrannical power; but Kant, who recognizes that Hobbes's principle of sovereign power is at once "terrifying" (8: 304) and unimpeachable, cannot follow suit. He therefore makes a compromise: he momentarily arrests his own cognitive processes. Better not think at certain times than think as a tyrannical authority orders. Something of this compromise may play a role in Kant's complaint. But at least two circumstances make this interpretation implausible: the death of the king and the beginning of Kant's illness are roughly contemporaneous; and this illness only affects his ability to work on theoretical philosophy, which the king had no interest in controlling, whereas he never found himself at a loss when it came to the reflections on religion for which he was censured.

These circumstances do not preclude a more subtle version of the same line of interpretation, however. Kant may have arrested his own cognitive processes as a punishment for having – ambiguously – violated his word. In 1794 he declares to the king that he will henceforth refrain from lecturing or publishing anything concerning religion and then, as though he always harbored a "mental reservation," he declares in the Preface to *The Conflict of the Faculties* that this promise applies only to the duration of the king's life, not to that of his own. He therefore grants himself the right to publish whatever he wishes, including – against his own policy – private correspondence. During the most acrimonious period of the so-called "pantheism conflict" Kant refuses Marcus Herz's request to publish some of his letters to Mendelssohn (10: 441). In 1798, by contrast, he publishes his correspondence with the king (7: 6–10). Going against both a public promise and a private policy, he punishes himself in kind: while he is able to write about religion, he cannot develop his thoughts concerning theoretical philosophy. In an often-cited letter of 1798 to Christian Garve, Kant indicates that his illness prevents him from closing "a gap [*eine Lücke*] in the system of crit[ical] philos[ophy]" (12: 257). He therefore compares his mental condition to the physical situation of Tantalus in Tartarus: both desperately seek to grasp what lies beyond their reach. The crime for which Kant pays would not consist in revealing divine secrets but, rather, in running afoul of the king by maintaining that the mysteries of God remain hidden even in light of the Gospels – and then breaking his promise to maintain his silence about religious matters. Far from being an independent insight, Wasianski's assertion that "Kant, the great thinker, now stopped thinking" is only a witless parody of the great thinker's complaint.

Kant, of course, does not interpret his peculiar illness as self-inflicted punishment for duplicity in his dealings with the king – saying one thing ("I will henceforth desist from writing or lecturing on religion . . .") while meaning another (". . . as long as you are alive"). In his letter to Friedrich Wilhelm II, he includes the expression "as a *most loyal subject* of Yo[ur] Roy[al] Maj[esty]" (7: 10), about which he writes in a footnote to the Preface to *The Conflict of the Faculties*: "Also this expression I chose carefully, so that I would not renounce *forever* my freedom to judge in this trial of religion [*Religionsprozeß*], but only as long as H[is] Maj[esty] would still be alive" (7: 10). Had this *clausula salvatoria* (8: 343) appeared in the letter sent to the king, it is unlikely that his "*most loyal subject*" would have been spared another royal reproof – or worse. And so the footnote effectively functions as a *reservatio mentalis* (8: 384). This may not have sat well with his conscience. Or perhaps Kant produced "blue vapor" (6: 38) that cleared his conscience, for, after all, no one can be expected to renounce his or her freedom to judge forever – especially if the king is dead. Nevertheless, regardless of the proper judgment in this case, in the "Conclusion" to the final part of *The Conflict of the Faculties* Kant concedes that he is largely responsible for the "oppression" (*Bedrückung*) under which he now lives: his philosophical method of mastering illness by sheer resolution not only did not cure the illness; the method made it incurable. But this confession, which makes no mention of his difficulties with the king, is evidence of another form of duplicity with regard to his illness. Whereas he publicly takes responsibility for his debility, he denies in private that he has anything to do with his "oppression" under which he suffers.

By accepting responsibility for his illness, Kant shows the limits of philosophy in medical matters: he can recommend that one master ill feelings by sheer resolution; but in certain cases – notably, his own – this recommendation produces the opposite of what it intends. He cannot accomplish what he wants to accomplish merely by willing to do so, and the source of his failure of the will lies in the very will to will.[27] The philosophical method of treating his condition only makes the condition intractable and untreatable:

Conclusion

All cases of illness with regard to which the mind possesses the capacity to become the master of their feelings by steadfast will alone, as the superior power of a rational animal, are of the spastic (cramp-like) kind; but one cannot say in reverse that all illnesses of this kind can be checked or stopped by firm resolution alone. – For some of them are of such a nature that the attempt [*Versuche*] to subject them to the force of resolution actually increases the cramp-like suffering: as is the case with myself, since the illness that was described about a year ago in the *Copenhagen Newspaper* as "an epidemic of catarrh connected with *oppression in the head*" [I consider it a kind of gout that has partly cast itself onto the brain] (in my case it is a year older, but there is nevertheless a similar sensation) disorganized me, as it were, for my own labors of the head; at the very least it has weakened and dulled me, and since this oppression [*Bedrückung*] has cast itself onto the natural weakness of age, it will only end when life itself does.

(7: 112)

Kant proceeds to describe the "disorganization" in which the "oppression" has placed him: "the unity of consciousness" disintegrates into irrevocable distraction. Kant does not quite turn into a so-called "split personality," but a distracted plurality of persona overtakes his consciousness at the precise moment when he insists on its unity. And this plurality expresses itself in the very description of his "disorganization": Kant begins in third person, with reference to an anonymous "patient," and then, without warning, the account changes into a first-person narrative. At the point of transition from first to third person he records the following failure of consciousness to maintain its constitutive unity: "in any discourse (oral or written), the very resolution to secure against distraction [*Zerstreuung*] the connectedness of representations in their temporal sequence produces an involuntary spasmatic condition of the brain, as an incapacity [*Unvermögen*] to maintain the unity of consciousness [*Einheit des Bewußtseins*] during the alteration of representations, as one follows upon the next. Therefore I encounter this . . ." (7: 113). Nothing is perhaps more ironic than this: the attempt to do away with distraction produces distraction *in extremis*, which challenges the very anchor of "my entire critical enterprise" (5: 170), namely the unity of apperception. In the second edition of the *Critique of Pure Reason* Kant conjures up an image of radical distraction: "only because I comprehend their manifold in a consciousness do I call them all together *my* representations; for otherwise I would have as multicolored, diverse a self as I have representations of which I am conscious" (B: 134). Late in his life, as a function of the peculiar incapacity from which he suffered, Kant begins to appear to himself as the "multicolored, diverse self" he once imagined. By presenting himself first as "he" and then as "I" in the same paragraph, he both exemplifies and confirms this self-diversification.

One curious detail of the "Conclusion" to *The Conflict of the Faculties* accords with the account of his illness that he tells his friends: its reference to Copenhagen.[28] It is unclear why Kant would have read a "Copenhagen Newspaper," even if there were such a thing; and it is equally unclear whether he would even be able to read papers printed in Copenhagen, since he does not know the local language. The capital of Denmark is, however, the place where cats were reputed to be dying in large numbers: "He dated this revolution from the time of the death of cats in Copenhagen, about which there was, a few years ago, much to read in the newspapers."[29] Only friends are privy to this explanation for his illness, however. In public forums he claims responsibility for his failure to master his morbid feelings, as well he should, for any attempt to deny responsibility would amount to a worse failure: he would be failing in his responsibility as a professor of philosophy to teach others to take responsibility for their failings. Because he is responsible – and he cannot change himself – the situation is hopeless: the illness "will only end when life itself does." In private, by contrast, he denies responsibility and entertains certain hopes. Besides the fragmentary note preserved in the *Opus postumum* (21: 89–90), there is only a single surviving account of his illness, written from his own hand, that also mentions the death of cats. It appears in a letter of December 1799 addressed to Johann Benjamin

Erhard, whose *Über das Recht des Volkes zur Revolution* Kant had cited in the subsection of *The Conflict of the Faculties* entitled "Soothsaying History of Humanity." As a physician, Erhard would have been receptive to Kant's complaints. And as a friend, he might also have been receptive to the subtle similarity between the political revolution that elicits discussion everywhere in Europe and the atmospheric transformation about which Kant never tires of talking:

> What concerns the first [the dreary condition of Kant's health], it consists in a spastic oppression of the head, a brain cramp, so to speak, about which I flatter myself that, since it has lasted throughout the extraordinarily long period in which an electrification of the air has been widely propagated, from the 1796 until now (as it was reported in the *Erlanger gelehrte Zeitung* and was connected with the death of cats), and since this property of the air must finally change [*umsetzen*], I can still hope to see myself freed [*befreit*].
>
> (12: 294)[30]

In private, Kant denies responsibility for the "oppression" under which he lives out the last days of his life. Neither his mind nor even the fragile state of his body can be held accountable for his state of unfreedom. Physicians are of no help; nor are his own philosophical methods of curing mental illnesses. But his preferred method of cure is not at fault either. Kant could scarcely be more inconsistent – and this, too, accords with the illness from which he suffers. Inconsistency is its constitutive feature. At one moment he describes himself as "he," at the next as "I." In public, he abandons all hope of recovery; in private he maintains his hopes. The consistency of his own inconsistency is an impressive demonstration of his capacity to grasp his incapacity. In two of his late works Kant quotes Abbé Coyer's dictum: "poor mortals, among you nothing is constant except inconstancy" (7: 83; 8: 336). Late Kant is an exemplum of impoverished mortality.

Transitions

According to the Introduction to the *Critique of Pure Reason*, which launches the "critical enterprise," receptivity contrasts with spontaneity among human beings (B: 33). That Kant is hyper-receptive means that he is correspondingly hypo-spontaneous; in his own terms, he suffers from a "brain cramp." None of this would matter much, even perhaps to Kant himself, if the confident claim with which he closes the Preface to the last *Critique* – "With this I thus bring my entire critical enterprise to an end" (5: 170) – were true. But from his own perspective, such is not the case. His inconsistency in this regard has often been noted. The famous letter to Garve is sufficient evidence: a "gap" remains, and a "Transition from the Metaphysical Foundations of Natural Science to Physics" is required for the "system of critical philosophy" to secure its completion. In the meantime there is only the impatience of perpetual postponement: "The claims of reason will not let up: the consciousness of the ability to do so will not do so either; but the satisfaction of these claims is delayed to the utmost degree of impatience [*aufgeschoben zur höchstens Ungeduld*], if not by the total paralysis of vital powers, then by their ever increasing inhibition" (12: 254). As Kant composes draft after draft of the project that aims to fill in the gap, the idea of "transition" (*Übergang*) stretches far beyond its original function. One of the drafts of the project outlines three transitions, each of which is more encompassing than the last, until the proposed work concludes with the "universal connection of the living forces of all things in reciprocal relation[.] God and the world" (21: 17). Another draft aims even higher and proposes a "transition to the limit of all cognition" (21: 9). And still another draft, reversing directions, momentarily speaks of illness as a "constant transition":

> We experience organic forces in our own body; and by means of the analogy with them, with a part of their principle, we achieve the concept of a vegetation of the body, by leaving out its animality. − In both cases, a continuing duration of the species and an alteration of death and life of individuals is the phenomenon of a genus that preserves itself in space and time, between which illness constitutes the constant transition [*bestandigen Ubergang*].
>
> (22: 373)

The use of the term *transition* in the context of illness is exceptional. Almost all of the other uses of *transition* in Kant's last theoretical exercise are metaphorical − or metaphorical to the second power − since the term has, itself, made a transition from the field of perceptible transitions from one state or place to another, to the field of cognition that accounts for the possibility of the totality of moving forces that manifest themselves as transitions from one state or place to another. One of the two principal points of reference for this account is ether, which is to say, according to its original meaning, "air." Another principal point of reference is the body, which, as a machine, is always already inserted into the totality of moving forces and, as a machine we ourselves control, allows for a division between organic and non-organic bodies. The fact that organic bodies suddenly appear to turn into inorganic ones runs counter to the principle of this division, however. The exposition of illness as "constant transition" seeks to safeguard the legitimacy of this principle. An organic body is neither precisely alive nor precisely dead but is always, from beginning to end, in "constant transition" from life to death. Only the species of which an organic body is a member is permanently alive.

The common conception of death as an incomprehensible leap "from time into eternity" (8: 327) is thus rendered untenable − without any appeal to

155

palingenesis. Every passage of every individual from one state to another is transitional: "only a step (*passus*), not a leap (*salto*)" (21: 387). Even death constitutes a transition to the second power: "The organic body can be healthy or sick, and the exhaustion of its powers is death[.] [W]ith this, however, a transition [*Übergang*] into the chemical operation of dissolution into matter that makes a transition [*übergeht*] to new formations" (22: 505). And in keeping with the motif of transition, the presentation of illness as "constant transition" is itself transitional: it allows Kant to pass from a problem that appears unsolvable to an unproblematic a priori proposition. The problem is stated in various ways but never more forcefully than in a draft that has been dated around 1799:

> In the division of the moving forces of matter that belongs to the transition from the metaph[ysical] found[ations] o[f] n[atural] s[cience] to physics the division into organic and inorganic cannot be missing; and, indeed, this division must be thought *a priori* in it, without previously having to be taught by experience of the exist-ence of such bodies, for the transition from the metaph[ysical] f[oundations] o[f] n[atural] s[cience] to physics necessarily leads to this concept [of organic bodies]. – The latter, however, does not appear to be attainable, for how could one ever come up with the idea of a production of such bodies, which resembles that of the highest form of art, in order even only to picture [*wähnen*] them problematically, and how could one think *a priori* of a plant or animal regime, whose internal and external purposive combination always must demand of us new disclosures into its possibility[?]*

In a less detailed draft Kant drops all qualification.[31] The problem of discovering an a priori principle of division cannot be solved, nor can anyone demonstrate that organic bodies must be ordered into sexuated species: "One cannot think *a priori* of the *possibility* of organic bodies, still less the matter of an organizing body (through procreation a[nd] propagation by means of two sexes). To this belongs experience. – But there can be an organization of a system of organized beings, for example, the deer for the wolf, the moss for the trees, even the human being for the different races according to the climate, and so the entire earth-globe can be organized" (22: 505). The foot-note Kant adds to the question posed in the more detailed draft represents precisely such a "system of organized beings":

> *One can *a priori* classify classes of organic bodies, organized for the sake of one another but specifically different as required for its existence and preservation, for example, the plant regime for the sake of the animal regime, and the latter for the human genus [*Menschengattung*]; thus all of them together as organic in the first,

156

second, or third degree. The highest level of classification would be that which organized the human species [*Menschenspecies*] according to the different levels of its nature, for one another and on behalf of the perfection of the genus; an event that may have perhaps occurred many times through terrestrial revolutions [*Erdrevolutionen*] and about which we do not know whether or not a new revolution is in prospect for our globe and its inhabitants.

(21: 211–12)[32]

None of the difficulties involved in discovering an a priori principle of division compromises the a priori character of the proposed system of classification. All classes of organic bodies must be organized according to the governing principle of organization: "this for the sake of that." As Kant notes in a draft devoted to the natural system of organic bodies, "The organization of the system of organized bodies also belongs, in turn, to the transition from the metaphys[ical] foun[dations] of [n]atural [s]cience to physics as a division that can be made *a priori* with concepts, according to which, in the order of classes, a species of creatures exists *for the sake of another*" (21: 566). Nothing exists solely for its own sake – not even the "highest level of classification." This is to say, however, that there is no "highest level of classification." Any identification of such a level is a function of impoverished experience. Kant obviously realizes the empirical character of his remark concerning the "highest level of classification" and so corrects himself by emphasizing its contingency. The question with which he then closes his footnote – "whether or not a new revolution is in prospect for our globe and its inhabitants" – is entirely different from the problem from which it sprang, for the problem can be solved a priori; the question, by contrast, can be answered only by waiting for a "new revolution." The a priori classification of classes of organic beings, nevertheless, does overcome the prejudice that Kant expresses in a moment of thoughtlessness: the prejudice, namely, that the species of which he is still a member constitutes the "highest level of classification."

Perhaps Kant's "brain cramp" is responsible for this moment of thoughtlessness; perhaps it is only a momentary relapse, which Kant elsewhere repudiates by entertaining the possibility of extraterrestrial forms of intelligent life. But, in any case, the question assumes here a certain degree of urgency, for it concerns the organization of the earth itself. Just as individuals are in "constant transition" from life to death, so, too, are the species of which they are members, and the "terrestrial revolutions" are only the events – like the birth and death of individuals – in which gradual steps appear as sudden leaps. To use the term Kant adopts from his young physician friend J. B. Erhard, defender of the people's right to revolution, every terrestrial revolution is, properly speaking, a "phenomenon of evolution" (7: 87).[33] And, as Erhard himself may have recognized, this may be true of the atmospheric revolution from which Kant suffers. His pains, in other words, may be something other than the failings of old age; they may be the birth-pangs of another "world epoch" (21: 566).

Going further

The moment of thoughtlessness in which Kant identifies the human species as the "highest level of classification" is merely transitory. He returns to his senses – or comes fully to his senses for the first time, as he periodically labors on his late works. The last residues of the ancient prejudice that the human species is the undisputed master of the earth are reduced. The point of this prejudice consists in ennobling one class of organic beings at the expense of all others. Kant, whose supplement to the *Doctrine of Right* recognizes the possibility that a writ of nobility may be temporarily valid (6: 369–70), unambiguously attacks any presumption that a noble class can be established in perpetuity. Asserting something to this effect in East Prussia during the era of the French Revolution may not be a revolutionary act; but it opposes the basic disposition of those in power. Kant, moreover goes even further and disputes the claim that the human species as a whole constitutes the permanent nobility of the earth, who, without having to enter into civil union with any other class of organism, can claim the surface of the planet as its own. Only once – in a dense footnote – does this thought appear in a text published under Kant's supervision. The text in question is, ironically, devoted to the study of the human species from a "pragmatic point of view." In the concluding section Kant adds a footnote to a remark that explains the tendency for human beings to ennoble themselves. Not only do human beings claim independence from one another; each member of the species also seeks "mastery over other beings that are his equal by nature, which can already be noticed even in the smallest child" (7: 328). As if he were adding a footnote to a footnote, he then goes even further and asserts, in effect, that human beings may be forced by circumstances to share the surface of the earth with other species of rational beings, at which time their undisputed domination of the planet will be over:

> The cry that a new-born child lets out does not have the tone of distress but, rather, of indignation and sudden rage – not because he is in pain but because something distresses him, presumably the fact that he cannot move about at will and feels his incapacity as a fetter by means of which his freedom has been taken away from him. – What intention might nature have had in letting the child come into the world with a loud cry, which is extremely dangerous for him and his mother *in the state of raw nature*? For a wolf or even a pig would thereby be signaled to eat the child during the absence of the mother or simply during her exhaustion from childbirth. But no animal other

than human beings (as they are now) *loudly announces* its existence at birth, which seems to be so arranged by the wisdom of nature to preserve the kind. One must therefore assume that in the early epoch of nature [*frühen Epoche der Natur*], with respect to this class of animal (during the period of its rawness) the child did not yet cry at the moment of birth; only later did a second epoch arrive when both parents had reached the state of culture that is necessary for domestic life, although we do not know how, and with which efficient causes, nature is arranged such a development. This remark leads further – for example, to the following thought: whether a third epoch might not follow upon the second with great revolutions of nature [*bei großen Naturrevolutionen*]. Then the orangutan or the chimpanzee would build up the organs for walking, for handling objects, and for speaking, until it had the structural features of a human being, whose interior would contain an organ for the use of the understanding and would gradually develop through social culture.

(7: 328)

The cry of the new-born human being is the trace of an epochal transition. It runs counter to the principle of purposiveness, since it endangers the infant along with its exhausted mother; but the very counterpurposiveness of this self-exposure is the original expression of a nescient rationality, which, from beginning to end, consists in the demand that the agent alone should be in charge of its moving forces. The cry can be heard to say: another "epoch of nature" has made its entrance.[34] Not only is a new individual let loose upon the world, so, too, is a species that will learn to say, in effect, "I am in control of myself." The only way of securing this control is by taking possession of the space upon which it is played out. And if this transition from inarticulate cry to articulate discourse could happen once, there is no reason to suppose that it could not happen again. In the same section of the *Anthropology*, Kant refuses to take sides in the dispute between Pieter Camper and Carl von Linné concerning the question "whether the gibbon, orangutan, and chimpanzee and so forth are destined [to walk on two feet or four]" (7: 322); but only a few pages later, with no greater insight into the anatomy of these animals, he implicitly accepts Camper's view of the gibbon and explicitly sides with Linné's view of the orangutan.[35] The question at hand is less anatomical than epochal. Chimpanzees and orangutans do not yet maintain a stature that bears comparison to that of human beings; but after a turbulent era of "natural revolutions" they may raise themselves to a position where they could dispute the claims of human beings to mastery over the earth.

And Kant goes further still – not in a published text, but in certain drafts of the *Opus postumum*, especially the one in which he defends the a priori character of the division of physical bodies into organic and inorganic:

One can take the classification of organic and living beings further, since not only does the plant regime exist for the sake of the animal regime and its increase and diversification; but human beings, as rational beings, exist for the sake of other human beings of a different species (race) [*Menschen als Vernünftige um anderer der Species (Race) nach verschiedenen Menschen willen da sind*], which stands at a higher level of humanity, either next to each other [*neben einander*], something like the Americans and Europeans, or after each other [*nach einander*]. If our terrestrial globe, which had once been dissolved into chaos but organized itself and now regenerated, were to bring forth, by terrestrial revolutions [*Erdrevolutionen*], differently organized creatures, which, in turn, make a place for others after their destruction, organic nature could be conceived as a sequence of different sequential world-epochs [*Weltepochen*], reproducing themselves in different forms, and our world-body [*Weltkörper*] not only a mechanical but also as an organically formed body.

(21: 214–15)[36]

That, late in his life – Adickes dates this draft to around the winter of 1799 – Kant still considers Europeans superior to "Americans" cannot be doubted, for he indicates as much in this passage. Yet the point of the passage is otherwise oriented. Not only does it fail to support any claim to superiority that Europeans might raise; it nullifies all claim of human superiority. Least of all can members of the human species claim undisputed dominion over the surface of the globe. On the contrary, as Kant asserts without the slightest degree of hesitation and without any qualifying conditions: "human beings, as rational beings, exist for the sake of other human beings of a different species (race)." Which is to say: the members of the human species, who must consider themselves ends-in-themselves by virtue of their personality, are nevertheless in service to a late-coming "species (race)" about which they – for now and perhaps forever – know nothing. Without quite saying so, the project of filling the "gap" in the critical system of philosophy by developing a "science of transition" discovers that the species to which the exponent of this system belongs may itself be only a transition.

The revolution in the air may come to an end. Such at least is the hope that Kant expresses in private: the "oppression" under which he suffers will be alleviated once the level of atmospheric electricity returns to the status quo ante. By restoring his freedom of thought, this "contra revolution" (21: 90) will give him a chance to finish the "transition" project and thereby complete the system of transcendental philosophy. The last sketches of this project indicate the degree to which the "entire critical enterprise" (5: 170) becomes progressively bound up with the ambiguous status of atmospheric electricity. Three propositions from the first "convolute" of the *Opus postumum*, which represents the last thoughts of Immanuel Kant, are particularly noteworthy:

1   "Galvanism [is] nothing other than atmospheric electricity" (21: 118);
2   "Transcendental philosophy is a galvanism" (21: 133);
3   "What one calls *galvanism* is, properly speaking [*eigentlich*], transcendental philosophy" (21: 136).

Only one conclusion can be drawn from these propositions: galvanism = atmospheric electricity; galvanism = transcendental philosophy; *ergo*, transcendental philosophy = atmospheric electricity. Which is to say: transcendental philosophy "is" what prevents its completion. Such a proposition, which Kant never quite articulates, captures its constitutive inconsistency. Nevertheless, something of this proposition can be seen in the series into which the first "convolute" of the *Opus postumum* finally issues: "The galvanism of nerve receptivity in the entire universe without which the human being would not even posit itself intuitively [*anschaulich*] in the universe — (Trans[cendental] philos[ophy] + galvanism + atmospheric electricity + nerves + a universe of light and warmth)" (21: 137).[37] An atmospheric revolution not only affects Kant, in other words; it has the potential to alter every term in this series — from transcendental philosophy to the universe in which the human being can posit itself. And this revolution may alter the human being in turn. Kant says nothing of the kind; on the contrary, he places all his hope on a *contra revolution* in nature. Beyond this last hope, however, there may lie in store another kind of human being, who, instead of positing itself in the universe, inconsistently desists from all self-positional acts.

CONCLUSION

Making way for another law of the earth

The thesis of radical mean-ness

Kant's failure to work out the "gap" in his "critical system of philosophy" (12: 257) during the last years of his life meant that the following thesis remained hidden among the loose bundle of papers that the editors of his leftovers called – for want of a better title[1] – *Opus postumum*: "human beings, as rational beings, exist for the sake of other human beings of a different species (race) [*Menschen als Vernünftige um anderer der Species (Race) nach verschiedenen Menschen willen da sind*]" (21: 214). The clause is neither in the subjunctive mood nor the future tense: humankind, as a class of rational beings, exists for the sake of another species of the same genus or another race of the same species – which is to say: humankind is, by nature, a means whose end lies in another, late-coming kind of human being. The lateness of this other kind may be the occasion for natural-historical speculation; but the thesis of radical mean-ness is not; it is based on an a priori principle of classification: "The organization of the system of organized bodies also belongs, in turn, to the transition from the metaphys[ical] foun[dations] of n[atural] s[cience] to physics as a division that can be made *a priori* with concepts, according to which, in the order of classes, a species of creatures exists *for the sake of another*" (21: 566). Human beings enjoy no special status; they are not exempt from the system of organized bodies, and so it must be asserted that they, too, exist for the sake of another. By nature, the species is a means like every other.

What to make of the thesis of radical mean-ness is, however, far from certain. It is worlds apart from a similar sounding proposition that Fichte formulates in his contemporaneous *System of Ethical Doctrine According to the Principles of the Wissenschaftslehre* (1798): "*Every human being is an end*, says Kant. . . . He is an end as a *means* to realize reason."[2] Even though the realization of reason is, for Fichte, infinitely remote, it is an end that human beings should aim to accomplish by wholly turning themselves into the means toward this end. For late Kant, by contrast, the mean-ness of human beings has nothing to do with an end that they themselves should aim to

162

accomplish: human beings do not exist so that reason can be realized but for the sake of another "species (race)" of human being, whose entrance on earth is an entirely contingent matter. In the meantime – which, for all we know, lasts forever – the mean-ness of human beings is without a corresponding end.[3]

Kant's reluctance to classify the kind of human beings for whose sake human beings exist is therefore fully justified. Until the late-comers arrive – if they ever do so – there is no basis for an answer to the question: do they constitute a different species or a different race? A similar hesitation expresses itself in the disjunction through which Kant represents the possible relations between the two kinds of human being: "human beings, as rational beings, exist for the sake of other human beings of a different species (race), which stands at a higher level of humanity, either next to each other [*neben einander*], something like the Americans and Europeans, or after each other [*nach einander*]" (21: 215). On the one hand, "after each other" presents the human being as something to be surpassed – as if Kant had anticipated Nietzsche's famous pronouncement in the Prologue to *Thus Spoke Zarathustra*: "what is great about the human being is that he is a bridge and not an end; what can be loved about the human being is that he is a *transition* and a *transience* [*ein* Übergang *und ein* Untergang]."[4] This representation of human mean-ness resonates, to a certain extent, with the thesis of radical mean-ness; but, for Kant, the other kind of being remains, despite all, entirely "human." On the other hand, the phrase "next to each other" presents the human being as subordinate to the other kind of human being in the same manner as the "Americans" are subordinate to the "Europeans" – as if the other race were to arrive on earth, colonize all of the continents, and make their original inhabitants, including Europeans, into a subject race. Slavery is perhaps ruled out, but colonial servitude is not. This representation of the for-the-sake-of structure of the species also resonates with Kant's thesis: the image of Europe suddenly colonized by a race that treats its inhabitants as they have treated the inhabitants of the other continents may express a fear that corresponds to Nietzsche's hope.

Neither of these two representations of the human species – as a bridge that disappears, as a subject race that remains – can be entirely dismissed, and yet neither can be altogether affirmed. Experience alone can answer these questions. Only this much is known, for it is knowable a priori: members of the species are by nature means for something other than themselves – but not *altogether* other. Nothing could be further from the thesis of radical mean-ness than the pietistic doctrine from which Kant freed himself in his youth. Human beings are not servants of a god who mysteriously reveals himself in human flesh; they are in service to human beings of another kind, who, for their part, may remain forever *in absentia*. The mean-ness of human beings cannot therefore be assimilated into conventional images of the role that human beings are supposed to play on earth – as passionate participants in a sacred history, for example, or, in reverse, as active agents in the construction of an artifice of culture.

Consequences

A series of negative consequences follows from the thesis of radical meanness. One of these consequences is explicitly formulated in the second part of *The Conflict of the Faculties*. Kant begins this part by emphasizing that the question he has "renewed" – "whether the human species [*Geschlecht*] is constantly progressing to the better?" – should not be confused with the similar-sounding question "whether new races [*neue Rassen*] of the human being might arise in the future" (7: 79). But the question of new races does not vanish entirely from the "Renewed Question." Whereas the question under discussion revolves around an affect generated by a real revolution in the political order of a particular people, the other question concerns the effect of a possible revolution in the natural order of all terrestrial things. Kant closes his "Soothsaying History of Humanity" by insisting that the despotic character of natural power must not be used to justify an action in which a sovereign treats his subjects as means for the attainment of his ends:

> It is not therefore merely a well-intentioned thesis that is also recommended for practical purposes but is also a thesis that can be maintained by the most rigorous theory, despite all disbelief: the human species has always been progressing toward the better and will continue to do so henceforth. If one does not simply look at what happens with a particular people but also looks at the spread across all the peoples of the earth who gradually may take part in the progress, this opens up a prospect into an unforeseeable time; insofar as a second epoch does not follow upon the first epoch of a natural revolution [*erste Epoche einer Naturrevolution*], which (according to Camper and Blumenbach) buried the kingdom of animals and plants alone, before any human beings existed – a second epoch that plays the very same game with human beings so that other creatures can make their entrance, and so forth. For, from the perspective of omnipotence of nature [*Allgewalt der Natur*] or, rather, from its supreme cause, which is inaccessible to us, the human being is only a trifle [*Kleinigkeit*]. But that the rulers of his own species also take him for one and treat him as such, partly by burdening him as an animal, as a mere tool of their intentions, partly by exposing him in conflicts with one another in order to have him massacred – that is no trifle but an overturning of the *final end* of creation itself.
>
> (7: 88–89)[5]

The following consequence, therefore, cannot be drawn from the prospect of a new epoch of the earth: that a ruler, who enjoys exemption from legal proceedings, can also claim exception from the moral law. The same thing can be said of any thesis developed under the auspices of theoretical reason: none can compromise the command that human beings treat themselves and every other member of the species as ends-in-themselves. But the thesis of radical mean-ness, unlike the declarations of war pronounced by princes of non-republican states, does not contradict this command, for, in Kant's formulation, the command concerns solely the humanity "in" the person of the human being – not human beings as members of a particular species: "Act so that you use humanity, whether in your own person or in the person of any other, always at the same time as an end, never merely as a means" (4: 429). Human beings can, therefore, be at once ends-in-themselves and means by nature: ends-in-themselves from the perspective of practical reason, which recognizes the humanity in their person, and radical means from the perspective of theoretical reason, which recognizes that organic beings are necessarily organized in accordance with the formula "each kind for the sake of another." This, however, means that another negative consequence can be drawn from the thesis of radical mean-ness: the "natural revolution" cannot be the work of human beings; nothing can or should be done to produce the other "species (race)" for whose sake human beings exist. Making any efforts in this direction – and Kant is familiar with at least one, which he rejects[6] – is not only comparable to the despotic acts of princes who use their subjects as means to their own particular ends; it is also doomed to failure, for every "natural revolution" must be entirely natural.

And a third consequence of the thesis can be derived as well: neither the species as a whole nor any class composed of its members can claim membership in the nobility of creation. To this extent, the thesis of radical mean-ness is the satirist's delight: no representation of the mean-ness of human beings is out of the question. For all its satiric potential, however, the thesis is neither a demotion nor a humiliation of the species; still less is it a collective punishment for the crimes that humankind has committed, including the original crime of having chosen the prospect of happiness over the principle of pure practical reason. In other words, the mean-ness of human beings is not a consequence of their radical evil. After having proposed the thesis that human beings are evil by nature in an essay of 1792 and then reprinted the essay in *Religion Within the Limits of Mere Reason* a year later, Kant subsequently ignores it – not entirely, of course, for the human race is still distinguished by a "foul spot," which consists in make false assertions in the court of conscience. But the stain that stamps the species is no longer interpreted in terms of an "intelligible act," and in certain places, most notably in drafts of the *Opus postumum*, he denies the very possibility of a genuinely radical evil.[7] If the thesis of radical evil were to be maintained in its original form, the thesis of radical mean-ness would naturally present itself as a corresponding condemnation. The creator of the world – whom Kant, flirting with gnosticism, calls the "demiurge," in contrast to God himself[8] – could then say something like this: "because you have chosen to use others of your kind – and even your own self – as mere means, you will be made *en masse* into mere means for the use of another kind of human being." From this perspective, a philosophical attempt at theodicy might prove fairly successful: human beings would get what they deserve, and justice would be served in the end. There might be some lingering questions about the wisdom of the demiurge – for, after all, a better race of human being could have been created from the beginning – but there would be no doubts about its justice.

This last philosophical attempt at theodicy is also a failure, however, since the mean-ness of the species has nothing to do with any "intelligible act" its members may have performed.[9] And God, for his part, is not the author of the world-book: "God is not the world-author (demiurge) from whom all evils as mere sensible objects have proceeded" (22: 52). Perhaps Kant set aside the thesis of radical evil in order to make room for the thesis of radical mean-ness – without fear that the latter would be understood as a consequence of the former. In a "Remark" added to section of the *Doctrine of Virtue* that concerns the vice of hatred for human beings, Kant cautiously endorses Albrecht von Haller's representation of humankind as an "'ambiguous middle-thing [*zweideutig Mittelding*] made of angel and beast'" (6: 461) but then adds this caveat:

> Dividing something composite into two heterogeneous things yields no definite concept at all and can lead to none in the order of beings whose class distinctions are unknown to us. The first comparison [of angelic virtue and devilish vice] is an exaggeration. The second, although human beings do – unfortunately! – fall into brutish vices, does not justify attributing to them a predisposition to these vices *belonging to their species*, any more than the stunting of a few trees in a forest is the basis for making them into a special *kind* of plant.
>
> (6: 461)

The thesis of radical mean-ness expands on this "Remark": instead of being a *Mittelding* (middle-thing), the human species is simply a *Mittel* (means). The determination of its mean-ness, moreover, is entirely a function of theoretical philosophy: it does not derive from a melancholic reflection on the stuntedness of the species – its lack of uprightness, its tendency to succumb to its inclinations – but, rather, from an attempt to develop an a priori system of classifying organic beings, with a view toward discovering a principle for the division of all moving forces, in an attempt to make a transition from the metaphysical foundations of natural science to physics, so that the "entire critical enterprise" (5: 170) can at least be completed. Organic classes are structured according to the formula "each kind for the sake of another" – and this goes for human beings as well. To think otherwise is thoughtless.

Concession

The thesis of radical mean-ness must, nevertheless, have troubled Kant. The complicated sentence of the *Opus postumum* in which it is expressed undergoes numerous alterations. Of particular significance is the following series of clauses, which, according to the Akademie editors, Kant deleted immediately after describing the two manners in which the relation between the two human regimes can be represented – either "next to each other" or "after each other":

> only although rational creatures nevertheless preferably make a place [*Platz zu machen*] for other, still more perfectly organized ones – not merely [*de*] *facto* (with respect to their political existence) but rather [*de*] *jure* because of their now innately greater specific perfection, so that it would be organized after the earlier ones have conceded them their place [*nachdem die vorige ihnen ihren Platz geräumt haben*], until finally a universal unity [*allgemeine Einheit*] of the final purpose of all organic bodies in a supreme world cause (which here may be called *demiurge*, since it is not here considered from a moral perspective[)] brings forth a complete organization. Earth-globe now now [breaks off]
>
> (21: 214)

The replacement for this remark, according to the editors of the text, runs as follows: "If our earth-globe, which once had been dissolved into chaos but organized itself and is now regenerated, were to bring forth, by terrestrial revolutions, differently organized creatures, which, in turn, made a place [*Platz machten*] for others after their destruction, organic nature could be conceived as a sequence of different sequential world epochs" (21: 214–15). Although the two versions use similar-sounding language – "making a place," "making room," "conceding space" (*Platz machen, Platz räumen*) – there is a decisive difference between the manner in which this act of place-making takes place: according to the version printed in the body of the text, nature alone makes a place for the other kind of human being; according to the version printed in the footnotes, by contrast, both nature and human beings make a place. So emphatic is Kant about this point in the deleted version that he repeats it: not only do human beings "preferably make a place," they also "concede them their place." And, regardless of the editors' decision to place this series of clauses in a footnote – which may be philologically

167

justified but could also be a sign of editorial timidity – there is good reason to suppose that it constitutes the legitimate continuation of the sentence under consideration. For it makes sense of the qualifying phrase "as rational beings" in the thesis of radical mean-ness. The rationality of human beings makes them aware that they *should* concede their place to those for whom they exist. "Making a place" is not simply a natural process but a political one as well.

To speak of a "political process" in this context is misleading, however, since Kant keeps a careful distance from the term *political* in the relevant clause: "rational creatures nevertheless preferably make a place for other, still more perfectly organized ones – not merely [*de*] *facto* (with respect to their political existence)." The act of making a place for another body in a *de facto* manner follows from the recognition that this body is powerful enough to keep its territory intact. The "political existence" of this newly formed body is acknowledged out of fear for the consequences of not doing so. The division of the earth into political regimes has hitherto proceeded in this *de facto* manner: a place on the surface is made for any regime that is strong enough to maintain the unity and integrity of a contiguous territory. The original meaning of the Greek word *nomos* is "division," especially the division and distribution of the land for the purpose of its occupation and cultivation.[10] The division and distribution of land is the *nomos* on the basis of which all the positive laws of any given particular political body rest. Unless a legal order can specify its space, dividing itself from its exterior and distributing the territory over which it disposes, there is no legal order, properly speaking. Insofar as the *nomos* of the earth is more original than any particular legal order, there is no position from which it can be judged right or wrong: it is a matter of fact, not of right. The earth, accordingly, is divided among those regimes that are sufficiently powerful to maintain their "political existence." *Toward Eternal Peace* addresses the lawless character of this *nomos* of the earth.

So, too, in a very different vein, does the next clause of the supposedly deleted sentence from the *Opus postumum*: "rational creatures . . . make a place for other, still more perfectly organized ones . . . [*de*] *jure* because of their now innately greater specific perfection, so that it would be organized after the earlier ones have conceded them their place." The only place in *Toward Eternal Peace* that comes close to this thought is the brief passage where Kant proposes that a remnant "race," which survives the "game [*Spiel*]" of mutual destruction, might interpret the catastrophe of its terrestrial ancestors as "a warning example [*ein warnendes Beispiel*]" and, to this extent, justify "providence" (8: 380). But the passage in the *Opus postumum* is far more exacting than this remark. It makes no reference to mutual destruction; human beings, by virtue of their rationality, do something that the plants and animals could not: concede their place to others. This concession accords with a law that they give themselves, a law that is beyond any *nomos* of the earth and that pays no attention to the "political existence" of its inhabitants. And this concession does not take place in some hypothetical future, after the other kind of human being has arrived on earth. The term *after* in the phrase "so that [the earth] would be organized after the earlier ones have conceded them their place" does not mean: only after the other kind enters is the concession made. Rather, the concession makes way for their entrance; it follows from the *now* in "their now innately greater specific perfection." Now is the time for concession. Any concession that would take place upon their arrival would be indistinguishable from a pragmatic recognition of their "political existence." Kant breaks off the clause with "Earth-globe now now," as if he himself could hardly get over the imperative he almost formulates: concede the "earth-globe" now.

Even before the break, however, Kant begins to register certain misgivings about the imperative he comes close to articulating. These misgivings may have led him to complete the sentence along the lines that he developed in the "Soothsaying History of Humanity": natural revolutions "make a place" for another kind of human being; human beings are merely passive spectators and helpless victims of this process. As Kant begins to complete the series of clauses printed in the editorial apparatus, he notes that his exposition of the epochal organization of the world contains no reference to practical reason: "so that it would be organized after the earlier ones had conceded them their place, until finally a universal unity of the final purpose of all organic bodies in a supreme world cause (which here may be called *demiurge*, since it is not here considered from a moral perspective[)] brings forth a complete organization." The distinction between God and demiurge in the parenthetical remark allows Kant to retain the consistency of his general argument, which derives from a purely theoretical exposition of the transition from the metaphysics of nature to physics; it has nothing to do with the metaphysics of morals. Yet, as Kant is doubtless aware, this simply cannot be right. He can legitimately describe the demiurge as the "supreme cause of the world," who makes use of natural revolutions for the purpose of organizing his work; but when Kant speaks of a "concession" whereby human beings make room for another kind of human being, he cannot deny that he has entered into the sphere of practical reason. The very distinction between *de facto* and *de jure* is unthinkable outside of this context: if there is no difference between physical necessity and moral necessitation, all talk of "right" or "virtue" is idle chatter. The simple fact that "concession" is an act – and not simply a natural occurrence – makes it into a moral matter. If the editors' reconstruction of the text accurately reflects the manuscript, the following conclusion is therefore inevitable: Kant decided against including any reference to "concession" in order to make sure that his exposition of the epochal transition of the earth would not be confused with a theodicy. Natural revolutions, so the final version would run, make a place for another kind of human being, for whose sake humankind exists; but human beings need do nothing in turn. The phrase "as rational beings" in the thesis of radical mean-ness could just as well be erased along with the reference to the "concession" that follows.

Another delay

If Kant did, indeed, decide to delete any reference to an act of concession – which cannot be decided without thoroughly investigating the relevant pages of the manuscript – he retreated from his own insight into the single positive consequence that can be drawn from the thesis of radical mean-ness. This thesis, for Kant, cannot be seriously doubted, inasmuch as it derives from an a priori principle of classification. One of the reasons Kant might have wished to shield himself from his own insight is fairly clear: it would require a fundamental and thorough reworking of the *Doctrine of Right*, espe-cially those sections of this much-delayed work that, according to the concluding paragraph of its Preface, are developed in greatest detail, namely the exposition of "private right" (6: 209).[11] The old law of the earth grants human beings the right to claim portions of "land" (*Boden*) as their own in accordance with the fundamental right of the species, taken as a whole, to possess the surface of the planet:

> All human beings are originally in *common possession* [Gesammt-Besitz] of the land of the entire earth (*communio fundi originaria*), along with the *will* (of everyone) by nature to use it (*lex iusti*), which, because of the naturally inevitable opposition between two different capacities to make choices, would cancel [*aufheben*] any use of the land in question, if this will did not at the same time contain the law according to which a *particular* possession for each human being on the common land could be determined (*lex iuridca*). . . . There is also a rightful *capacity* [*rechtliches* Vermögen] of the will to bind everyone to acknowledge the act of taking possession and of appropriation as valid, although it is only unilateral. Provisional acquisition of land, together with all its rightful consequences, is possible.
>
> (6: 267)

Since the right to possess a portion of land is the original right of acqui-sition, upon which all others are based, any concession of this right would require a complete revision of all "acquired right." And this revision would be only the beginning, for "public right," too, would have to be reformu-lated as well. Whereas "private right" lays out the principles for distributing portions of earth into mine and yours, "public right" demonstrates the principles by which a contiguous segment of the earth can be claimed, ordered, and protected for the purpose of instituting and maintaining a self-consistent legal order. The entire *Doctrine of Right* is jeopardized by the mere suggestion that human beings must concede their place to another kind of human being for whose sake they exist. Members of species, taken together, cannot rightfully claim possession of the earth, even if the other "species (race)" remains forever *in absentia*. "Our earth world" is not ours after all. A sovereign sentence pronounced by another "species (race)" has the power – out of the blue, at any moment – to interrupt legal procedures and revoke legally valid decisions.

The last laugh

The only action that remains immune from the threat of a sovereign sentence pronounced by another kind of human being is that of making room for this other kind. If Kant's proposal for "international right" guaranteed by a confederation of states appears "ridiculous" (8: 313) to those who are in charge of political affairs, imagine the laughter that would ensue from the far more radical proposal that human beings concede the earth to those for whose sake they exist. Kant could protect himself from ridicule in *Toward Eternal Peace* by presenting the treatise as a mere game of pins. Such an apotropaic strategy would be of little use in making the other proposal, however: instead of being taken as a joke, it would be interpreted as a sign of permanent mental breakdown. Judging that the whole thing is only a joke might almost be an act of charity. There is no question that "practical politicians" (8: 343) would take the demand for the concession of the earth less seriously than the proposal for a confederation of republican states. And it is equally certain that this would not matter in the least. Concession is not an act that any legal order could perform without destroying itself as such. Nor, however, can individual members of the species concede the earth to another kind of human being. Concession, in other words, cannot be understood in terms either of "public right" or "private right." Something beyond these categories of legal reasoning is required in order to answer the question: how is it possible to concede – and not simply make space after the fact, as a prudential response to the "political existence" of an opposing body?

Kant does not pose this question in so many words; it remains implicit in the distinction between the terms "facto" and "jure." The concession of the earth to the other kind of human being must be prepared in advance of its arrival; otherwise, *de jure* concession cannot be distinguished from *de facto* acceptance. Concession, then, is not so much a matter of receding from some already established dominion as a matter of abstaining from all right-positing actions in the right manner. Concession is, in this sense, constitutively inconsistent: the abstention from all right-positing actions is done for the sake of right. The agent who concedes must admit that, regardless of its autonomy, it is not its own master, for it must obey a law of the earth that another kind of agent is alone capable of setting down. Nothing is, perhaps, more

difficult than this: autonomous agents must admit that they are, nevertheless, subject to another law, which divides "their" space of action – and
divides themselves in turn. They must concede a space "inside" themselves,
in other words, admitting that they are already inhabited by another "species
(race)" before it appears in "outer sense." By making a place for another kind
of human being, human beings make themselves into their own remnant.
For this reason, no one, strictly speaking, can concede – and remain "one."
The draft of the *Opus postumum* indicates, moreover, the direction of this
self-division: toward a difference internal to being human. Human beings
differ from themselves – and exist for the sake of this, their internal difference. Very little separates this statement from the thesis that Kant
unambiguously proposes: "human beings, as rational beings, exist for the
sake of other human beings of a different species (race)." Admitting this self-
difference – making space for another kind – is the condition under which
the concession of the earth is possible.

No one, however, can admit purely and simply this self-difference – by
saying, for example, "I am different from myself." Any statement to this
effect is constitutively inconsistent, as Kant would doubtless insist. The unity
of apperception runs counter to the act of concession: whereas the former
consists in the capacity to call all my representations "my own," the latter
makes a place for what could never be mine; whereas the former shows the
legitimacy of certain claims to ownership – such is the basic function of a
"deduction" (B: 113) – the latter admits to the illegitimacy of all such claims;
and whereas the former is the self-unifying unity that founds numerical
oneness, the latter consists in a self-division that subtracts the remnant self
from the order of extensive magnitudes. This is to say, once again: no one,
strictly speaking, can concede. Only a "no one" can do so. The only "thing"
that cannot be considered some-one-thing is a constitutively inconsistent
plurality. As such, this "thing" cannot be placed within any consistent
scheme of classification, including the a priori ordering of organic beings.

No wonder Kant vacillates between the terms *species* and *race* for the taxo-
nomic description of the kind of human being for the sake of which human
beings exist. An even greater degree of indecisiveness can be expected for
any attempt to classify the "no one" that concedes its place to the other kind
of human being. One possible name for this "no one" is "the friend" – under
the condition that, as Kant repeatedly writes and reportedly says, "there is
no such thing." Since, however, few "so-called friends" (23: 85) are willing
to admit that there are none, this name is of limited use. An even better
name momentarily appears in the second version edition of the "Transcendental Deduction": "only because I comprehend their manifold in a
consciousness do I call them all together *my* representations; for otherwise I
would have as multicolored, diverse a self [*vielfärbiges, verschiedenes Selbst*] as
I have representations of which I am conscious" (B: 134). The "multicolored,
diverse self" is not one: it is not *a* self, the self-same self, on the basis of

which manifolds can be ordered, counted, and classified. Yet it is not altogether self-less either. The "multicolored, diverse self" is distracted, not chaotic. And in the last years of his life Kant "himself" admits that he suffers from a constitutive distraction – "as an incapacity [*Unvermögen*] to maintain the unity of consciousness" (7: 113).

By virtue of this incapacity, late Kant comes close to becoming the self-divided self that, by admitting an internal difference from itself, makes way for another law of the earth. To the public at large he claims responsibility for his ailing condition: his technique of mastering ill feelings by sheer resolution ironically mastered him. To his friends, by contrast, he denies that he can be held accountable for the oppression under which he suffers: the rebellious atmosphere of the earth is accountable. Kant, in short, is not one: he is not himself, as he readily admits, and he cannot keep track of the representations that he can nevertheless call "his own." A community of "late Kants" – and late Kant is "himself" one – prepares the earth for its rightful division. A community of this kind cannot, however, recognize itself as such. Without the possibility of self-recognition, any expectation of cognition is dashed. Bursts of laughter, therefore, from all those who are able to recognize themselves as members of the human species, as members of one of its races, and as non-diverse, colorless selves.

At the end of the Preface to *Doctrine of Right*, Kant indicates that, despite the long delay in its publication, the later sections of the work, which concern "public right," have not been developed in sufficient detail. But "a decisive judgment" (6: 209) on questions of "public right" can be postponed, he argues, because these highly consequential questions have come under intense discussion of late. Immediately before announcing this last delay, which strongly suggests that certain questions of "public right" cannot simply be derived from the principles of law that he proposes – otherwise, there would be no excuse for delay other than a wholly "personal" incapacity – Kant impatiently responds to a satirical attack that had been launched at the "critical enterprise":

> If, as Shaftesbury asserts, the capacity of a doctrine (especially a practical one) to withstand *laughter* [Belachen] is not a contemptible touchstone of its truth, then, with time, the critical philosopher must take his turn and laugh *last* – and therefore laugh *best* – when he sees the paper systems of those who talk big for a long time fall, one after the other, and all their adherents scatter: a fate that will inevitably stand before them.
>
> (6: 208–09)

Kant sets no date for the last laugh. Presumably it coincides with the rendering of a "decisive judgment" on those questions of public law that the *Doctrine of Right* leaves in sketchy shape. The "decisive judgment" may, however, be this: a "decisive judgment" must wait for the arrival of the "species (race)" of human being for whose sake human beings exist. In the meantime, without making the slightest attempt to hasten the arrival of these late-comers, human beings must make way for them nevertheless. A distracted recognition of this tense situation yields the last – and best – laugh.

NOTES

INTRODUCTION

1 See Jenisch's discussion of Green as model for Orbil in his edition of Theodor Gottlieb von Hippel's play, *Der Mann nach der Uhr*, pp. 18–21. Jenisch also discusses – and dismisses – the suggestion that Kant serves as the model for the learned pedant, Magister Blasius, pp. 21–22.

2 Pia Reimen's detailed analysis of Hippel's play concludes that Kant is the model for Hippel's play; see Reimen, "Struktur und Figurenkonstellationen," esp. pp. 224–26. One of Kant's earliest biographers, Rheinhold Bernhard Jachmann, claimed that Green was the model; see J. B. Jachmann, *Immanuel Kant geschildert in Briefen an einen Freund* (1804), reprinted in *Immanuel Kant*, ed. Felix Groß, p. 154: "Hippel wrote his *Man by the Clock* in order that you might get to know him better." This is an odd comment, to say the least, since it is unclear why a comedy of character (à la Moliére) would be written to make a particular individual better known. On the contrary, it seeks to represent a universal type: "the orderly man." Green's life is, in any case, comparable to that of Orbil, the protagonist of the play, only at the point of their punctuality. For a study of Hippel's relation to Kant, see Hamilton Beck, *The Elusive "I" in the Novel*.

3 See Heinrich Heine, *Zur Geschichte der Religion und Philosophie in Deutschland* (second edition, 1852), reprinted in Heine, *Werke*, 4: 123.

4 Needless to say, I do not consider all of Kant's writings after he completed the third *Critique* and, indeed, some of the texts that have direct bearing on my analysis are largely ignored; elsewhere I have treated Kant's "On the Newly Arisen Superior Tone in Philosophy" (1796) and related writings; see *Raising the Tone of Philosophy*, ed. Fenves, pp. 1–30; and the central section of *The Conflict of the Faculties* (1798), entitled "Renewed Question: Whether the Human Race is Constantly Progressing Toward the Better"; see Fenves, *A Peculiar Fate*, pp. 170–285.

5 The conflict over the chronology has been waged long ago; see Arthur Warda, "Der Streit um den 'Streit der Fakultäten,'" Otto Schöndorfer, "Zur Entstehungsgeschichte des 'Streit der Fakultäten,'" and Karl Vorländer's notes to his edition of the Akademie edition (7: 337–43).

6 Thus Johann Gottfried Hasse records Kant's words in his generally unremarkable *Merkwürdige Äußerungen Kant's von einem seiner Tischgenossen* (1805); reprinted in *Der alte Kant*, ed. Buchenau and Lehmann, pp. 18–19.

7 Friedrich Theodor Rink, *Ansichten aus Immanuel Kant's Leben* (1805), p. 109.

8 See Kant's essay of 1754 entitled "Die Frage, ob die Erde veralte, physikalisch erwogen" (1: 193–214).

1 THE PLEASURES OF FAILURE

1 See the section of the *Phänomenologie des Geistes* entitled "Die Lust und die Notwendigkeit"; reprinted in G. W. F. Hegel, *Werke*, 3: 270–75.

2 For a detailed account of the complex set of reflections that ultimately took shape as the third *Critique*, see John Zammito, *Genesis of the "Critique of Judgment."*

3 See especially Aristotle, *Nicomachean Ethics*, Books 7 and 10. For an illuminating discussion of the difficulties Aristotle encounters as he seeks to come to terms with pleasure (*hedonai*), see Amélie Rorty, "Akrasia and Pleasure."

4 On Epicureanism in the eighteenth century, with particular attention to England, see Richard Kroll, *The Material World*; for a similar study that pays attention to Germany, see Dorothee Kimmich, *Epikureische Aufklärungen*. See also *Atoms, Pneuma, and Tranquillity*, ed. Margaret J. Osler; and Howard Jones, *The Epicurean Tradition*. Of particular interest is the singularly insightful study of W. R. Johnson, *Lucretius and the Modern World*.

5 See the section of the Analytic of Principles entitled "Anticipations of Perception," esp. A: 116; B: 208: "One can call all knowledge by means of I can know and determine *a priori* what belongs to empirical knowledge an anticipation, and this is doubtless the meaning of Epicurus attributed to his expression *prolepsis* [in Greek letters in the original]."

6 Kant does not attempt to distinguish among the various atomists. The first attempt to separate early Greek atomism from its later version can be rightly ascribed to Karl Marx's doctoral dissertation, *Differenz der demokratischen und epikureischen Naturphilosophie* (University of Jena, 1841), reprinted in *Marx-Engels Werke*, 40: 257–373. As I tried to show, Marx presents Democritus as a (flawed) Kantian and Epicurus as a (failed) Hegelian; see my essay, "Marx's Doctoral Thesis on Two Greek Atomists and the Post-Kantian Interpretations."

7 The poem quoted in his own prose translation in section 49 of the *Critique of Judgment* (5: 315–16) is entitled "Au Maréchal Keith, Imitation du troisième livre de Lucrèce: 'Sur les vaines terreurs de la mort et les frayeurs d'une autre vie'" (originally published in 1762). Regardless of the poetic quality of the lines Kant quotes (which can be found in *Ouevres de Fredéric II*, 10: 203), they accurately capture an Epicurean–Lucretian conviction that this life is the only one and that, for this reason, there should be no fear of another. No "postulate" of an afterlife, in other words, is required in order to strengthen one's resolve to live a life in accordance with rationally controlled desires.

8 Friedrich II of Prussia, *Briefe*, 2: 62; for an analysis of Friedrich's Epicureanism in the context of contemporaneous Epicurean and anti-Epicurean discourse, see Kimmich, *Epikureische Aufklärungen*, pp. 228–30.

9 Lucretius, *De rerum natura*, Book 1, lines 78–79. Many years later, Kant quotes these lines, as he once again defends himself against "defenders of religion" (1: 223): see the essay of 1796 entitled "On a Newly Arisen Superior Tone in Philosophy" (8: 404).

10 In the third edition of the third *Critique*, "*voraus sagte*" is replaced by "*voraussagte*," which more strongly associated the phrase with "prophecy": the foretelling of a disastrous future.

11 Paul Guyer has drawn attention to this proposition and extensively discussed its presuppositions and consequences; see, in particular, *Kant and the Claims of Taste*, pp. 70–88; see also "Beauty and Utility in Eighteenth-Century Aesthetics." For a critique of Guyer's position, see Henry Allison, *Kant's Theory of Taste*, pp. 55–59. Allison, to my mind, correctly perceives the transitional function of the proposition he mistranslates (see note 13 below); but his refutation of the proposition in question fails to take into account Kant's own explanation for the pleasure in unexpected events:

> It [the law that every attainment of an intention is connected to pleasure] is inherently implausible because there seem to be clear cases of pleasure that are unconnected with the satisfaction of an aim, namely those that are totally unexpected. Suppose, for example, I just happen to meet and converse with my favorite female movie actress at a cocktail party. Not only did I not intend to meet her there, but I may never even have entertained the idea of meeting her at all. Such an encounter, one might say, was "beyond my wildest dreams." Nonetheless, this would hardly preclude the possibility of my taking pleasure in such an encounter, were it perchance to occur. Indeed, it might be claimed that some of life's greatest pleasures fall into this category.
>
> (Allison, *Kant's Theory of Taste*, p. 56)

The unnumbered "Remark" between sections 53 and 55 of the third *Critique* provides Kant's response to this scenario, which certainly does not involve a universally communicable pleasure: the pleasure in meeting the movie star is only "satisfaction," and it is caused by the sudden convulsion of the body, which, as it communicates itself to the mind, promotes one's life as a whole. For a lengthy discussion of this "Remark," see the last three sections of this chapter.

12 See Kant, *Critique of Judgment*, trans. Werner Pluhar, p. 27. Pluhar adds "always" into the sentence: "The attainment of an aim is always connected with the feeling of pleasure."

13 Allison, *Kant's Theory of Taste*, p. 55.

14 For an investigation of Kant's appeal to "life" in the third *Critique*, see Rudolf Makkreel, *Imagination and Interpretation in Kant*.

15 For a discussion of Kant's shifting conception of the "mind-body problem," see Shell, *The Embodiment of Reason*, esp. p. 402 (which briefly discusses this passage).

16 As is his custom, Kant adds some "remarks" to the Dialectic of Aesthetic Judgment (5: 341–46), which serve as addenda to paragraph 57. The unnumbered paragraph between 53 and 55, however, is the last independent remark of the Critique of Aesthetic Judgment. It corresponds to the magnificent paragraph 76 in the Critique of Teleological Judgment, which is also simply called "Remark." No passage of the *Critiques* is more consequential for the development of post-critical thought than section 76, as Heidegger suggests in "Kants These über das Sein," in *Wegmarken*, p. 463. From another direction, Eckart Förster has shown its consequences in "Die Bedeutung von §§76, 77 der 'Kritik der Urteilskraft' für die Entwicklung der nachkantischen Philosophie."

17 That Kant makes almost no mention of wit in the *Critique of Judgment* is surprising for this reason. Throughout the eighteenth century, inquiries in the mental powers that were modeled on Locke's regularly took up his distinction between wit and judgment,

including the *Critique of Pure Reason*, which lightly touches on "mother wit [*Mutterwitz*], the lack of which cannot be repaired by schooling" (A: 133; B: 172). In the so-called Blomberg Logic (from the early 1770s) Kant has further remarks on *Mutterwitz* as a "natural capacity of healthy understanding and healthy reason" (23: 22–23). For some general comments about the relation between the *Critique of Judgment* and the corresponding sections in the *Anthropology*, see Wolfgang Ritzel, "Kant über den Witz und Kants Witz."

18 For Plato, see A: 314; B: 370; for Leibniz, see 8: 251.

19 There is no better evidence of this than the lengthy footnote through which Werner Pluhar seeks to make sense of this term (*Critique of Judgment*, p. 205). The point of the note is to save Kant from an inconsistency, for he unambiguously states that "intellectual feeling" is a contradiction *in abjectio* (5: 75).

2 THE SOVEREIGN SENTENCE

1 The terms "infelicity" and "speech act" are drawn, of course, from the work of John Austin, who characteristically would not concern himself with any "uncommon" – noble or especially sovereign – speech acts; see Austin, *How To Do Things With Words*.

2 Hans Hattenhauer, *Die geistesgeschichtlichen Grundlagen des deutschen Rechts*, p. 20.

3 For a brief analysis of the term *Machtspruch*, see Jacob and Wilhelm Grimm, *Deutsches Wörterbuch*, 13: 1415.

4 See Adolf Stölzel, *Brandenburg-Preußens Rechtsverwaltung und Rechtsverfassung*, 2: 15. Stölzel's work is an indispensable resource for research into the character of Prussian law. An abbreviated account of the concept of the *Machtspruch* can be found in the last two chapters of Stölzel's *Fünfzehn Vorträge aus der Brandenburglich-Preußischen Rechts- und Staatsgeschichte*, pp. 157–82. See also Eberhard Schmidt, "Rechtssprüche und Machtsprüche der preussischen Könige des 18. Jahrhunderts." Schmidt's study, which relies heavily on Stölzel's documentation, is compromised by its premises, which largely correspond to those of the regime under which it was written. Stölzel is an unabashed and outspoken antagonist of the sovereign sentence. Near the end of his voluminous work he blames much of the ills of the Prussian administration of justice on its tendency to admit sovereign sentences (or executive mandates) into its calculations: "Those '*Machtsprüche*,' which in the course of the eighteenth century convulsed the structure of the Prussian legal state, produced the demand for complete separation of supreme-judicial and royal powers. This demand found nourishment partly from France, partly from the Rhein, which exercised its influence eastward" (Stölzel, *Rechtsverwaltung und Rechtsverfassung*, 2: 684–85). Schmidt criticizes Stölzel for misunderstanding the character of sovereign sentences in the early decades of the eighteenth century and, more generally, for failing to discern the reason for their initial acceptance and gradual rejection: beginning with Friedrich II, Prussian kings lost their self-confidence and forgot that they alone could speak in the name of "popular" justice.

5 Anonymous (attributed to Philipp Joseph von Jariges), *Réflections philosophiques et historiques d'un jurisconsulte*, p. 22; quoted in Stölzel, p. 249. (Decker is the court publisher.) The attribution of the pamphlet to Jariges, who also served as the secretary for the Prussian Royal Academy of Sciences, derives from Johann Ludwig Klüber, *Oeffentliches Recht des Teutschen Bundes und der Bundes-Staaten*, p. 888.

6 Quoted in Stölzel, *Fünfzehn Vorträge*, p. 178.

7 See *Allgemeines Landrecht für die Preussischen Staaten von 1794*, ed. Hans Hattenhauer. For analyses of the conditions and consequences of the *Allgemeines Landrecht*, see Hattenhauer's introduction to his edition; Reinhart Koselleck, *Preußen zwischen Reform und Revolution*; and more briefly, Theodore Ziolkowski, *The Mirror of Justice*, pp. 187–214.

8 Quoted from Adolf Stölzel, *Carl Gottlieb Svarez*, pp. 312–14.

9 Hattenhauer, *Die geistesgeschichtlichen Grundlagen*, p. 20. The most famous case of a royal *Machtspruch* is the one with which Friedrich II concluded the trial of the miller, Günther Arnold, resident of Pommerzig (Neumark), against Count Schmettau. The king was of the opinion that the judges in the case were partial to the Count, nullified their decision, and when it was reinstated, had them imprisoned (1779). After the king's death in 1786 the trial was resumed, and they were set free. The negative connotations of *Machtspruch* in the latter part of the eighteenth century were, in large measure, due to the controversy over the Arnold affair; see Stölzel, *Fünfzehn Vorträge*, pp. 170–82.

10 In the second edition of the *Critique of Pure Reason* Kant emphasizes the legal character of the term "deduction" (B: 113): in the course of a legal action, the *quid juris* (unlike the *quid facti*) proceeds as a "deduction." For an explication of Kant's remarks on the legal (as opposed to logical) provenance of "deduction," see Dieter Henrich, "Kant's Notion of a Deduction and the Methodological Background of the First *Critique*."

11 As early as 1765, Kant mentions to Lambert that he plans to publish shortly a "metaphysical first principles of practical world-wisdom [*Weltweisheit*]" (10: 53). A detailed account of Kant's changes in plans for a treatment of moral topics from 1765 to the publication of the second *Critique* in 1787 can be found in Lewis White Beck, *Commentary on Kant's "Critique of Practical Reason,"* pp. 1–18; a succinct presentation of the many delays between the letter to Lambert and the eventual appearance of the *Doctrine of Right* can be found in Bernd Ludwig's edition of the *Metaphysische Anfängsgründe der Rechtslehre*, esp. pp. xiv–xxv.

12 For a lucid analysis of Kant's doctrine of punishment, see Susan Shell, *The Rights of Reason*, esp. pp. 160–62.

13 The term *correi* derives from *correus*, "partaker in guilt, joint criminal," and it is defined in the *Digest* of Justinian (34, 3, 3, §3).

14 On the zone of indetermination and its relation to life (understood in a manner quite different from its exposition in Kant's work in general and his *Doctrine of Right* in particular), see the provocative study of Giorgio Agamben, *Homo Sacer*.

15 Elsewhere in the *Doctrine of Right* Kant associates certain royal actions with cannibalism (6: 345); even more devastating remarks can be found in *Toward Eternal Peace* (8: 354–55). For further discussion of these passages see Susan Shell, "Cannibals All: The Grave Wit of Kant's Perpetual Peace." See also the fourth section of Chapter 6 below.

16 For Kant's most extensive analysis of republicanism, see the "first definitive article for eternal peace" in *Toward Eternal Peace*: "*Republicanism* is the political principle of separation of the executive power (the government) from the legislative power" (8: 352). In this brief discussion Kant does not mention juridical power. His silence corresponds to a curious passage in Montesquieu's *L'Esprit des Loix* (from whom he derives this definition), according to which the juridical power should be "invisible et nulle" (cited in Carl Schmitt, *Die Diktatur*, pp. 109–110; see also Schmitt's discussion of the separation of powers in *Verfassungslehre*, pp. 182–87). Kant takes

Montesquieu's enigmatic remark concerning the invisibility of juridical power literally, so to speak, for he, too, makes it invisible, as it – in keeping with its basic obligation – merely subsumes cases under laws that are elsewhere legislated and enforced.

17 For an analysis of "On the Supposed Right to Lie," see Chapter 6 of this volume.

18 For a more extensive analysis of this remarkable footnote in the *Doctrine of Right*, see Fenves, *A Peculiar Fate*, pp. 271–76.

19 Hannah Arendt, *The Origins of Totalitarianism*, p. 243; on the relation of the linguistic mode of decree and imperial expansion, see Susannah Gottlieb, *Regions of Sorrow*, pp. 44–50.

20 For Kant's identification of the "historical sign," which is likewise its interpretation *as* a sign, see the second section of the *Conflict of the Faculties* (7: 49–94); on the character of this sign and its interpretation, see Michel Foucault, "Un cours inédit," in *Dits et écrits*, 4: 679–88; Jean-François Lyotard, *L'Enthousiasme*; and Fenves, *A Peculiar Fate*, pp. 170–285.

21 See the sub-section of the *Conflict of the Faculties* that responds to the question "What Proceeds [*Ertrag*] Will Progress Toward the Better Throw Forth?": "Not an ever-growing quantity of *morality* with regard to intentions but an increase in the products of *legality* in dutiful actions whatever their driving springs" (7: 91).

3 THE OTHER SOVEREIGN SENTENCE

1 Johann Gottlieb Fichte, *Grundlage der gesammten Wissenschaftslehre* (1794), reprinted in Fichte, *Werke*, 1: 105.

2 Having announced at the opening of his treatise that a "sovereign sentence of reason" will appear at the precise moment when the "deduction" comes to a halt – as the arresting of the process – Fichte proceeds to make good on his promise:

> The actual, supreme task that embraces all others is: how can the I operate immediately on the not-I, or the not-I on the I, when both are held to be utterly opposed to each other? We slip some X between them, on which both may act, so that they also act mediately upon one another. But we soon discover that there must again be some point in this X, at which the I and the not-I immediately meet. To prevent this, one slips a new link Y between them as a replacement for the sharp boundary. But it soon appears that here too, as in X, there must be a point at which the two opponents immediately touch each other. And so it would go on forever, if the knot were not, to be sure, not untied but rather torn apart by an absolute sovereign sentence of reason, which the philosopher does not pronounce but which, instead, he only shows – through which [it is declared]: *let there be* no not-I at all, for the not-I does not allow itself be united with the I in any manner whatsoever [*Und so würde es ins unendliche fortgehen, wenn nicht durch einen absoluten Machtspruch der Vernunft, den nicht etwa der Philosoph thut, sondern den er nur aufzeigt – durch den: es soll, da das Nicht-Ich mit dem Ich auf keine Art sich vereinigen lässt, überhaupt kein Nicht-Ich seyn, der Knoten zwar nicht gelöst, aber zerschnitten würde*].
>
> (Fichte, *Werke*, 1: 143–44)

Later in the *Foundation* Fichte recalls Kant's ban on sovereign sentences and indeed submits himself to this meta-philosophical command:

The demand that everything should agree with the self, that all reality should be posited absolutely by the self, is the demand of what is called – and with justice – practical reason. Such a practical capacity of reason has previously been postulated, but not proved. . . . Now such a proof must be carried out in agreement with theoretical reason itself, and the latter should not be ousted from the case by a sovereign sentence [*Machtspruch*]. This can be achieved no otherwise than by showing that reason cannot even be theoretical if it is not practical; that there can be no intelligence in human beings if they do not possess a practical capacity; the possibility of all representation is founded on the latter.

(Fichte, *Werke*, 1: 264)

3 Fichte, *Werke*, 1: 105–06.
4 See especially Fichte, "Über Geist und Buchstab in der Philosophie: In einer Reihe von Briefen" (written 1795, published 1800), *Werke*, 8: 270–300. The letters were intended for Schiller's *Horen*, but, to Fichte's dismay, were rejected; see the informative introductory remarks of Daniel Breazeale to his translation of the letters in Fichte, *Early Philosophical Writings*, pp. 185–91.
5 Kant makes a similar remark about Leibniz at the end of "On a Discovery" (8: 251); for a more extensive examination of the hermeneutics Kant briefly sketches in this remark, see Fenves, *A Peculiar Fate*, pp. 137–42.
6 On the multiple senses of *Versuch* in Kant's earlier work, see Willi Goetschel, *Kant als Schriftsteller*.
7 For Leibniz's reference to the "bathos of Paul," see the concluding Latin resumé of *Essais de Théodicée sur la bonté de Dieu, la liberté de l'homme et l'origine du mal* (1710), reprinted in *Die philosophischen Schriften*, 6: 459–60. On Leibniz's invention of the term *théodicée*, see Fenves, *Arresting Language*, pp. 59–60.
8 For detailed accounts of the growing dissatisfaction with theodicy, see Carl-Friedrich Geyer, "Das 'Jahrhundert der Theodizee'"; Stefan Lorenz, *De Mundo Optimo*; and especially Thomas Saine, *The Problem of Being Modern*.
9 Johann Erich Biester, "Über Hrn. Kants Aufsatz, in Betref der Theodicee," p. 418.
10 G. L. Spalding, "Über die Quellen, aus welchen eine Theodicee zu fließen pfleget." A far more interesting contribution to the reconsideration of theodicy that was doubtless prompted by Kant's essay is Solomon Maimon, "Über die Theodicee."
11 As was their custom, La Académie Royal des Sciences et Belles-Lettres in Berlin posed its prize contests in French. An account of the prize contest, which was posted in 1788 and given the term of 1791 (later delayed to 1795), can be found in Karl Rosenkranz, *Geschichte der Kant'schen Philosophie*, pp. 350–55.
12 The anti-Leibnizian character of the theme may be a result of Maupertius' unmistakable inclinations. The director of the Royal Academy and good friend of Friedrich II, he was also an opponent of Leibnizianism. Lessing and Mendelssohn, both of whom defended Leibniz from beginning (almost) to the end, collaborated on a satirical response to the Academy's theme: *Pope ein Metaphysiker!* reprinted in Lessing, *Werke*, 3: 631–70.
13 Kant had written a series of sketches for a response to the prize contest of 1755 (17: 230–39). Instead of developing these notes into a finished work, however, he publishes the *Universal Natural History*, which not only quotes Pope but also explains in its own way why "the all" is good, even as all its parts collapse into nothingness.

"Attempt at a Few Considerations of Optimism" (1759) defends certain aspects of theodicical reasoning but comes to life, so to speak, when its conclusion celebrates the sanctity of mere being: "Hail us! We are! [*Heil uns! Wir sind!*]" (2: 35).

14 For an incisive analysis of authentic interpretation in "On the Failure" as transcendental hermeneutics in miniature, see Werner Hamacher, "The Promise of Interpretation," in *Premises*, pp. 85–99.

15 See also Kant's analysis of Plato's failure in the *Critique of Pure Reason* (A: 312; B: 371). Various commentators have used these two passages as interpretative keys to Kant's theoretical program, especially Gerold Prauss, *Kant, zur Deutung seiner Theorie von Erkennen und Handeln*. It is, therefore, an error to assert that the basic concepts of "On the Failure" were only developed in the second and third *Critiques*; see Christoph Schulte, "Zweckwidriges in der Erfahrung."

16 See, for example, Friedrich Schelling, *Weltalter* (1815), reprinted in *Sämmtliche Werke*, 1, 7: 337–39.

17 As Kant clearly explains in the *Anthropology from a Pragmatic Point of View*, which reproduces the argument of numerous earlier works and brings together decades of lectures on the topic, speaking to oneself aloud is the "general mark of madness [*Verrücktheit*]": "the loss of *common sense* [Gemeinsinn] (*sensus communis*) and the onset of *logical private sense* [logische Eigensinn] (*senses privatus*)" (7: 219).

18 In subsequent texts devoted specifically to the relation between philosophical and sectarian modes of interpreting Scripture, Kant returns to the opposition between authentic and doctrinal interpretation; but much of the complexity of the original exposition is lost – for two closely related reasons: authentic interpretation aims at elucidating a written text rather than the "letter" of creation; and it becomes a strictly philosophical cause, whereas in the attack on philosophical attempts at theodicy, it is allegorically expressed in a decidedly non-philosophical text, to wit, a book of Scripture. The other discussions of authentic interpretation can be found in *Religion Within the Limits of Bare Reason* (6: 114) and more extensively in the *Conflict of the Faculties* (7: 48, 66–67). Of greater interest is Kant's use of the opposition between authentic and doctrinal interpretation in a draft of the *Opus postumum*, as he seeks to elucidate the relation between physics and the metaphysical foundations of natural science (22: 172–73).

19 Carl Schmitt, *Der Leviathan*, p. 123.

20 Thomas Hobbes, *Leviathan*, p. 227; Book 2, Chapter 17.

21 Hobbes, *Leviathan*, p. 362; Book 2, Chapter 28. In addition to the lengthy descriptions of the sea monster in Chapters 40 and 41 of *Job*, Leviathan appears in four other places in the Hebrew Bible: Isaiah 27: 1; Ps. 74: 14; Ps. 104: 26; and Job 3: 8: "Let those who curse the day curse it, who are ready to rouse up Leviathan" – which is to say, let creation as a whole collapse.

22 Despite its patent and prominent display of vicious and obsequious anti-Jewishness, Schmitt's reflections on *Leviathan* make clear the degree to which Hobbes is silently indebted to both Jewish and Christian interpretations of the sea monster. As he would tell Hansjörg Viesel many years later, the source of his investigation into the meaning of this "political symbol" was Walter Benjamin's *Origin of the German Mourning-Play*, which, according to Schmitt, should have included its own study of the allegorical figure of Leviathan; see H. Viesel, *Jawohl, der Schmitt*, pp. 14, 16. On the relation of Schmitt to Benjamin in this context, see Giorgio Agamben, "On the State of Exception: the Debate between Walter Benjamin and Carl Schmitt."

23 See the remarks of Marvin H. Pope in his informative translation and commentary, *The Anchor Bible: Job*, pp. 276–78.

24 A slight trace of another form of madness makes itself known in "On the Failure": the madness of ancient *atê*, which strikes unawares and makes one do otherwise unthinkable deeds. For *authentês* originally meant "murderer." Kant may have known little Greek and paid even less attention to the original sense of the term, but the passing reference to the Furies (8: 261), who pursue the *authentês* in lieu of an "Areopagus" (1: 222), indicates that the original sense is not entirely lost. Orestes, who is the authentic *authentês*, so to speak, appears in rather prominent place in the *Doctrine of Virtue* – as one of the two friends (along with Pylades) who make up a "perfect friendship." *Authentês* as "murderer," came to mean the doer of the deed, its "perpetrator," whoever can be held responsible for a death and can, in turn, claim responsibility for other deeds, especially the linguistic deed of "authorship." To my knowledge, the only reader of "On the Failure" who has drawn attention to the original sense of *authentês* is Thomas Schestag, "Komische Authentizität."

25 See Hans Saner, *Kants Weg vom Krieg zum Frieden*.

26 See Kant, *Doctrine of Right*, 6: 334; Chapter 2 of this volume is principally concerned with this passage.

27 Friedrich II, who had at times dismissed juridical findings by declaring sovereign sentences (to his great regret), said in 1780: "I am very far from presuming to render immediate decisions. That would be a sovereign sentence, and you know that I abhor them" (quoted in Adolf Stölzel, *Fünfzehn Vorträge*, p. 178); see Chapter 2 above.

28 Ehregott Andreas Christoph Wasianski, *Immanuel Kant in seinen letzten Lebensjahren* (1804); reprinted in *Immanuel Kant*, ed. Felix Groß, pp. 245–46: "Kant adopted the blinding paradox of Aristotle: My dear friends, there is no such thing as a friend." For further discussion of Wasianksi's remarks, see Chapter 7 of this volume.

29 For no particular reason, the Akademie edition drops the signature line of the essay. With few exceptions Kant generally signed himself simply "I. Kant" when publishing in the *Berlinische Monatsschrift*. Here, however, he – or Biester, the editor – sees fit to include his locale as well. Other contributors would simply sign themselves by their last name.

30 It is of some interest to note that the most recent translation of "On the Failure" into English gives incorrect – or even misleading – renditions of the last two passages quoted here. Instead of translating "in dem Bewußtsein: ob ich in der That glaube Recht zu haben" (8: 268) as "in the consciousness whether I in fact believe myself to be right," George di Giovanni proposes the (ungrammatical) phrase "in the judgment whether I in fact believe to be right" (Kant, *Religion and Rational Theology*, p. 34); and instead of translating the last sentence in the passage above (8: 270) in such a manner that it follows from the previous one, de Giovanni writes "it must then be that, although we are all aware of the falsity of the coin with which we trade, that coin still manages to maintain itself in circulation [*es müßte denn dieses sein, daß, obzwar ein jeder von der Falschheit der Münze belehrt ist, mit der er Verkehr treibt, sie sich dennoch immer so gut im Umlaufe erhalten kann*]" (Kant, *Religion and Rational Theology*, p. 36). The latter translation may be grammatical, but it makes no sense why Kant would write such a sentence. Even more unfortunate, however, is the mistranslation of the title of the essay as "On the Miscarriage of All Philosophical Trials in Theodicy." Only two things can be said to miscarry: pregnancies and justice. "Attempts," "essays," and "experiments" (*Versuche*) do not miscarry; they fail to reach

183

their goal. Obviously di Giovanni wants to suggest that the trial (in the juridical sense of the term, which the German term does not carry) is a miscarriage of justice, but this, too, is mistaken, since a miscarriage could take place only if the trial produced a verdict – which it does not in this case, except perhaps in the "Concluding Remark," where Kant judges human beings guilty of a refined penchant for deceptiveness.

31 Jonathan Swift, *A Tale of the Tub* (1704), reprinted in *The Writings of Jonathan Swift*, 304. For a longer discussion of Kant's relation to Swift, see Chapter 6.

32 Walter Benjamin, *Ursprung des deutschen Trauerspiels* (1928), reprinted in *Gesammelte Schriften*, 1: 350. The idea of allegorical expression developed here is, of course, indebted to Benjamin's great study of the baroque *Trauerspiel*, in which he – perhaps not by chance – briefly touches on Kant's conception of melancholia in the *Observations on the Feeling of the Beautiful and the Sublime* (Benjamin, *Gesammelte Schriften*, 1: 326): "Kant still paints the image of the melancholic in the colors in which it appears in the older theoreticians." Benjamin would doubtless have been familiar with "On the Failure," given the fact that he had originally planned to write his dissertation on Kant's theory of history.

33 Translated from Luther's translation: "Das ist aber alles geschehen, damit erfüllt würde, was der Herr durch den Propheten gesagt hat, der da spricht (Jesaja 7, 14): 'Siehe, eine Jungfrau wird schwanger sein und einen Sohn gebären, und sie werden ihm den Namen Immanuel geben,' das heißt übersetzt: Gott mit uns."

34 Kant studied Hebrew in his years at the Albertina (University in Königsberg) and was reported to be more interested in philology than philosophy; see Karl Vorländer, *Immanuel Kant*, 1: 26–43.

35 This last quotation, taken from the *Religion Within the Limits of Bare Reason* (1793), very likely does not represent an opinion Kant held before he had knowledge of Bishop Warburton's *Divine Legation of Moses* (1737–41), on the one hand, and Mendelssohn's *Jerusalem* (1783), on the other. The other two quotations do not depend on any learned references.

36 See Vorländer, *Kants Leben*, pp. 14 and 29. Nevertheless, the title page of the *Gedanken von der wahren Schätzung der lebendigen Kräften* (Königsberg: Dern, 1746) calls him "Emmanuel Kant" (reproduced in Norbert Weis, *Königsberg*, p. 30). The Akademie edition "corrects" this spelling (1: 1). The original spelling of Kant's name did not disappear for good, however; it reappeared late in his life, first in the French edition of *Toward Eternal Peace* published by Nicolovius in 1796 and four years later in Jäsche's edition of Kant's lectures on logic. And John Richardson's translation of his essays (1798) calls Kant "Emanuel" (see Kant, *Four Neglected Essays*, p. 1).

37 Anonymous, *Wöchentliche-Königsberger Frag- und Anzeigungs- Nachrichten*, no. 24 (1755); reproduced in Steffen Dietzsch, "Kant, die Juden und das akademische Bürgerrecht in Königsberg," p. 111.

38 Johann Gottfried Hasse, *Merkwürdige Äußerungen Kant's von einem seiner Tischgenossen* (1804); reprinted in *Der alte Kant*, ed. Artur Buchenau and Gerhard Lehmann, p. 21. Hasse also reports the following about his name:

> He showed a particular affection for his first name *Immanuel*, and he spoke with delight – and often – about it. More than once he flattered me by saying that "he had otherwise written *Emanuel*; but having learned from

me what it meant, and how it must be written, he constantly writes *Immanuel*." I replied that I would never had dared teach him anything, since he taught me; that, to my knowledge, he had written *Immanuel* long before I came to Königsberg and was lucky enough to become acquainted with him (let me add that Emanuel is not, according to my opinion, false; one could also read the first letter (*ain*) as *e*, as contemporary Jews do, and the doubling of the *m* is not essential; it means the same nevertheless); but none of this helped; he remained steadfast.

(Hasse, Der alte Kant, p. 21)

For a brief discussion of the change from *Emanuel* to *Immanuel*, see Manfred Kuehn, *Kant: A Biography*, p. 26: "It is perhaps meaningful that he found it necessary to critically evaluate and correct[!] the very name given to him, but it is noteworthy that the literal meaning of his name provided him with comfort and confidence throughout his life." It is entirely unclear how Kuehn, who gives no evidence of knowing Hebrew, is certain that the change from *Emanuel* to *Immanuel* is a "correction," still less a correction based on a critical evaluation. Had he ever encountered a sign in the contemporary world that said something like "Temple Emanuel" – or indeed had he simply read Hasse's correct assessment of the Ashkenazi transcription – he would be less sure, one would hope, that Kant was making a correction. Kuehn, in short, never even considers that Kant may have changed his first name so that he would be as little associated with the Jews of his day as possible. This is of a piece with Kuehn's deeply flawed account of Kant's profoundly ambivalent relation to Judaism.

A full examination of Kuehn's failure in this regard would require more space than a note, but two points may suffice. (1) Of Mendelssohn's rejection of the idea that humanity progresses, he writes, "His position was motivated, at least in part, by Jewish ideas of human corruption" (p. 375). Needless to say, there is no footnote here that would substantiate this false claim. (All one need do is reflect on the significance of the term *mensh* in Yiddish to cast doubts on it.) Mendelssohn had very good reasons to suspect that talk of human progress – and indeed any proposal for a "philosophy of history" – is a dangerous occupation: in the case of Lessing's essay, in particular, it means that Judaism is an obsolete relic of primitive minds. (2) A careful evaluation of Kant's relation to Marcus Herz is necessary for any thoughtful consideration of Kant's relation to Judaism, and one of the facts of this relation is that Kant contemptuously dismissed Herz's study *Über den Schwindel* (On vertigo). According to Kuehn, the reason for this surprising show of contempt is simple: "Kant's indifference was the result of his lack of interest in purely psychological questions" (p. 320). Anyone who has even glanced over the table of contents in Herz's work would know that it does not concern itself with "purely psychological questions" and, indeed, in the context of eighteenth-century medicine, talk of "pure psychology" is sheer nonsense. In any case, according to Kuehn, Kant's own *Anthropology* "presents a great deal of empirical psychology" (p. 407), to which he might have added: including numerous remarks on vertigo that would have benefited from a reading of Herz's study (see, for example, 7: 166, 178, 264). The reason for Kant's surprising contempt for his former student and apparent friend has to lie elsewhere. That it has something to do with his ambivalence toward the Jews-Palestinians, which seemed to have intensified with age, cannot be seriously doubted.

4 OUT OF THE BLUE

1 Kant, "Vom radicalen Bösen in der Menschennatur," *Berlinische Monatsschrift* (April 1792): 323–85; reprinted as the first chapter of *Religion innerhalb der Grenzen der bloßen Vernunft* (1793); references are to the Akademie edition of *Religion*, although the quotations follow the *Monatsschrift* version.

2 There are numerous accounts of Kant's conflict of the censor, all of which are indebted to Dilthey's detailed study, "Der Streit Kants mit der Zensur über das Recht freier Religionsforschung" (1890), republished in Wilhelm Dilthey, *Gesammelte Schriften* 4: 265–309.

3 See the discussion of self-fulfilling prophecy in Chapter 5 of this volume.

4 A fairly large literature has grown around the issue of more-than-radical-evil. Among the milestones of this debate John Silber, "The Ethical Significance of Kant's *Religion*," and Emil Fackenheim, "Kant and Radical Evil," *University of Toronto Quarterly* 23 (1954): 339–53; Jean-Luc Nancy, "Le Katègorein de l'excès," in *L'Impératif catégorique*, pp. 5–32; and Sharon Anderson-Gold, "Kant's Rejection of Devilishness" and Gordon Michalson, *Fallen Freedom*, esp. pp. 73–88. See also Slavoj Žižek, "On Radical Evil and Related Matters," in *Tarrying with the Negative*, pp. 83–124. The last-named essay proposes the following answer to its own question: "what, precisely, *is* Evil?" Here is Žižek's answer: "Evil is another name for the 'death-drive,' for the fixation on some Thing which derails our customary life-circuit" (p. 96) – which sounds rather like the moral law, as Kant describes its effect on those whom it affects. It is unclear whether Žižek means such comments as commentary or critique, and it is equally unclear whether this definition has anything to do with either radical or diabolical evil.

5 At times Kant speaks of the "sole fact of pure reason" (e.g. 5: 31); at others, of the "fact, as it were, of pure reason" (e.g. 5: 47), and at others still, of "practical data of reason" (e.g. *Critique of Pure Reason*, B: xviii and xxii). For a helpful commentary on the difficulties surrounding the genitive construction "Faktum der Vernunft," see Lewis White Beck, *A Commentary on Kant's "Critique of Practical Reason,"* pp. 166–70.

6 This note has been overlooked by Henry Allison in his interpretation of Kant's thesis of radical evil; see Henry Allison, *Kant's Theory of Freedom*, pp. 146–61. Allison tries to resolve the aporias of Kant's text by supplementing it: "The claim [radical evil], then, is to be taken as a priori; indeed, as a postulate [this is Allison's term, not Kant's], it must be synthetic a priori. Consequently, it requires some sort of deduction or justification; and since Kant fails to provide one, we must attempt to do so" (p. 155). Kant's failure would seem to be a worthy topic of consideration: it may slow down the course of the argument, but so much the worse for argumentation. In any case, Allison proceeds as follows: "Instead of offering a 'formal proof' of the universality of the propensity to evil, he simply asserts the necessity for such a proof is obviated by 'the multitude of crying examples which experience *of the actions* of men put before our eyes' . . . In short, he seems to treat it as an unproblematic empirical generalization" (p. 154). But in the sentence immediately preceding the one Allison quotes, Kant makes clear that he leaves the matter of empirical generalization to the only authoritative – that is, scientific – mode of addressing this question, namely "anthropological research" (6: 25). His "generalization," in other words, is far from "unproblematic." And immediately after the sentence Allison quotes, Kant writes: "even if the existence of this propensity to evil in human nature can be demonstrated by experiential proofs of the real opposition, in time, of man's elective will,

such proofs do not reach the essential character of that propensity or the ground of this opposition" (6: 35) – which indicates how problematic Kant understood the thesis of radical to be. So little does Kant "obviate" the necessity of a "formal proof" that he adds a footnote to the section from which Allison draws his quotation: "The proper proof of this sentence of condemnation by morally judging reason is to be found in the preceding section rather than in this one" (6: 39). Finally, at the very end of the section in which Kant, according to Allison, offers only an empirical generalization, he asks his readers to decide by themselves whether "everyone has his price" (6: 38) – which makes any talk of an "*unproblematic* generalization" highly unlikely.

7 See, for example, Goethe's spirited letter to Herder of 7 June 1793: "Kant required a long lifetime to purify his philosophical mantle of many impurities and prejudices. And now he has wantonly tainted [*beschlabbert*] it with the shameful stain [*Schandfleck*] of radical evil, in order that Christians, too, might be attracted to kiss its hem" (Goethe, *Goethes Briefe*, 2: 166); see also Fackenheim's discussion in "Kant and Radical Evil," p. 340. The question how this *Schandfleck* dissolves the "purity" of Kant's "philosophical mantle" will occupy us below, but at least this much can be said: Goethe is one of the very few who read Kant's thesis in terms of a "taint" (*Fleck*).

8 Ehregott Andreas Christoph Wasianski, *Immanuel Kant in seinen letzten Lebensjahren* (1804); reprinted in *Immanuel Kant*, ed. Felix Groß, pp. 245–46; for further consideration of this "paradox," see Chapter 5 of this volume.

9 See Schopenhauer's polemic against academic philosophy, "Über die Universitätsphilosophie," *Werke*, 4: 139–99. Nietzsche learned at least this much from Schopenhauer "as educator": "A scholar can never become a philosopher; for even Kant was unable to do so" ("Schopenhauer als Erzieher," in *Unzeitgemässige Betrachtungen*, reprinted in Nietzsche, *Sämtliche Werke*, 1: 409; §7). Although neither Schopenhauer nor Nietzsche acknowledged it, the most rigorous attack on Kant's honesty takes place in Hegel's famous discussion of the hypocrisy at the heart of moral consciousness; see Hegel, *Grundlinien der Philosophie des Rechts*, reprinted in Schopenhauer, *Werke*, 7: 265–86; §140.

10 For an analysis of another moment when Kant resorts to the word *Verstimmung*, a moment, like this one, that concerns secrecy and self-deception, see Derrida, "On a Newly Arisen Apocalyptic Tone in Philosophy," in *Raising the Tone of Philosophy*, ed. P. Fenves, pp. 131–33.

11 The origin and meaning of the old, and still frequently used, expression "blauen Dunst vormachen" (to generate blue vapor, fool, humbug, hoodwink, blow smoke in one's face) remains unclear, as befits its meaning; but there is a general agreement that the sense of this expression owes much to dust used by magicians, alchemical fumes, and the smoke of tobacco. According to Keith Spalding, "the blue mist produced by mediaeval entertainers during their conjuring tricks contributed to this phrase" (Spalding, *Historical Dictionary of German Figurative Usage*, 1: 334). See also the entry on *Dunst* in Grimm's *Deutsches Wörterbuch*, 6: 1525: "einbildung, vortäuschung phantasiegebilde; oft verstärkt durch das adjektiv *blau*" (with citations from the fifteenth century onward); cf. *Duden*, 12: 163. The blueness of the "blue vapor" opens up other dimensions of this expression, as Spalding indicates: "presumably the blueness of distance" contributes to the sense of the expression. Moreover, in certain other phrases – *blaue Ente*, *blauer Nebel*, and *blaues Märchen*, for example – "blue" indicates lying, deception, and invention, although blue is also the sign of loyalty and fidelity in many color symbolisms. Finally, blue not only indicates

indeterminateness and openness; it also conjures up the closely related sense of something unusual, out of the ordinary or exceptional, as in the expression "once in a blue moon" and "out of the blue" (*aus blauer Luft*). For one of Kant's infrequent uses of "blue" as indicative of something indeterminate and thus "hazy," see the essay entitled "Announcement of a Near Conclusion of a Treaty for Eternal Peace in Philosophy": "[critical philosophy] begins its conquest with the investigation of the faculty of human reason . . . and does not ratiocinate into the blue heavens [*ins Blaue hinein vernünftelt*] when discussion comes around to philosophemes that no possible experience could vouchsafe" (8: 416).

12 See, especially, Kant's first discussion of *Stimmung* in the *Critique of Judgment*: "But if cognitions are to be communicated, then the mental state, that is, the mood [*Stimmung*] of the cognitive powers that is required for cognition in general – namely, that proportion suitable for turning a presentation (by which an object is given to us) into cognition – must also be universally communicable. For this mood is the subjective condition of cognition, and without it cognition could not arise" (5: 238). On the fleeting moments in which the *Stimmung* of moral receptivity makes itself felt and gives rise to an otherwise unaccountable sense of thanks and praise, see 5: 445–46.

13 See, in particular, Kant's application of the concept of "negative quantities," which he first introduced in an essay by this name, (2: 165–204) to moral problems in a lengthy footnote to the opening subsection of *Religion*, 6: 23.

14 Kant uses the same image in another, closely related connection – the end of philosophy: "Lying ('from the father of lies, through which all evil has come into the world') is the actual foul spot on human nature" (8: 422).

15 For Kant's discussion of skin color, see especially his response to Georg Foster in "On the Use of Teleological Principles in Philosophy" (8: 93). For further discussion of race in late Kant, see the next chapter.

5 UNDER THE SIGN OF FAILURE

1 Throughout this book the title of the text is italicized, since Kant first published it as a self-standing work. Furthermore, I translate *ewig* by "eternal," although there are also good philological reasons to choose the more traditional translation "perpetual." Kant's opening remarks clearly take their point of departure from Leibniz's *Codex Juris Gentium Diplomaticus* (1693), Praefatio, III. In the opening paragraph of his introduction to this collection of documents Leibniz makes reference to the image of a graveyard above which is written the words *pax perpetua*, and he subsequently refers to the same image in a letter of 1712 to Jean Leonor le Gallois de Grimarest (translated in Leibniz, *Political Writings*, p. 183). The Latin term gave way to its French equivalent in Fontenelle's eulogy for Leibniz in 1716, Saint-Pierre's *Project pour rendre la paix perpétuelle en Europe* (1713), and Rousseau's "extracts" from the latter "project" (which he published in 1761). Finally, Kant's own publisher, Nicolovius, printed a French translation of *Zum ewigen Frieden* in 1796 under the title *Projets de paix perpétuelle*. But even in this last and apparently decisive case there are reasons to prefer the less idiomatic translation, *Toward Eternal Peace*. For the French translation was, itself, announced under the telling title "paix eternelle," and this same phrase, which was used to translate the Dutch innkeeper's sign, was apparently the one Kant preferred; indeed, he was irritated by the appearance of

"paix perpétuelle" as a translation for "ewigen Frieden" (see Kant, *Über den Gemeinspruch*, p. lvii; see also Volker Gerhardt, *Immanuel Kants Entwurf "Zum Ewigen Frieden,"* p. 42). Furthermore, the phrase *ewigen Frieden* obviously pre-dates Leibniz's *Codex*. One of the tracts from the Thirty Year's War proposes the question "under what conditions the Swedish crown could bring about eternal peace?" And in the context of this war – which was precisely the kind of war Leibniz set out to prevent – the eschatological character of the phrase is unmistakable; see the anonymous pamphlet entitled *Politischer, auss göttlicher vnd erbarn Völckern Rechten kürtzlich verfaster Discurs*. The eschatological character of the term *Ewigkeit* is, finally, the point of departure for the essay Kant published only a few months before *Toward Eternal Peace*, namely "The End of All Things." And within the treatise itself Kant use *stehende* (standing) to translate the Latin word *perpetuus*. If one of the preconditions of peace is the disbanding of *miles perpetuus* (standing armies), then the peaceful condition toward which Kant aims should not be so quickly assimilated to the balance of forces represented in its ideal form by a *perpetuum mobile*, and the word *ewig*, in turn, should be dissociated from *perpetuus*. But Kant's peace should not be *completely* dissociated from the image of the perpetual motion machine (see 8: 367), and so the translation of *ewig* by "eternal" is also wanting. As Hansjürgen Verweyen points out, finally, the preposition "zu" can also function as the shield for a tavern, and the title could thus be rendered: "At the Inn of Eternal (or Perpetual) Peace"; see Verweyen, "Social Contract Among Devils," p. 201.

2 In a letter to Kiesewetter (October 15, 1795) Kant speaks of the treatise as "Meine reveries" (12: 45), and in one of the preliminary drafts to the treatise Kant explicitly states that, for "practical men" (*Praktiker*), metaphysics is "idle theory and empty dreaming [*leere Träumerey*]" (23: 155).

3 Of the many studies devoted to *Toward Eternal Peace* very few have, to my knowledge, sufficiently acknowledged the interpretive difficulties posed by the title, although Kant's opening words are concerned with nothing else. In his extensive and incisive analysis of the treatise Hans Saner, who has done more than anyone else to show the significance of the idea of peace and polemics in Kant, describes the prologue as "ironic" (Saner, "Die Negative Bedingungen des Friedens," p. 46). Klemme uses the same term (Klemme, *Über den Gemeinspruch*, p. xxvii). Similar terms are often used in discussions of the treatise. Hannah Arendt, for example, opens her lectures on Kant and politics with the following remark: "the ironical tone of Perpetual Peace . . . shows clearly that Kant himself did not take them [his writings on politics] too seriously" (Arendt, *Lectures on Kant's Political Philosophy*, p. 7).

It is by no means obvious that the concept of irony can be so easily mastered, however, especially in the context of Germany in the 1790s. Indeed, the writer who, perhaps more than anyone else, made irony into an indispensable term of criticism – Friedrich Schlegel – has more than an incidental relation to the text under consideration. His extraordinary review of *Toward Eternal Peace* may have played a significant, perhaps even decisive, role in Kant's "renewal" of the "old question" in *The Conflict of the Faculties*, and this review, in turn, may have played a decisive role in his own recognition of the critical potential of irony. Schlegel's review appeared in the first volume of *Deutschland* (1796) and has been reprinted, among other places, in the useful collection *Friedensutopien*, eds Z. Batscha and R. Saage, pp. 93–110. To my knowledge, the first one to recognize the relation between *The Conflict of the Faculties* and Schlegel's review is Klaus Reich; see the introduction to his edition of

Der Streit der Fakultäten, esp. pp. xv–xxiv. Schlegel's review is named in Refl., 6340; immediately below, Kant associates Schegel's analysis with the thesis of radical evil, understood in terms of insincerity: "Die Unredlichkeit der Menschen als das radikale Böse" – a line, however, which, as Reich notes, appears in Reicke's *Lose Blätter aus Kants Nachlass* (2: 107), but for some strange reason is not reproduced in the Akademie edition.

For an analysis of the process by which *Toward Eternal Peace* came into its final form, see Kant, "Ein neu aufgefundenes Reinschriftfragment Kants mit den Anfangstexten seines Entwurfs 'Zum ewigen Frieden.'"

4 Kant opens the contemporaneous essay "The End of All Things" (1795) with the following words: "It is a common expression, especially when speaking piously, for a dying man to say he is passing *from time into eternity* [*er gehe* aus der Zeit in die Ewigkeit]" (8: 327).

5 For an examination of the relation between passages across borders, non-passages, and the passage from life to death, see Jacques Derrida, *Aporias*, pp. 84–86 (a long footnote concerning *Toward Eternal Peace*); see also the incisive investigation of Geoffrey Bennington, *Frontière kantiennes*, esp. pp. 131–63.

6 In his powerful condemnation of European imperialism Kant mentions only a single nationality: the Dutch, whom the Chinese and Japanese rulers wisely keep well apart from their own people (8: 359).

7 See Emmanuel Kant, *Projet de paix perpétuelle*.

8 Kant begins the letter of April 10, 1794, which is addressed to J. E. Biester and includes the fair copy of "Something on the Influence of the Moon on the Wind and the Weather," with a revealing remark: "Here you have, most worthy friend, for your M. S. [*Berlinische Monatsschrift*] something that may serve, like Swift's [*Tale of a*] *Tub*, to create a momentary diversion from the constant noise about the same thing" (11: 495); at the end of same letter, Kant promises to deliver "The End of All Things." Clearly, he had recently read Swift's work, which he then quotes in a foot-note to *Toward Eternal Peace* (8: 353). He also quotes *A Tale of the Tub* in the section of the *Anthropology* devoted to the tricky topic of "Permissible Moral Semblance [*Schein*]" (7: 152–53). Kant probably knew the eight-volume *Satyrische und ernsthafte Schriften von Dr. Jonathan Swift*.

9 Kant attributes this insight to Samuel Butler's *Hudabris*, but it is far more power-fully formulated in *A Tale of the Tub*, especially section eight, which discusses "that Renowned *Cabbalist, Bumbastus*" (Swift, *The Writings of Jonathan Swift*, p. 341), and section nine, which is a digression "concerning the Original, the Use and Improve-ment of Madness in a Commonwealth" (p. 345). Kant, similarly, concludes his "Essay on the Sicknesses of the Head" with Swift's observation that a bad poem is "merely the purification of the brain" (2: 271).

10 Swift, "Introduction" to *A Tale of the Tub*, reprinted in *The Writings of Jonathan Swift*, p. 298. Kant truncates the quote: "cracked a nut and was rewarded by a worm" (8: 353).

11 Kant considers Maupertius's proposal for creating a stock of intelligent, diligent, and righteous people "feasible" (*tunlich*); but "a wise nature hinders it quite well, for the great driving springs, which set the sleeping powers of humanity into play and compel them to develop all of their talents and to approach the perfection of their determination, lie precisely in the mixing of evil with good" (2: 241). It is worth noting that the passage of *Toward Eternal Peace* where Kant speaks of nature hindering

the plans of princes for world domination repeats the phrasing of this passage from "On the Different Human Races." The erasure of *race* in the former is therefore all the more remarkable.

12 Susan Shell has emphasized the close connection between *Toward Eternal Peace* and cannibalism, especially with respect to the term *Kegel*; see "Cannibals All" and "Bowling Alone."

13 See the first chapter in this volume for a more extensive discussion of Kant's reflections on naïveté. A contemporaneous – and highly influential – account of satire, which owes its origin to Kantian aesthetics, can be found in Friedrich Schiller's "On Naïve and Sentimental Poetry" (originally published in *Die Horen*, 1795–96). According to Schiller, sentimental poetry is either satirical or elegiac: "The poet is satirical if he makes the distance from nature and the contradiction between actuality and the ideal (in their effect upon the mind both amount to the same) as his subject-matter" (Schiller, *Über das Schöne und die Kunst*, p. 255). Among the satirists Schiller names are Juvenal, Rousseau, Swift, and von Haller. Schiller's extensive analysis of satire can be considered a Kantian-inflected summit of eighteenth-century reflection on this important genre of enlightenment. The *Berlinische Monatsschrift* welcomed satirical works, and the journal was also a forum for the consideration of the question whether satire contributes to the advancement of enlightenment. Just after Moses Mendelssohn proposed an answer to the question "what is enlightenment?" he raised anew the less well-known but equally troubling question: satire or state intervention?; more exactly, mockery of religious fanaticism or coercive control of fanatics? See the brief essay he published in 1785 in the *Berlinische Monatsschrift*, "Soll man der einreißenden Schwärmerei durch Satyre oder durch äußerliche Verbindung entgegenarbeiten?" (reprinted in Mendelssohn, *Gesammelte Schriften*, 12: 137–41). Wieland, whom Kant places in the company of Homer (5: 309), had earlier posed the same question as Mendelssohn, and Lessing proposed a remarkable answer; see his essay, "Über eine zeitige Aufgabe: Wird durch die Bemühung kaltblutiger Philosophen und Lucianischer Geister gegen das, was Enthusiasmus und Schwärmerei nennen, mehr Böses als Gutes gestiftet Und in welchen Schranken müssen die Antiplatoniker halten um nützlich zu sein?" in Gotthold Ephraim Lessing, *Sämtliche Werke*, 16: 297. In the remarks he made in conjunction with his *Observations of the Feeling of the Beautiful and the Sublime*, Kant had responded to the same question with a decisive "no": "Satire never improves anything, so even if I had the talent for it, I would not use it" (Kant, *Bemerkungen in den "Beobachtungen über das Gefühl des Schönen und des Erhabenen,"* p. 81). Two recent commentators have tried to discover the reason Kant, having written this remark, went on to write the *Dreams of a Spirit Seer*: see Allison Laywine, *Kant's Early Metaphysics and the Origins of the Critical Philosophy*, esp. pp. 78–80; and John Zammito, *Kant, Herder, and the Birth of Anthropology*, esp. pp. 208–12. Having recently experienced the sting of royal reproof, which was motivated by religious fanaticism, Kant may have changed his mind about the validity of satire. He writes to Carl Stäudlin on December 4, 1794: "I beg of you most ardently: give my warmest thanks to your excellent Privy Councillor *Lichtenberg*; his clear head, his righteous mode of thinking, and unsurpassable humor [*Laune*] can perhaps work against the evil of a miserable coercion of faith than others with their demonstrations" (11: 534). In the same letter Kant says that the "approaching peace [of Basel] may also bring with it an increased freedom for innocent judgments" (11: 533–34). Kant dedicates *The Conflict of the Faculties* to Stäudlin.

14 Walter Benjamin, "Karl Kraus," reprinted in Benjamin, *Gesammelte Schriften*, 2: 355.

15 Swift, "Preface of the Author" to *The Battel of the Books* (1710), reprinted in Swift, *The Writings of Jonathan Swift*, p. 375.

16 See Johann Christoph Girtanner, *Über das Kantische Princip für die Naturgeschichte*.

17 An important indication of Kant's reticence to use the term *race* in the 1790s can be found near the conclusion of "Something Concerning the Influence of the Moon on the Wind and the Weather" (1794): "Perhaps to this [community of jovial and volcanic air] belongs also the make-up of the air that renders some illnesses in certain countries at a certain time *epidemic* (actually, ravaging) and that shows its influence not merely on a *people* [Volk] of human beings but also on a people of certain species of animals or plants" (8: 323). Instead of using *Race* or *Rasse*, Kant prefers *Volk*, even though it requires that he describe "a people" of animals and plants. The term *race* does, however, play a function in Kant's description of organic terrestrial species in various versions of *Physische Geographie*, all of which derive from a variety of note-books from different periods in Kant's academic career.

18 Kant refuses to enter into the controversy concerning the origin of language. The closest he comes to making a contribution to this topic is his counter-Herderian "Conjectural Beginning of Human History," where the first human beings could already "*talk* (Gen. 2: 20), and even *converse*, that is, speak in coherence concepts (Gen. 2: 23), consequently *think*" (8: 110). Nevertheless, in footnotes to some of his late writings, especially "The End of All Things" and *Toward Eternal Peace*, he shows an interest in developing a genealogy of moral terms, which would indicate a direction for linguistic-moral research (8: 328, 359–60).

19 All of Kant's essays on race seek to show that, although race does not figure into "natural description," it still is valid for "natural history." As a result of Georg Forster's critique of his earlier formulations of his concept of race, Kant unambig-uously states in the last of his race-oriented essays, "On the Use of Teleological Principles in Philosophy," that differences in race are based on teleological judg-ment; see John Zammito, *The Genesis of Kant's "Critique of Judgment,"* esp. pp. 213–18.

20 For analyses of Kant's conceptualization of race, see Erich Adickes, *Kant als Naturforscher*, 2: 406–59; Monika Firla, "Kants Thesen von 'Nationalcharakter' der Afrikaner"; Emmanuel Eze, "The Color of Reason"; Mark Larrimore, "Sublime Waste"; and Robert Bernasconi, "Who Invented the Concept of Race? Kant's Role in the Enlightenment Construction of Race."

21 Among the notes gathered in the section of the anthropology *Reflexionen* is the following: "All races will be wiped away (Americans and Negroes cannot govern themselves. To serve therefore only as slaves), only not that of the whites [*Alle racen werden ausgerotten werden (Amerikaner und Neger können sich nicht selbst regiren. Dienen also nur zu Sclaven), nur nicht die der Weissen*]" (15: 878).

22 See Eric Voegelin, *Die Rassenidee in der Geistesgeschichte von Ray bis Carus*.

23 A recent English translation of "The End of All Things" has sought to remove any trace of this conclusion by translating "*weil Christentum allgemeine Weltreligion zu sein zwar bestimmt . . . sein würde* [because Christianity would indeed be destined to be a universal world religion]" by "because Christianity, though supposedly destined to be the world religion" (translated by Allen Wood, in Kant, *Religion and Rational Theology*, p. 231); but the word *supposedly* does not capture the positive character of the assertion, which, regardless of the use of a subjunctive, is emphasized by *zwar* (indeed).

24 The term *clausula salvatoria* does not appear in Adolf Berger's comprehensive *Encyclopedic Dictionary of Roman Law*. According to Klenner's informative note, a *clausula salvatoria* was introduced into the Preface of Karl V's penal code (1532): the new legal code did not supercede "old, well adapted, legal, and fair practices." This concept was also used to protect scholars from accusations that they wrote something against Christian doctrine. Grotius concludes the Preface to his *De jure belli ac pacis* (1625) in this manner; see Kant, *Rechtslehre*, p. 510.

25 Géza von Molnár has shown that the passage of the first *Critique* devoted to belief and betting (A: 824–25; B: 852–53) decisively shaped Goethe's conception of the pact scene in *Faust*; see von Molnár, "'Die Wette biet' ich.'"

26 Although Kant had little interest in the phenomenon of luck (beyond some remarks on gambling and the discussion of wagering in the Canon of Pure Reason), he takes note of the Epicurean concept of the *clinamen* in his exposition of universal natural history in his early writings and universal human history in his later ones: "Should one expect that by virtue of some *Epicurean* confluence of efficient causes, states, like minute particles of matter randomly colliding with one another, should experiment with all sorts of organizations that will be destroyed by new collisions, until they finally succeed *by chance* upon an organization that can maintain itself in its own form (a lucky accident [*Glückzufall*] that is surely very unlikely ever to happen)?" (8: 25).

27 Kant may have no trouble naming nature as guarantor of eternal peace; but the same cannot be said of the point of view from which "the great artist nature" is to be regarded: "If we regard this design as a compulsion resulting from one of its [nature's] causes whose laws of operation are unknown to us, we call it fate [*Schicksal*], whereas, if we reflect on nature's purposiveness in the flow of world events, and consider the underlying wisdom of a higher cause that directs the human race toward its objective goal and predetermines the world's cause, we call it providence" (8: 360–61). By the end of the paragraph Kant admits that the word "providence" is too high, and compares those who speak in this way to Icarus. Although the term "nature" is therefore more "appropriate" (*schicklich*) than "providence" – and in this way closer to *Schicksal* – Kant declines to return to the earlier term, except in the often-repeated quotation from Seneca's *Epistles* (8: 365; 8: 313).

28 Otherwise, Kant would not have found it necessary to append a "Secret Article to Eternal Peace" to the second edition of the treatise. This article takes up the challenge of the treatise's Preface: philosophers should be allowed to publish treatises on eternal peace precisely because the word of philosophers – or "theoretical politicians" – has no immediate impact. But there is at least one peculiarity of this doubly supplementary article that should be noted. Kant concludes the "secret article" of 1796 with these words: "because this class [i.e. the philosophical] is by nature incapable of sedition and forming clubs, it cannot be suspected of disseminating *propaganda*" (8: 369). In the opening lines of another treatise he published in 1796 he says something quite different. Once again, however, the silence and secrecy of philosophers is under discussion:

> Since it relinquished its first meaning, scientific wisdom of life, the name of philosophy has very early on come into demand as a title that would adorn the minds of uncommon thinkers who now imagine it to be a mode whereby secrets are revealed. – To the ascetics in the Marcarian

desert, philosophy means their monasticism. The alchemist called himself *philosophus per ignem*. Tradition has made the Masons of ancient and
modern times adepts of a secret about which they jealously want to say
nothing (*philosophus per initiationem*). The newest owners of this secret
are, finally, those who have in themselves but unfortunately cannot
express and universally communicate it through language (*philosophus per
inspirationem*).

(8: 389)

Masons, of course, are not only members of a club; they were widely suspected of
being members of a revolutionary organization in which sedition was propagated.
Kant must therefore deny these club-members the status of philosopher; but he does
so in the context of an attack on Schlosser, a rather harmless conservative official
whose edition of Plato's letters from Syracuse are a thinly disguised attack on the
French Revolution. Nothing more is heard of (leftist) club-members. By the time
Kant received Schlosser's reply to his polemic, he must revoke his statement in the
closing lines of the "Secret Article": philosophers do, after all, tend to unite "into
a huge mass [and] *to lead an open war* against one another (school against school as
army against army)" (8: 414). Only by acknowledging this tendency on the part
of philosophers toward forming factions can Kant announce "the Near Conclusion
of a Treaty for Eternal Peace in Philosophy."

29 In his *Universal Natural History and Theory of the Heavens* (1755), eternity manifests
itself at a moment of interruption. When the universe collapses and begins to re-
ignite itself, like a Phoenix, eternity is, as it were, brought into view – but only "as
it were" or in the "imagination" (1: 321). At these moments of interruption Kant
repeatedly returns to Albrecht von Haller's "Unvollkommenes Gedicht über die
Ewigkeit" (1736; reprinted in *Die Alpen und andere Gedichte*, pp. 75–79). In "The
End of All Things" (8: 327), which Kant writes almost forty years later, the
same poem functions in the same way: it shows eternity to be "frightfully-sublime"
(8: 327). This presentation of eternity in terms of sublimity associates it once again
with an untimely interruption of time. For, according to paragraph 27 of Kant's
Analytic of the Sublime, the attempt to comprehend "in one instant what is apprehended successively" – which is required for any presentation of eternity – "is a regression that cancels [*aufhebt*] the condition of time in the imagination's progression"
(5: 258–59).

30 One of the few commentators who has shown the centrality of self-fulfilling prophecy
to Kant's reflections on history is Margherita von Brentano, "Kants Theorie der
Geschichte und der bürgerlichen Gesellschaft."

31 In the "Secret Article for Eternal Peace," Kant insists that the words of the philosopher should not have the kind of authority that accrues to those of the king.
Philosophers are, from this perspective, "silent" (8: 369), regardless of how often
they speak in the public realm; indeed, their public speech is a form of silence. By
appending this "secret article" to the appendix of the treatise "On the Guarantee of
Eternal Peace," Kant indicates that this guarantor, *natura daedala rerum*, cannot carry
out its assignment: mute nature must be supplemented by "silent" – yet articulate
– philosophers.

32 In a final footnote to the "Second Definitive Article for Eternal Peace: The Right of
States Shall be Based on a Confederation of Free States," Kant suggests that the end

of any conflict should include a day of atonement after the festival of celebration. The Jews in general, and the prophets in particular, go in the opposite direction: "The festivals of thanksgiving for victories during the war, the hymns that are sung (in good Israelite fashion [*auf gut israelitisch*]) to the *Lord of Hosts*, could not stand in greater contrast with the idea of the father of human beings" (8: 375). At the opening of the second section of *The Conflict of the Faculties* Kant explicitly denounces the prophets:

> Jewish prophets could well prophesy that sooner or later not merely decadence but complete dissolution awaited their state, for they were themselves the authors of this fate. — As national leaders, they had weighed down their constitution with so many ecclesiastical burdens, along with all the incumbent civil ones, that their state became utterly unfit to subsist of itself and especially so in conjunction with neighboring states, and the jeremiads of their priests therefore were spoken in vain to the winds; because the priest obstinately [*hartnäckicht*] persisted in the untenable constitution that they had themselves created; and thus they could, without fail, foresee the outcome.
>
> (7: 80)

In a draft version of these remarks, Kant discusses Moses Mendelssohn instead of the Jewish prophets, presumably because Mendelssohn's *Jerusalem* does not recommend the "euthanasia of Judaism" (7: 53); see Kant, "Ein Reinschriftsfragment zu Kants 'Streit der Fakultäten.'"

33 The concept of "the remnant of Israel" (*she'ar* or *she'erit Yisrael*) is first developed in *Isaiah*: "And it shall come to pass in that day, that the remnant of Israel, and such of the house of Jacob who have escaped, shall no more again rely upon him who struck them; but shall rely upon the Lord, the Holy One of Israel, in truth. The remnant shall return, the remnant of Jacob, to the mighty God" (Isaiah 10: 20–21). Jeremiah speaks of the "remnant of Judah" that outlives the Babylonian exile (Jer. 40–44). For a short exposition of the phrase, see Nahum Glatzer, "Remnant of Israel"; see also Giorgio Agamben, *Le Temps qui reste*, esp. pp. 90–97.

34 Similar considerations are probably at the basis of Kant's use of the term *race* in the second part of the *Conflict of the Faculties*. He parenthetically notes that the question that this section seeks to answer – "whether the human species [*Geschlecht*] is constantly progressing toward the better?" – should not be construed as an inquiry into "whether new races could somehow emerge" (7: 79); and he briefly reflects on this question later in the section (7: 89). For an extensive consideration of these passages and similar ones in the *Opus postumum*, see Chapter 7 and the Conclusion.

35 See Norman O. Brown, *Life Against Death*, pp. 179–201.

36 See Friedrich Schiller, *Über die ästhetische Erziehung des Menschen in einer Reihe von Briefe* (1795), reprinted and translated in *On the Aesthetic Education of Man*. Kant makes a promise to Schiller that he will "study and give you my thoughts" about the first of the *Aesthetic Letters* (12: 11); he may have done the former, but there is no evidence that he did the latter.

37 Kant thus associates himself with the poet, who, unlike the orator, "announces merely an entertaining play with ideas" (5: 321).

38 Hölderlin, "Wie wenn am Feiertage," *Sämtliche Werke*, 2: 120.

6 IN THE NAME OF FRIENDSHIP

1 The earliest drafts of the so-called *Opus postumum* probably date from 1796; for a lively and informative account of its impetus, see Eckart Förster's "Introduction" to his edition of the *Opus postumum*, esp. pp. xxxvi–xxxviii. See also Förster, "Fichte, Beck, and Schelling in Kant's *Opus postumum*," esp. pp. 158–62.

2 Kant's famous letter of September 21, 1798 to Christian Garve (who, incidentally, can hardly be considered one of Kant's truest friends) reiterates his equally famous letter to Fichte, in which he complains of acute mental paralysis (12: 257).

3 A full account of Kant's practices as a friend is beyond the scope of a note; indeed, it would occupy a large volume, particularly if it paid close attention to his friendship with Joseph Green. By the time he had completed the *Critiques*, all of his friendships were with men. Such is not the case in his pre-critical years. Of particular significance is his friendship with Charlotte Amalie von Knobloch in the early 1760s (see 10: 43–44). In a letter she wrote to Kant after she had married, Charlotte Amalie addresses him as "worthy friend" and proceeds to outline a theory of friendship according to which the philosopher is less prone than other kinds of people to become colder to friends who have departed for long stretches of time; see 10: 127–28. She also reminds Kant that he had sent her a copy of Christoph Martin Wieland's *Erinnerungen an eine Freundin* (Remembrances of a female friend), although strangely enough – but perhaps this is by design – she misremembers the author of these "remembrances" and attributes them to a certain "v. Kleist" (10: 128), presumably Ewald von Kleist. Kant's gift could mean many things: Wieland's *Erinnerungen an eine Freundin* is, on the one hand, a conventional presentation of the idealized woman who has learned that inward beauty is more important than the outward variety and, on the other, a strange projection of a loss to come. The "remembrances" are, therefore, not those of the male poet but of the female friend who remembers herself – or how she was supposed to have been – in anticipation of the departure, perhaps even the death of her friend; see C. M. Wieland, *Erinnerungen an eine Freundin* (Zürich: Orel, 1754); reprinted in Wieland, *Gesammelte Schriften*, 2: 205–14.

4 The most likely explanation is that of Eckart Förster, who attributes Kant's anger to his colleague Johann Schultz's decision not respond to Gottlob Ernst Schulze's *Aenesidemus*; see note 110 to his edition of the *Opus postumum*, 278. By contrast, the circumstances that led to the dismissal of Fichte from Jena are quite clear; for a succinct exposition and analysis, see Daniel Breazeale's introduction to Fichte, *Early Philosophical Writings*, esp. pp. 40–46.

5 Originally published as Immanuel Kant, "Über ein vermeintes Recht aus Menschenliebe zu lügen," *Berliner Blätter*, 10 (September 6, 1797): 301–14. Kant quotes from K. F. Cramer's translation of Benjamin Constant, *Des réactions politiques* (1796); reprinted in B. Constant, *De la force du gouvernement actuel de la France*, p. 136. Two guides to the controversy between Kant and Constant have recently appeared: François Boituzat, *Un Droit de mentir? Constant ou Kant* and Andrea Tagliapietra, *La verità e la menzogna*; see also Robert Benton, "Political Expediency and Lying" and Jules Vuillman, "On Lying: Kant and Benjamin Constant."

6 Ehregott Andreas Christoph Wasianski, *Immanuel Kant in seinen letzten Lebensjahren* (1804); reprinted in *Immanuel Kant*, ed. Felix Groß, pp. 252–53.

7 For Kant's attempts to distinguish the two senses of *Menschenliebe*, see 6: 401 and especially 6: 450. A particularly revealing use of the term can be found in Kant's

retelling of Carazan's dream of utter isolation in the *Observations on the Feelings of the Beautiful and the Sublime* (2: 209); and Kant discusses in passing the duty of *Menschenliebe* in *Toward Eternal Peace* (8: 385). According to Dagobert de Levie, who has undertaken a thorough investigation into the history of the word, *Menschenliebe* first began to play a significant role in ethical discourse in Johann Christoph Gottsched's *Erste Gründe der gesammten Weltweisheit*, §222; see D. de Levie, *Die Menschenliebe im Zeitalter der Aufklärung*, pp. 69–75; cf. Wolfgang Fleischhauer, "Zur Geschichte des Wortes 'Menschenliebe.'" Taking over and translating Christian Wolff's idea of *amor universalis omnim huminum*, which serves as a counter-weight to an otherwise "egoistic" ethic of individual perfection, Gottsched further developed the concept of *Menschenliebe* in his treatises on literature, which, in turn, gave direction to much of the literary activity during the middle years of the century, even among those who contested Gottsched's methods and models; see also Regina John, *Vernünftige Menschenliebe*. Johann Jakob Dusch defines the term in a way that accords with the general precepts of Enlightenment ethical theory: "*Menschenliebe* is the universal and fundamental command of virtue out of which all social duties can be derived" (J. J. Dusch, *Moralische Briefe zur Bildung des Herzens*, vol. 1, letter 17). But as the ideas of the *Aufklärung* fell into disfavor, so too did the ideal of *Menschenliebe*; thus, as de Levie shows, Justus Möser's *Patriotische Phantasien*, which began to be published in 1766, not only casts doubts on this ideal but ridicules the word as a "term of fashion" (de Levie, *Die Menschenliebe im Zeitalter der Aufklärung*, p. 29). By the time Kant employed the term for his title, it had fallen out of favor.

8 Later in the essay Kant demonstrates Constant's inconstancy by first quoting him against himself: "'A principle recognized as true must therefore never be abandoned, however apparent is the danger present in it.' (And yet the good man himself had abandoned the unconditional principle of truthfulness because of the danger to society it brought with it)" (8: 428). As Philippe Raynaud notes, some of Constant's biographers, especially, Henri Guillemin, often refer to him as "inconstant Benjamin" (Constant, *De la force du gouvernement actuel*, p. 8).

9 See Constant, *De la force du gouvernement actuel*, pp. 131–39.

10 When Constant retells the story, he replaces "votre ami" with "autrui" (Constant, *De la force du gouvernement actuel*, p. 137). Much more could be said about Constant's theory and practice of friendship, and one place to begin an investigation into this theme is *Des réactions politiques*, for, as Constant emphasizes, his intervention into the debates about the character and validity of the post-Thermidorian regime begins with an assessment of "the resources that remain to the friends of freedom and enlightenment [ressources qui restent aux amis de la liberté et des lumières]" (title of Chapter 8, *Des réactions politiques*, in Constant, *De la force du gouvernement actuel*, p. 123). Constant's liberalism as well as his literary activity can perhaps be best understood as a constant assessment of the resources, including those of friendship, that remain to the "friends of freedom."

11 See Aristotle, *Nicomachean Ethics*, pp. 192–247 (1155a–72a); and Marcus Tullius Cicero, *Laelius de amicitia*.

12 A thorough analysis of the theme "Kant and friendship," which cannot be undertaken here, would not only have to examine his lectures on ethics, anthropology, and pedagogy, but would also have to trace his various circles of friends within the context of East Prussian social history. For a translation and an extensive discussion of the

sections of the "doctrine of virtue" dedicated to the question of friendship, see H. J. Paton, "Kant on Friendship." See also Maria Fasching, *Zum Begriff der Freundschaft bei Aristoteles und Kant*, and Stephen Watson, *Tradition(s)*, pp. 121–30. Of particular importance for an assessment of Kant's discussion of friendship in the *Doctrine of Virtue* is the analysis Derrida undertakes in *Politiques de l'amitié*, pp. 282–94.

13 Quoted in Wolfdietrich Rasch, *Freundschaftskult und Freundschaftsdichtung*, p. 181. Rasch's work is thoroughly compromised by his attempt to demonstrate (in 1936) that the German *Volk* was engaged in a struggle, during the eighteenth century, to recognize itself and discover its proper mission; but as a study of the cult and culture of friendship in eighteenth-century German literature it is still valuable.

14 On Kant's conception of "moral enthusiasm" (*moralische Schwärmerei*), see Fenves, *Arresting Language*, pp. 103–14.

15 The use of the term "hobby horse" (*Steckenpferd*) points toward one particular writer of novels – Laurence Sterne – and toward a friendship that may have been, for Kant, perfect: Tristram's father and his uncle Toby. Not surprisingly, this friendship is between brothers. In his discussion of "weaknesses and sicknesses of the head" in his *Anthropology from a Pragmatic Point of View* (1798) Kant calls hobby horses "the mildest of all transgressions over the borderline of a sound mind" and concludes with a quotation from *Tristram Shandy* (7: 204).

16 See the section of the *Doctrine of Virtue* devoted to the "Duties of Virtue Toward Other Human Beings Arising from the *Respect* Due to Them": "The *respect* that I have for others or that another can require from me (*observantia aliis praestanda*) is therefore recognition of the dignity (*dignitas*) in other human beings, that is, of a worth that has no price, no equivalent for which the object evaluated (*aestimii*) could be exchanged" (6: 462).

17 Thus Mary Gregor writes: "The context of 'even the fact' would make *gemeistert* (finds fault with) seem to be a misprint for *gemustert* (examines)" (Kant, *Practical Philosophy*, p. 585).

18 See Wilhelm Dilthey, "Der Streit Kants mit der Zensur über das Recht freier Religionsforschung" (1890), republished in Wilhelm Dilthey, *Gesammelte Schriften*, 4: 265–309.

19 *Die Bibel nach der Übersetzung Martin Luthers*: "einer ist euer Meister; ihr aber seid alle Brüder."

20 For a detailed discussion of the spectators who "border on enthusiasm," see Fenves, *A Peculiar Fate*, pp. 170–285.

21 Johann Heinrich Kant was nine years younger than his famous brother. It is perhaps odd that the younger brother received the father's name, while Kant was given one that he would later change (see the discussion in the final section of Chapter 3). Immanuel and Johann rarely saw each other and, as Karl Vorländer notes, "the letters of the younger Kant came more often and bore a cordial tone, like the notes of his wife and children; Immanuel seldom wrote and then only briefly and rather coldly" (Vorländer, *Kants Leben*, p. 196); but Kant was generous to his brother's family, giving them not what he explicitly owed them but what he implicitly, perhaps "in his heart," felt obligated to offer. Kant's relations to his sisters were similarly distant. For an insightful presentation of the relation between the two brothers, see Walter Benjamin's remarks on a letter Johann, his wife, and eldest daughter wrote to their famous relative; Detlev Holz (pseudonym), *Deutsche Menschen, eine Folge von Briefen*, reprinted in W. Benjamin, *Gesammelte Schriften*, 4: 156–59.

22 Under certain circumstances the command "love thy neighbor" and the pronouncement "all ye are brethren" have been interpreted in terms of friendship, and it is even
possible to propose a formula for the determination of these circumstances: the more
violently a community rejects any office or institution that claims the right
to represent the divinity in whose name it defines itself, the more likely it will
interpret these sayings in terms of friendship. More specifically, an inquiry into the
history of friendship and fraternity in the seventeenth and eighteenth centuries would
have to ask why a Christian community would understand itself as a "Society of
Friends" and why certain other ones, like the communities founded and sponsored
by Count von Zinzendorf, would organize themselves according to a "brotherly agreement" (of Herrnhut) and proclaim that the ultimate aim of both every new brotherhood and every brother in such a brotherhood is "to be a friend of God, enemy to the
world [Gottes Freund, der Welt Feind zu sein]" (quoted in August Gottlieb
Spangenberg, *Leben des Herrn Nicolaus Ludwig Grafen und Herrn von Zinzendorf und
Pottendorf*, pp. 50–52). For a wide-ranging investigation into the significance of the
Christian principle of universal brotherhood, see the remarkable collection of essays
by Marc Shell, *Children of the Earth*. At the conclusion of the last essay, "Tribal
Brotherhood and Universal Otherhood," Shell emphasizes what is at stake in the principle of universal brotherhood: "Chamfort, pondering the French republican promise
of 'liberty, equality, fraternity' and the French revolutionary slogan of 'fraternity, or
death!,' commented thus: '"Fraternity or Death?" Yes: be my brother or I will kill
you!' 'If I had a brother,' quipped Metternich, 'I would call him cousin.' . . . If a person cannot or will not become a brother, then he is not human and may as well be
treated as such. The promise of universal brotherhood – even a united nations – turns
all too easily into the individual and fatal fraternity of Cain and Abel" (p. 192).

23 See, for two prominent examples, Lilian Faderman, *Surpassing the Love of Men* and
Janice Raymond, *A Passion for Friends*.

24 An early inquiry into male friendship in German literature that does not shy away
from questions of sexuality is that of Hans Dietrich (pseudonym of Hans Dietrich
Hellbach), *Die Freundesliebe in der deutschen Literatur*. More recent analyses of male
friendships and sexuality include the collection of Alice Kuzniar, *Outing Goethe and
His Age*; Simon Richter, "The Ins and Outs of Intimacy."

25 Michel Foucault, "Sex, Power, and the Politics of Identity," in *Ethics, Subjectivity, and
Truth*, p. 171; see also "Friendship as a Way of Life," *Ethics, Subjectivity, and Truth*,
pp. 135–40. In an earlier interview Foucault suggests that in the culture of ancient
Greece friendship and sexuality were, if not mutually exclusive, then certainly at
odds with each other: "Friendship is reciprocal, and sexual relations are not reciprocal: in sexual relations you can penetrate or you are penetrated. . . . [I]f you have
friendship, it is difficult to have sexual relations" (Foucault, *Ethics, Subjectivity, and
Truth*, p. 257). On these remarks of Foucault, see the closing pages of Maurice
Blanchot, *Michel Foucault tel que je l'imagine*, pp. 63–64; "Michel Foucault as I Imagine
Him," in Foucault, *Foucault/Blanchot*, pp. 108–09: "it was thus he would be tempted
to call on the ancients for a revalorization of the practices of friendship, which,
although never lost, have not again recaptured, except for a few of us, their exalted
virtue. . . . Friendship was perhaps promised to Foucault as a posthumous gift." On
the aporetic character of these remarks, see Derrida, PA: 332–74.

26 Wasianski, *Immanuel Kant in seinen letzten Lebensjahren*; reprinted in *Immanuel Kant*,
ed. Felix Groß, p. 245.

27 For a discussion of this and similar formulas, which Derrida draws (with certain hesitations and reservations) from the writings of Blanchot and Jean-Luc Nancy, see PA: 98–100.

28 On the massive philosophical and philological difficulties of these words, which Diogenes Laertius first attributes to Aristotle, see PA: 219–52.

29 At the conclusion of a thorough analysis of the concept of community in Kant, Susan Shell, like Derrida, emphasizes the predominance of distance over closeness: "This insistence on a certain 'pathos of distance' – even, and perhaps especially, within the bonds of friendship – provides a sort of anticipatory, democratic answer to Nietzsche's later animadversions against the 'last men,' who like 'to rub against one another for warmth.' Indeed, there is in Kant's and Nietzsche's common fastidiousness a curious aesthetic convergence; both are nauseously repelled by common intimacies – Nietzsche, in the name of 'aristocracy,' Kant in the name of a nobility consistent with equality" (Shell, *The Embodiment of Reason*, p. 160).

30 Blanchot, "Lettre à Salomon Malka," 68; quoted in Derrida, PA: 337.

31 See Gotthold Ephraim Lessing and Moses Mendelssohn, *Pope ein Metaphysiker!* (1755), reprinted in Lessing, *Werke*, 3: 631–70. For further considerations of Kant's response to this prize contest, which sought to evaluate Leibniz's theodicy but, as Lessing and Mendelssohn forcefully argue, had the temerity to replace his thesis (that this is the best of all possible worlds) with Pope's (which claims in a poetic context that the world is good), see Chapter 3 above.

32 Hannah Arendt, *Von der Menschlichkeit in finsteren Zeiten: Rede über Lessing* ("On Humanity in Dark Times: Thoughts about Lessing"). Arendt delivered this lecture upon being awarded the Lessing Prize by the city of Hamburg in 1959. For a consideration of the circumstances of the award and the lecture, see Elizabeth Petuchowski, "'Von der Menschlichkeit in finsteren Zeiten.'"; see also Lisa Disch, "On Friendship in 'Dark Times.'" Neither Petuchowski nor Disch places Arendt's lecture in the tradition with which Arendt associates herself, a tradition much older than the Hamburg prize and one to which she alludes when she subtitles the address "Rede über Lessing" and "Thoughts on Lessing." Of particular importance in this tradition, beyond what Franz Mehring famously called "the Lessing legend," are Friedrich Schlegel's "Über Lessing" (On Lessing, 1797), which she quotes at the end of her lecture, and Søren Kierkegaard's "Noget om Lessing" (Something about Lessing, which is the opening section of the *Concluding Unscientific Postrcript*), to which her discussion of Lessing's *Selbstdenken* is indebted. For a discussion of Arendt's lecture on Lessing in the context of a thoughtful reflection on Aristotle, Kant, and the politics of friendship, see Ronald Beiner, *Political Judgment*, esp. pp. 119–25. For an inquiry into one of Arendt's friendships, which reproduces in chiastic form the relation between Mendelssohn and Lessing, see Susannah Gottlieb, *Regions of Sorrow*, pp. 11–13.

33 Arendt, VM: 19; MDT: 12: "Sei mein Freund" (Lessing, *Nathan der Weise*, Act 3, Scene 7; Lessing, *Werke*, 2: 280). Associating Lessing's conception of friendship with that of the classical world, Arendt says that *Nathan* "might with some justice be called the classical play of friendship" (VM: 42; MDT: 25).

34 Arendt, VM: 42; MDT: 25: "Wir müssen, müssen Freunde sein" (Lessing, *Nathan der Weise*, Act 2, Scene 5; Lessing, *Werke*, 2: 253).

35 Lessing, *Nathan der Weise*, Act 1, Scene 3; Lessing, *Werke*, 2: 219.

36 See Arthur Warda, *Kant's Bücher*, p. 22.

37 Friedrich Hölderlin, *Sämtliche Werke*, 4: 236: "In guten Zeiten giebt es selten Schwärmer."

38 In her address on Lessing Arendt indicates that she "cannot discuss here the mischief that compassion has introduced into modern revolutions because it tried to make the unhappy happier rather than establish justice for all" (VM: 24; MDT: 14; translation modified); but see Arendt, *On Revolution*, pp. 73–98. A more thorough investigation into Arendt's conception of fraternity would have to analyze her intricate discussion in *The Origins of Totalitarianism* of "race-thinking before racism" in relation to the image of the "family of man"; see Arendt, *The Origins of Totalitarianism*, pp. 158–84: "When they [early nineteenth-century philologists] overstepped the limits of pure reseach it was because they wanted to include in the same cultural brotherhood as many nations as possible . . . In other words, these men were still in the humanistic tradition of the eighteenth century" (Arendt, *Origins*, p. 160). Arendt emphatically returns to the same topic near the conclusion of her address when she says of Lessing that he would reject "any doctrine [religious or racial] that in principle barred the possibility of friendship between two human beings" (VM: 49; MDT: 29) – regardless of the proofs proffered to establish its validity.

39 At the opening of her address, Arendt argues that "of all the specific liberties which may come into our minds when we hear the word 'freedom,' freedom of movement is historically the oldest and also the most elementary . . . Freedom of movement is also the indispensable condition for action" (VM: 14–15; MDT: 9).

40 Arendt, of course, was particularly concerned with the relation of lying, truth, and politics. *The Origins of Totalitarianism* could be understood to be about nothing else; see also her essay, "Lying in Politics," in *Crises of the Republic*, pp. 3–47.

41 See Hannah Arendt, *Lectures on Kant's Political Philosophy*.

7 REVOLUTION IN THE AIR

1 Friedrich Theodor Rink, *Ansichten aus Immanuel Kant's Leben*, pp. 108–9. See also Kant's reflections on similar matters collected among the "Hand-written Declarations" (12: 407–08).

2 Rink, *Ansichten aus Immanuel Kant's Leben*, pp. 109–11.

3 Johann Gottfried Hasse, *Merkwürdige Äußerungen* (1804); reprinted in Hasse, *Der alte Kant*, ed. Buchenau and Lehmann, pp. 18–19.

4 Hasse, *Der alte Kant*, ed. Buchenau and Lehmann, p. 19.

5 Kant mentions the revolution of the air several times in the *Opus postumum* (see 21: 117, 139, 148; 22: 7, 449), although only the passage above (21: 89–90) connects it with the death of cats.

6 Ehregott Andreas Christoph Wasianski, *Immanuel Kant in seinen letzten Lebensjahren*; reprinted in *Immanuel Kant*, ed. Felix Groß, p. 235.

7 See Kuehn, *Immanuel Kant*, p. 416.

8 In the third part of *The Conflict of the Faculties* Kant includes a subsection on sleep that discusses the very same ailment about which he complains to his friends, namely "mental paralysis" or "brain cramp" (12: 294): "Everyone who has got into bed and gotten ready to sleep will occasionally not be able to fall asleep, even by leading his thoughts [in the way prescribed by doctors above]. In this case he will feel something *spastic* (cramp-like) in his brain" (7: 106). Kant then explains that he used an old Stoic remedy (fixing thoughts on an arbitrary object, which in his case was the

name *Cicero*), and this "dulled the sensation" (7: 107). For the results of this technique, see the discussion in the section entitled "Arrested Thought" below. Kant's obsessive concern with atmospheric electricity could also be understood in terms that he might have happily accepted – as a "hobby horse." And as Kant would have known, although he may have forgotten, the phenomenon of the hobby horse is intimately related to electrical charges: "A man and his HOBBY-HORSE, tho' I cannot say that they act and re-act exactly after the same manner in which the soul and the body do upon each other: Yet doubtless there is a communication between them of some kind, and my opinion rather is, that there is something in it more of the manner of electrified bodies" (Laurence Sterne, *The Life and Opinions of Tristram Shandy*, p. 77).

9 Wasianski, *Immanuel Kant in seinen letzten Lebensjahren*, reprinted in *Immanuel Kant*, ed. F. Groß, pp. 245–46.

10 Kant, *Physische Geographie*, "Mathematische Vorkenntnisse," 1: 19. Any exposition of Kant's *Physische Geographie* is fraught with textual problems, the first of which involves the text chosen for analysis. These problems occasioned one of the great monuments of Kant philology, namely Erich Adickes's *Untersuchungen zu Kants physische Geographie*, which, following Kant's repudiation of the edition prepared by Vollmer pére (1801) in a public declaration (12: 398), makes no use of it; see Adickes, *Untersuchungen*, pp. 12–13). But the Rink edition, which is largely drawn from some very early notebooks (around 1759), is significantly less detailed than the editions published by the Vollmer family. In his bibliography Adickes is less dismissive of the Vollmer volumes than in his *Untersuchungen*: "Arranged from 3 lecture manuscripts of the years 1778, 1782, and 1793" (Adickes, *German Kantian Bibliography*, p. 27).

11 Quoted in Erich Adickes, *Kants Ansichten über Geschichte und Bau der Erde*, 111; for the relation to Canterzani (and Buffon, who held similar views), see pp. 112–13, 179–80.

12 Quoted in Erich Adickes, *Ein neu augefundenes Kollegheft nach Kants Vorlesung über physische Geographie*, p. 79; from the lecture notes of a certain A. L. W. Werner, dated March 1793.

13 Wilhelm August Lampadius's *Versuche und Beobachtungen über die Elektrizität und Wärme der Atmosphäre* (1793), which, as the complete title indicates, discusses in an appendix Jean André de Luc's *Recherches sur la modifications de l'atmosphère* (1772), a German translation of which appeared between 1776 and 1778; see de Luc, *Untersuchungen über die Atmosphäre*. Kant cites de Luc's *Lettres physiques et morales sur les montagnes et sur l'histoire de la terre et de l'homme* in the conclusion to both "On the Failure of All Philosophical Attempts at Theodicy" (8: 271) and "Something on the Influence of the Moon on the Wind and the Weather" (8: 324). Lampadius, incidentally, became a major figure in early nineteenth-century meteorology.

14 For an extensive analysis of Kant's theory of hail storms and the meteorological sources from which it is drawn, see Adickes's note to Refl. 79 (14: 526–29).

15 Kant, *Physische Geographie*, 3: 70.

16 See Kant, *Physische Geographie*, 3: 68–69.

17 See Kant, *Physische Geographie*, 3: 76–84. A full account of Kant's theory of atmospheric electricity would have to take into account almost all of his reflections on fire, the caloric, and ether. Kant was, of course, by no means the only one of his contemporaries who emphasizes the role of "electrical material" in the atmosphere. One of his teachers, Christian August Crusius, as Adickes notes, "used the atmosphere in

order to make electrical phenomena comprehensible" (14: 303). And from the opposite end of Kant's life one of his last manuscripts describes the "ethereal atmosphere of the world body" (22: 495). Of particular importance in this context are the meteorological speculations of Friedrich Schelling, particularly the exposition of atmospheric electricity in *Ideen zu einer Philosophie der Natur* (1797), which Kant may have known through reviews in the *Erlanger Literatur Zeitung* (the same journal that, according to Kant, reports elevated levels of atmospheric electricity, 21: 89–90): "The more strongly the electrical matter gathers in the free space of the sky, the more palpable become these stirrings in the interior of the earth, and at this moment it even seems that the laws of gravity are not alone in drawing us toward the sun; so, too, are living, electrical forces. Years of thunderstorms are not infrequently years of great earthquakes, and in any case they are the most productive. . . . After all the inquiries that have been undertaken, however, the origin of atmospheric electricity still remains an enigma" (pp. 66–67). For a brief consideration of the possibility that Schelling exercised some influence on late Kant, see Eckart Förster, "Fichte, Beck and Schelling in Kant's *Opus postumum*," esp. pp. 167–68.

18 For Kant's theory of meteors, see *Physische Geographie*, esp. 3: 93–96.

19 Wasianski, *Immanuel Kant in seinen letzten Lebensjahren*, reprinted in *Immanuel Kant*, ed. F. Groß, p. 283.

20 The correction to "elaterometer" was first discovered by Paul Czygan while reviewing Wasianski's marginal comments on his biography; see Adickes's remarks to Refl. 79 (14: 531–32); see also Karl Vorländer, *Die älteste Kant-Biographie*, p. 29. As Kant would have known, Horace Bénédict de Saussure developed the first accurate electrometer, and Abraham Bennet invented the first gold-leaf electroscope in 1786. For a contemporaneous celebration of the meteorological advantages of the Bennet device, see Lampadius, *Versuche und Beobachtungen*, pp. 3–12.

21 Wasianski, *Immanuel Kant in seinen letzten Lebensjahren*, reprinted in *Immanuel Kant*, ed. F. Groß, pp. 281–83.

22 Exasperated by the thought that Kant's efforts to build an "electrometer" could have persisted so long, Lehmann doubts that Wasianski correctly remembers when Kant asked him to build the device (22: 818).

23 Precisely when Kant began to reflect on the possibility of a future revolution of the earth is a difficult matter to decide because of the largely unedited condition of the lectures on physical geography. Adickes, once again, who would have been able to answer this question, does not seem to have posed it in so many words. Having reviewed the relevant texts except those on physical geography, Reinhard Brandt concludes that "the reflection that nature could have other intentions than the perfection of our species only appears in his late work" (Brandt, *Kritischer Kommentar zu Kants "Anthropologie in pragmatischer Hinsicht,"* p. 499).

24 Jean André de Luc is also Kant's point of reference for the final paragraph of "On the Failure of All Philosophical Attempts at Theodicy." Kant concludes "Something Concerning the Influence" by noting that de Luc's proposal for the advancement of meteorology – that people observe weather conditions more diligently – is doomed to failure and is probably "cast as a stumbling block only for the antiphlogistics" (8: 324). For an account of Kant's own wavering position at this time with respect to the new chemistry of Lavoisier, see Michael Friedman, *Kant and the Exact Sciences*, pp. 264–90. Oddly enough, Friedman does not mention this passage.

25 See the first two principles that Franz Anton Mesmer proposes in his *Mémoire sur la découverte du magnetism animal* (1779): "1. Il existe une influence mutuelle entre les

corps célestes, la terre et les corps animés. 2. Un fluide universellement répandu, et continué de manière à souffrir aucun vide, dont la subtilité ne permet aucune comparaison, et qui, de sa nature, est susceptible de recevoir, propager et communiquer toutes les impressions du mouvement, est le moyen de cette influence" (quoted in Maria Tatar, *Spellbound*, p. 273; the early chapters of Tatar's study, especially "Salvation by Electricity," provide a vivid picture of the atmosphere in which Mesmer exerted his remarkable influence). Kant was doubtless well aware of Mesmer's theory of "animal magnetism," which had become the subject of discussion in the *Berlinische Monatsschrift* as early as 1783; see Walter Artelt, *Der Mesmerismus in Berlin*, esp. pp. 13–15. Borowski, who would later write one of the early biographies of Kant, published a book entitled *Cagliostro, einer der merkwürdigsten Abendtheurer unsres Jahrhunderts* (1790), to which Kant replied in an extensive letter that Borowski appended to subsequent editions of his book. Alluding to the third of Mesmer's twenty-seven propositions on animal magnetism – "Cette action réciproque est soumise à des lois mécaniques inconnues jusqu'à présent" (Tatar, *Spellbound*, p. 273) – Kant makes the following recommendation:

> This is the usual trick of the trade whereby the enthusiasts [*Schwärmer*] give their ignorance the veneer of science: they ask, do you know the true cause of the magnetic force, or do you know the matter that produces such wonderful effects in electrical phenomena? Now, they believe they can discuss with good grounds something of whose inner constitution, in their opinion, the greatest natural scientists know as little as they do, even with respect to its most likely effects.... Against these shenanigans there is nothing to do but magnetize the animal magnetizers and grant space for disorganization, so long as it pleases them and others who are easily fooled.
>
> (11: 139–40)

26 Walter Artelt, *Mesmerismus in Berlin*, pp. 20–21; see also Maria Tatar, *Spellbound*, p. 75.

27 Two analyses of Kant's failure to will himself well are of particular interest, especially since they point in different directions; see Susan Shell, *The Embodiment of Reason*, pp. 294–97; and Jean-François Lyotard, "Judiciousness in Dispute, or Kant after Marx," in Lyotard, *The Lyotard Reader*, pp. 324–59. For a singularly impressive analysis of cognitive failure in Kant, which pays particular attention to his late writings, see Avital Ronell, *Stupidity*, pp. 280–310.

28 Karl Vorländer, editor of the Akademie edition, does not bother to annotate this reference. No one, so far as I have been able to discover, has even tried to identify the source.

29 Hasse, *Der alte Kant*, ed. Buchenau and Lehmann, p. 19.

30 The editors of the letters indicate that the article to which Kant refers has not been discovered (13: 502). In two other letters Kant relates his mental disability to atmospheric electricity but does not mention the cats; see the letter to Johann Georg Scheffner, January 24, 1799 (12: 273) and the draft of a letter to Samuel Thomas Sömmerring (12: 319).

31 The relation between the treatment of organic bodies in the *Opus postumum* and the Critique of Teleological Judgment is extraordinarily complex and would demand a correspondingly intricate investigation into both the philosophical problem that Kant sought to solve and the natural-historical sources of his reflection. Michael

Friedman declines to enter into the issue of organic bodies in the *Opus postumum*, presumably because it does not involve the "exact sciences"; see Friedman, *Kant and the Exact Sciences*, p. 213. An enormously helpful step in this direction is, however, taken by Eckart Förster, *Kant's Final Synthesis*, esp. pp. 24–28, which discusses the reasons for Kant's decision to devote renewed attention to organic bodies within the general project of a "science of transition": "it is not the human artifact and the realization of practical purposes that originally permits the formation of this concept [of natural purpose]. Rather, it is the experience of our own bodily organization, of our body's ability to exercise intentionally moving forces in accordance with the laws of mechanics" (p. 27). For an analysis of the *Opus postumum* in terms of Kant's own body, see Susan Shell, *The Embodiment of Reason*, pp. 298–305.

32 The first sentence of this note is an anacoluthon, since the verb "classify" (*classificiren*) includes here a reflexive (which indicates that Kant had begun with another verb in mind). Eckart Förster and Michael Rosen surmise that Kant intended to write something like "sich vorstellen" and therefore insert *imagine* (Kant, *Opus postumum*, p. 65). There is good reason for this interpretation; but it is also possible to suppose that the reflexive is an uncorrected oversight and that *classificiren* is the definite verb of the sentence. Elsewhere Kant makes it clear that he considers the classification of organic beings outlined in the footnote to be a priori, even if the principle by which nature is divided into organic and non-organic bodies may only be a priori in a problematic sense; see especially 21: 567–70 and 22: 505. I am, however, greatly indebted to Förster's edition, which makes the *Opus postumum* far more comprehensible than the Akademie edition.

33 For an analysis of the question of relation between Kant's remarks on natural revolution and Darwin's theory of natural selection, see especially Arthur Lovejoy, "Kant and Evolution"; see also the succinct comments of Reinhard Brandt, *Kritischer Kommentar zu Kants "Anthropologie in pragmatischer Hinsicht,"* pp. 494–95.

34 The term "epoch of nature" is clearly drawn from Buffon's *Époques de la nature*, which was translated in 1781.

35 Kant erases *gibbon* from the manuscript at this point. For a discussion of the dispute over the anatomy of the orangutan, see Adickes's discussion in *Untersuchungen zu Kants Physischer Geographie*, pp. 115–16; see also his footnote to Refl. 1498 (15: 778).

36 Adickes provides a lengthy analysis of the relevant sources in his notes on Refl. 102 (14: 619–20). Lehmann's note to the *Opus postumum*, which relies on Vorländer, is mistaken (22: 805).

37 All of these quotations are from the first "convolute" of the *Opus postumum*, which, according to Adickes, represent the last stages of Kant's thought (December 1800–February 1803). An adequate exposition of Kant's surprising attempts to represent transcendental philosophy in terms of "galvanism" would exceed the bounds of a note and would demand an inquiry into the complicated controversy between Galvani and Volta as it was represented in the various books and periodicals with which Kant familiarized himself about recent scientific discoveries; for an astute analysis of this controversy, which does not present Volta as the unambiguous champion of truth, see Marcello Pera, *The Ambiguous Frog*. Of particular importance, once again, is Schelling. Immediately after making the connection between transcendental philosophy and atmospheric electricity Kant writes the following note: "(Of a univ[ersal] world spirit, not world soul)" (21: 137) – which alludes to the title of Schelling's treatise of 1798, *Von der Weltseele*.

CONCLUSION

1 The remarkable story of the bundles of papers that make up Kant's last "work" is wonderfully related in Eckart Förster's "Introduction" to his edition of the *Opus postumum*, pp. xvi–xxiii.

2 Fichte, *Das System der Sittenlehre, nach den Prinzipien der Wissenschaftslehre*, reprinted in Fichte, *Werke*, 4: 255–56.

3 Kant is therefore closer to Walter Benjamin's concept of "pure means" than to Fichte's proposal that human beings be understood as means through which reason actualizes itself; see Benjamin, "Zur Kritik der Gewalt" (1921), reprinted in Benjamin, *Gesammelte Schriften*, 2: 179–203; see Hamacher, "Afformative, Strike."

Many years after publishing "Zur Kritik der Gewalt" – and without any reference to the thesis of radical mean-ness – Benjamin comes close to capturing the peculiarity of late Kant: "Denn das eben ist das sonderbare Schauspiel dieses Daseins, daß es in seniem völligen Verfall zugleich sich auslebt, im strengen Doppelsinne des Wortes [For this is precisely the peculiar spectacle of this existence, that in its complete collapse it at the same time outlives itself, in the strict ambiguity of the word]" (*Gesammelte Schriften*, 6: 155).

4 Nietzsche, *Sämtliche Werke*, 4: 16–17.

5 See note 36 to Chapter 7 for the relevant references.

6 See Kant's response to Maupertius's proposal for the establishment of state-controlled, human breeding farms in "On the Different Human Races": "a wise nature hinders [this proposal] quite well" (2: 241).

7 See especially 22: 123: "The evil principle would be a subjective practical principle without a principle [*Grundsatz ohne Prinzip*], indeed to act against all principle; it is therefore a *contradictio in abjecto*. Therefore merely *inclination* (instinct), that is, well-being (*in diem dicere: vixi*), to live for the day."

8 There are numerous references to the demiurge in the *Opus postumum*, of which the most important is probably at 21: 33–34; see also the remarks at the end of the *Anthropology*, 7: 331–32.

9 In a famous remark to the *Observations on the Feeling of the Beautiful and the Sublime*, Kant writes of his own conversion to the party of humanity, so to speak: as a "researcher by inclination," he once "despised the crowd that knows nothing. Rousseau set me straight . . . I learned to honor human beings" (Kant, *Bemerkungen*, p. 38). Just as the thesis that human beings are on earth for the sake of others does not amount to a theodicy, it cannot be considered a return to his early contempt for the common lot of humankind.

10 See the extensive treatise of Carl Schmitt, *Nomos der Erde* along with the more incisive "Nomos, Nahme, Name"; see also the even more concise note that Hannah Arendt appends to a discussion of "The Public and the Private Realm," in Arendt, *The Human Condition*, p. 63.

11 See note 11 to Chapter 2.

BIBLIOGRAPHY

Adickes, Erich. *Kants Ansichten über Geschichte und Bau der Erde*. Tübingen: Mohr, 1911.
——. *Untersuchungen zu Kants Physischer Geographie*. Tübingen: Mohr, 1911.
——. *Ein neu aufgefundenes Kollegheft nach Kants Vorlesung über physische Geographie*. Tübingen: Mohr, 1913.
——. *Kant als Naturforscher*. 2 vols. Berlin: De Gruyter, 1925.
——. *German Kantian Bibliography*. 1893–96. Reprinted, New York: Franklin, 1970.
Agamben, Giorgio. *Homo Sacer: Sovereign Power and Bare Life*. Trans. Daniel Heller-Roazen. Stanford: Stanford University Press, 1998.
——. *Means Without End: Notes on Politics*. Trans. Cesare Casarino. Minneapolis: University of Minnesota Press, 2000.
——. *Le Temps qui reste*. Trans. Judith Revel. Paris: Rivages, 2000.
——. "On the State of Exception: The Debate between Walter Benjamin and Carl Schmitt." Unpublished manuscript.
Allison, Henry. *Kant's Theory of Freedom*. Cambridge: Cambridge University Press, 1990.
——. *Kant's Theory of Taste: A Reading of the "Critique of Aesthetic Judgment."* Cambridge: Cambridge University Press, 2001.
The Anchor Bible: Job. Ed. and trans. Marvin H. Pope. New York: Doubleday, 1965.
Anderson-Gold, Sharon. "Kant's Rejection of Devilishness: The Limits of Human Volition," *Idealistic Studies* 14 (1984): 35–48.
Anonymous. *Politischer, auss göttlicher vnd erbarn Völckern Rechten kürtzlich verfaster Discurs*. n. pl.: n. pub., 1644.
Arendt, Hannah. *The Human Condition*. Chicago: University of Chicago Press, 1958.
——. *Von der Menschlichkeit in finsteren Zeiten: Rede über Lessing*. Munich: Piper, 1960.
——. *On Revolution*. Harmondsworth: Penguin, 1965.
——. *Crises of the Republic*. New York: Harcourt Brace & Company, 1972.
——. *The Origins of Totalitarianism*, rev. edn. New York: Harcourt Brace Jovanovich, 1979.
——. *Lectures on Kant's Political Philosophy*. Ed. Ronald Beiner. Chicago: University of Chicago Press, 1982.
——. *Men in Dark Times*. New York: Harcourt Brace Javonovich, 1983.
Aristotle. *Nicomachean Ethics*. Trans. D. Ross. Oxford: Oxford University Press, 1980.
——. *Ethica Nicomachea*. Ed. L. Bywater. Oxford: Clarendon, 1986.
Artelt, Walter. *Der Mesmerismus in Berlin*. Abhandlungen der geistes- und sozialwissenschaftlichen Klasse, vol. 6. Wiesbaden: Akademie der Wissenschaften und der Literatur in Mainz, 1965.

Austin, John. *How To Do Things With Words*. Ed. J. O. Urmson and Marina Sbisà. Cambridge, Mass.: Harvard University Press, 1975.

Batscha, Zwi and Richard Saage, eds. *Friedensutopien*. Frankfurt am Main: Suhrkamp, 1979.

Beck, Hamilton. *The Elusive "I" in the Novel: Hippel, Sterne, Diderot, and Kant*. New York: Lang, 1987.

Beck, Lewis White. *A Commentary on Kant's "Critique of Practical Reason."* Chicago: University of Chicago Press, 1960.

Beiner, Ronald. *Political Judgment*. Chicago: University of Chicago Press, 1983.

Benjamin, Walter. *Gesammelte Schriften*. 7 vols. Ed. Rolf Tiedemann and Hermann Schweppenhäuser. Frankfurt am Main: Suhrkamp, 1972–91.

Bennington, Geoffrey. *Frontière kantiennes*. Paris: Galilée, 2000.

Benton, Robert. "Political Expediency and Lying: Kant vs. Benjamin Constant," *Journal of the History of Ideas* 43 (1982): 135–44.

Berger, Adolf. *Encyclopedic Dictionary of Roman Law*. Philadelphia: American Philosophical Society, 1953.

Bernasconi, Robert. "Who Invented the Concept of Race? Kant's Role in the Enlightenment Construction of Race." In *Race*, ed. R. Bernasconi, 11–36. Oxford: Blackwell, 2001.

Biester, Johann Erich. "Über Hrn. Kants Aufsatz, in Betref der Theodicee," *Berlinische Monatsschrift* (1791): 411–20.

Blanchot, Maurice. *L'amitié*. Paris: Gallimard, 1971.

——— . *Michel Foucault tel que je l'imagine*. Paris: Fata Morgana, 1986.

——— . "Lettre à Salomon Malka," *L'Arche* 373 (May, 1988): 68.

Boituzat, François. *Un Droit de mentir? Constant ou Kant*. Paris: Presses Universitaires de France, 1993.

Borowski, L. Ernst. *Cagliostro, einer der merkwürdigsten Abendtheurer unsres Jahrhunderts. Seine Geschichte nebst Raisonnement über ihn und den schwärmerischen Unfug unsrer Zeit überhaupt*. Königsberg: Nicolivius, 1790.

Brandt, Reinhard. *Kritischer Kommentar zu Kants "Anthropologie in pragmatischer Hinsicht" (1798)*. Hamburg: Meiner, 1999.

Brentano, Margherita von. "Kants Theorie der Geschichte und der bürgerlichen Gesellschaft." In *Spiegel und Gleichnis*, ed. N. W. Bolz and W. Hübener, 205–14. Würzburg: Königshausen and Neumann, 1983.

Brown, Norman O. *Life Against Death: The Psychoanalytic Meaning of History*. Middletown, Conn.: Wesleyan University Press, 1959.

Buffon, Georges Louis Leclerc, Comte de. *Epochen der Natur*. St Petersburg: Logan, 1781.

Cicero, Marcus Tullius. *Laelius de amicitia*. Ed. and trans. J. G. F. Powell. Warminster: Aris & Phillips, 1990.

Constant, Benjamin. *De la force du gouvernement actuel de la France et de la nécessité de s'y rallier; Des réactions politiques; Des effets de la Terreur*. Ed. Philippe Raynaud. Paris: Flammarion, 1988.

Corngold, Stanley. *Complex Pleasures: Forms of Feeling in German Literature*. Stanford: Stanford University Press, 1998.

de Levie, Dagobert. *Die Menschenliebe im Zeitalter der Aufklärung: Säkularisation und Moral im 18. Jahrhundert*. Frankfurt am Main: Lang, 1975.

de Luc, Jean André. *Untersuchungen über die Atmosphäre und die zu Abmessung ihrer Veränderungen dienlichen Werkzeuge*. Leipzig: J. C. Müller, 1776–78.

Derrida, Jacques. *Aporias*. Trans. Thomas Dutoit. Stanford: Stanford University Press, 1993.

——. "On a Newly Arisen Apocalyptic Tone in Philosophy." In *Raising the Tone of Philosophy*, ed. Peter Fenves, trans. John Leavey, Jr. 117–68. Baltimore: Johns Hopkins University Press, 1993.

——. *Politiques de l'amitié*. Paris: Galilée, 1994.

Die Bibel nach der Übersetzung Martin Luthers. Trans. Martin Luther. Rev. edn. Stuttgart: Deutsche Bibelgesellschaft, 1985.

Dietzsch, Steffen. "Kant, die Juden und das akademische Bürgerrecht in Königsberg." In *Königsberg: Beiträge zu einem besonderen Kapital der deutschen Geistesgeschichte des 18. Jahrhunderts*, ed. Joseph Kohnen. 109–25. Frankfurt am Main: Lang, 1994.

Dilthey, Wilhelm. *Gesammelte Schriften*. 23 vols to date. Stuttgart and Göttingen: Teubner, Vandenhoech & Ruprecht, 1957–.

Disch, Lisa. "On Friendship in 'Dark Times,'" in *Feminist Interpretations of Hannah Arendt*, ed. Bonnie Honig. 285–311. University Park, Pa.: Pennsylvania State University Press, 1995.

Dusch, Johann Jakob. *Moralische Briefe zur Bildung des Herzens*. 2nd edn. Leipzig: Breitkopf, 1762–64.

Eze, Emmanuel. "The Color of Reason: The Idea of 'Race' in Kant's Anthropology," *Anthropology and the German Enlightenment*. Ed. Katherine Faull. 150–75. Lewisburg: Bucknell University Press, 1995.

Fackenheim, Emil. "Kant and Radical Evil," *University of Toronto Quarterly* 23 (1954): 339–53.

Faderman, Lilian. *Surpassing the Love of Men*. New York: Morrow, 1980.

Fasching, Maria. *Zum Begriff der Freundschaft bei Aristoteles und Kant*. Würzburg: Königshausen & Neumann, 1990.

Fenves, Peter. "Marx's Doctoral Thesis on Two Greek Atomists and the Post-Kantian Interpretations," *The Journal of the History of Ideas* 46 (1986): 433–52.

——. *A Peculiar Fate: Metaphysics and World-History in Kant*. Ithaca and London: Cornell University Press, 1991.

——, ed. *Raising the Tone of Philosophy: Late Essay by Kant, Transformative Critique by Derrida*. Baltimore: Johns Hopkins University Press, 1993.

——. *Arresting Language: From Leibniz to Benjamin*. Stanford: Stanford University Press, 2001.

Fichte, Johann Gottlieb. *Werke*. 8 vols. Ed. Immanuel Hermann Fichte. 1845–46. Reprinted, Berlin: De Gruyter, 1971.

——. *The Science of Knowledge* [*Foundation for the Entire Wissenschaftslehre*]. Ed. and trans. Peter Heath and John Lachs. Cambridge: Cambridge University Press, 1982.

——. *Early Philosophical Writings*. Ed. and trans. Daniel Breazeale. Ithaca and London: Cornell University Press, 1988.

Firla, Monika. "Kants Thesen vom 'Nationalcharakter' der Afrikaner, seine Quellen und der nicht vorhandene 'Zeitgeist.'" In *Rassismus und Kulturalismus*, ed. Ulrike Davey, 17–37. Vienna: Institut für Wissenschaft und Kunst, 1997.

Fleischhauer, Wolfgang. "Zur Geschichte des Wortes 'Menschenliebe,'" *Monatshefte: Für deutschen Unterricht, deutsche Sprache und Literatur* 57 (1965) 1–7.

Förster, Eckart. "Fichte, Beck and Schelling in Kant's *Opus postumum*." In *Kant and his Influence*, ed. George MacDonald Ross and Tony McWalter. 146–69. Bristol: Thoemmes, 1990.

———. *The Final Synthesis: An Essay on the "Opus postumum."* Cambridge, Mass.: Harvard University Press, 2000.

———. "Die Bedeutung von §§ 76, 77 der 'Kritik der Urteilskraft' für die Entwicklung der nachkantischen Philosophie," *Zeitschrift für philosophische Forschung* 56 (April–June, 2002): 169–90.

Foucault, Michel. *Foucault/Blanchot*. Trans. Jeffrey Mehlman and Brian Massumi. New York: Zone Books, 1987.

———. *Dits et écrits: 1954–1988*. Paris: Gallimard, 1994.

———. *Ethics, Subjectivity, and Truth: Essential Works of Michel Foucault, 1954–1984*. Ed. Paul Rabinow, trans. Robert Hurley. New York: New Press, 1997.

Friedman, Michael. *Kant and the Exact Sciences*. Cambridge, Mass.: Harvard University Press, 1992.

Friedrich II of Prussia. *Ouevres de Fredéric II*. 24 vols. Amsterdam: n.p., 1789–90.

———. *Briefe*. Ed. Max Hein. Berlin: Hobbing, 1914.

Gerhardt, Volker. *Immanuel Kants Entwurf "Zum Ewigen Frieden": Eine Theorie der Politik*. Darmstadt: Wissenschaftliche Buchgesellschaft, 1995.

Geyer, Carl-Friedrich. "Das 'Jahrhundert der Theodizee,'" *Kant-Studien* 73 (1982): 393–405.

Girtanner, Johann Christoph. *Über das Kantische Princip für die Naturgeschichte: Ein Versuch diese Wissenschaft philosophisch zu behandeln*. 1796. Reprinted, Brussels: Culture et Civilisation, 1968.

Glatzer, Nahum. "Remnant of Israel." In *Contemporary Jewish Religious Thought*, ed. Arthur Cohen and Paul Mendes-Flohr, 779–83. New York: Free Press, 1987.

Goethe, Wolfgang von. *Goethes Briefe*. Ed. K. R. Mandelkow. Hamburg: Wegner, 1964.

Goetschel, Willi. *Kant als Schriftsteller*. Wien: Passagen, 1990.

Gottlieb, Susannah Y. *Regions of Sorrow: Anxiety and Messianism in Hannah Arendt and W. H. Auden*. Stanford: Stanford University Press, 2003.

Gottsched, Johann Christoph. *Erste Gründe der gesammten Weltweisheit*. Leipzig: Breitkopf, 1733–34.

Grimm, Jacob and Wilhelm, eds. *Deutsches Wörterbuch*. Rev. ed. Gustav Rosenhagen and the Arbeitstelle des Deutschen Wörterbuches zu Berlin. Leipzig: Hirzel, 1954.

Groß, Felix, ed. *Immanuel Kant. Sein Leben in Darstellung von Zeitgenossen. Die Biographie von L. E. Borowski, R. B. Jachmann und A. Ch. Wasianski*. Berlin: Deutsche Bibliothek, 1912.

Guyer, Paul. *Kant and the Claims of Taste*. 2nd edn. Cambridge, Mass.: Cambridge University Press, 1997.

———. "Beauty and Utility in Eighteenth-Century Aesthetics," *Eighteenth-Century Studies* 35 (Spring 2002): 439–53.

Haller, Albrecht von. *Die Alpen und andere Gedichte*. Ed. Adalbert Elschenchroich. Stuttgart: Reclam, 1965.

Hamacher, Werner. "Afformative, Strike." In *Walter Benjamin's Philosophy: Destruction and Experience*, ed. Andrew Benjamin and Peter Osborne, trans. Dana Hollander. 110–38. London and New York: Routledge, 1994.

———. *Premises: Essays on Philosophy and Literature from Kant to Celan*. Trans. Peter Fenves. Stanford: Stanford University Press, 1999.

Hasse, Johann Gottfried. *Merkwürdige Äußerungen Kant's von einem seiner Tischgenossen*. Königsberg: Lebrecht, 1804.

———. *Der alte Kant. Hasse's Schrift: Letzte Äußerungen Kants und persönliche Notizen aus dem opus postumum*. Ed. Artur Buchenau and Gerhard Lehmann. Berlin: De Gruyter, 1925.

Hattenhauer, Hans, ed. *Allgemeines Landrecht für die Preussischen Staaten von 1794*. Frankfurt am Main: Metzner, 1970.

———. *Die geistesgeschichtlichen Grundlagen des deutschen Rechts*. 3rd edn. Heidelberg: Müller, 1983.

Hegel, G. W. F. *Werke*. Ed. Eva Moldenhauer and Karl Markus Michel. 20 vols. Frankfurt am Main: Suhrkamp, 1971.

Heidegger, Martin. *Wegmarken*. Frankfurt am Main: Klostermann, 1978.

Heine, Heinrich. *Werke*. 4 vols. Ed. Christoph Siegrist, Wolfgang Preisendanz, Eberhard Galley, and Helmut Schanze. Frankfurt am Main: Insel, 1968.

Hellbach, Hans Dietrich (under the pseudonym Hans Dietrich). *Die Freundesliebe in der deutschen Literatur*. Leipzig, 1931; rpt. Berlin: Winkel, 1996.

Henrich, Dieter. "Kant's Notion of a Deduction and the Methodological Background of the First *Critique*." In *Kant's Transcendental Deduction*, ed. Eckart Förster, 29–46. Stanford: Stanford University Press, 1989.

Herz, Marcus. *Versuch über den Schwindel*. Berlin: Voß, 1786.

Hippel, Theodor Gottlieb von. *Der Mann nach der Uhr; oder, Der ordentliche Mann*. Ed. Erich Jenisch. Halle: Niemeyer, 1928.

Hobbes, Thomas. *Leviathan*. Ed. C. B. MacPherson. Harmondsworth: Penguin, 1968.

Hölderlin, Friedrich. *Sämtliche Werke*. 8 vols. Ed. Friedrich Beißner *et al*. Stuttgart: Kohlhammer, 1943–85.

Howard, Jones. *The Epicurean Tradition*. London: Routledge, 1989.

Husserl, Edmund. *Husserliana. Gesammelte Werke*. 33 vols to date. Ed. Husserl-Archiv in Leuven under the directorship of H. L. van Breda. The Hague: Nijhoff, 1950–.

Jariges, Philipp Joseph von (published anonymously). *Réflections philosophiques et historiques d'un jurisconsulte, adressées à son ami à Turin sur l'ordre de la procédure et sur les décisions arbitraires et immédiates du souverain*. Berlin: Decker, 1765.

John, Regina. *Vernünftige Menschenliebe: Wohltat und Almosen in Drama und Roman der deutschen Aufklärung*. Frankfurt am Main: Lang, 1992.

Johnson, W. R. *Lucretius and the Modern World*. London: Duckworth, 2000.

Justinian. *Digest*. 4 vols. Ed. Theodor Mommsen and Paul Krueger, trans. Alan Watson. Philadelphia, Pa.: University of Pennsylvania Press, 1985.

Kafka, Franz. *Gesammelte Werke*. 12 vols. Ed. Hans-Gerd Koch. Frankfurt am Main: Fischer, 1994.

Kant, Immanuel. (under the name Emmanuel Kant). *Projet de paix perpétuelle* Königsberg: Nicolovius, 1796.

———. (under the name Emmanuel Kant). *Logik, ein Handbuch zu Vorlesungen*. Ed. Gottlob Benjamin Jäsche. Königsberg: Nicolovius, 1800.

———. *Physische Geographie*. 4 vols. Ed. G. Vollmer. Mainz and Hamburg: Vollmer, 1801–05.

———. *Lose Blätter aus Kants Nachlass*. 3 vols. Ed. Rudolf Reicke. Königsberg: Beyer, 1889.

———. *Gesammelte Schriften*. 29 vols to date. Ed. Königlich-Preußische [later Deutsche] Akademie der Wissenschaften zu Berlin. Berlin: Reimer; later, De Gruyter, 1900–.

———. *Der Streit der Fakultäten*. Ed. Klaus Reich. Hamburg: Meiner, 1959.

———. "Ein neu aufgefundenes Reinschriftfragment Kants mit den Anfangstexten seines Entwurfs 'Zum ewigen Frieden.'" Ed. Günther Baum, Wolfgang Bayerer, and Rudolph Malter, *Kant-Studien* 77 (1986): 316–137.

———. "Ein Reinschriftsfragment zu Kants 'Streit der Fakultäten.'" Ed. K. Weyand and G. Lehmann, *Kant-Studien* 51 (1959–60): 3–13.

———. *Metaphysische Anfängsgründe der Rechtslehre*. Ed. Bernd Ludwig. Hamburg: Meiner, 1986.

———. *Critique of Judgment*. Trans. Werner Pluhar. Indianapolis: Hackett, 1987.

———. *Rechtslehre*. Ed. Hermann Klenner. Berlin: Akademie, 1988.

——— *Bemerkungen in den "Beobachtungen über das Gefühl des Schönen und des Erhabenen."* Ed. Marie Rischmüller. Hamburg: Meiner, 1991.

———. *Über den Gemeinspruch . . . Zum ewigen Frieden*. Ed. Heiner Klemme. Hamburg: Meiner, 1992.

———. *Opus postumum*. Ed. Eckart Förster, trans. Eckart Förster and Michael Rosen. Cambridge: Cambridge University Press, 1993.

———. *Four Neglected Essays*. Trans. John Richardson (1798). Ed. and intro. Stephen Palmquist. Hong Kong: Philopsychy Press, 1994.

———. *Practical Philosophy*. Ed. and trans. Mary Gregor. Cambridge: Cambridge University Press, 1996.

———. *Religion and Rational Theology*. Ed. and trans. Allen Wood and George di Giovanni. Cambridge: Cambridge University Press, 1996.

Kimmich, Dorothee. *Epikureische Aufklärungen: Philosophische und poetische Konzepte der Selbstsorge*. Darmstadt: Wissenschaftliche Buchgesellschaft, 1993.

Klüber, Johann Ludwig. *Oeffentliches Recht des Teutschen Bundes und der Bundes-Staaten*. 2nd edn. Frankfurt am Main: Andreä, 1822.

Koselleck, Reinhart. *Preußen zwischen Reform und Revolution: Allgemeines Landrecht, Verwaltung, und soziale Bewegung zwischen 1791 bis 1848*. Stuttgart: Klett, 1967.

Kroll, Richard. *The Material World: Literate Culture in the Restoration and Early Eighteenth Century*. Baltimore: Johns Hopkins University Press, 1991.

Kuehn, Manfred. *Kant: A Biography*. Cambridge: Cambridge University Press, 2001.

Kuzniar, Alice. *Outing Goethe and His Age*. Stanford: Stanford University Press, 1996.

Lampadius, Wilhelm August. *Versuche und Beobachtungen über die Elektrizität und Wärme der Atmosphäre, angestellt im Jahr 1792: Nebst der Theorie der Luftelektrizität nach den Grundsätzen des Hern. de Lüc und einer Abhandlung über das Wasser*. Berlin and Stettin: Nicolai, 1793.

Larrimore, Mark. "Sublime Waste: Kant and the Destiny of the 'Races.'" In *Civilization and Oppression*, ed. Catherine Wilson, 99–125. Calgary: University of Calgary Press, 1999.

Laywine, Allison. *Kant's Early Metaphysics and the Origins of the Critical Philosophy*. Atascadero, Calif.: Ridgeview, 1993.

Leibniz, Gottfried Wilhelm. *Die philosophischen Schriften*. 7 vols. Ed. C. J. Gerhardt. 1875–90. Reprinted, Hildesheim: Olms, 1978.

———. *Political Writings*. Ed. and trans. Patrick Riley. Cambridge: Cambridge University Press, 1988.

Lessing, Gotthold Ephraim. *Sämtliche Werke*. 23 vols. Ed. Karl Lachmann and Franz Muncker. 1886–1924. Reprinted, Berlin: De Gruyter, 1979.

———. *Werke*. 8 vols. Ed. Karl Eibl, Karl and Herbert Georg Göpfert. Munich: Hanser, 1971.

Lorenz, Stefan. *De Mundo Optimo: Studien zu Leibniz' Theodizee und ihrer Rezeption in Deutschland (1710–1791), Studia Leibnitiana Supplementa*, vol. 31. Stuttgart: Steiner, 1977.

Lovejoy, Arthur. "Kant and Evolution." In *Forerunners of Darwin: 1745–1859*. Ed. Bentley Glass, Owsey Temkin, and William Strauss. 173–206. Baltimore: Johns Hopkins University Press, 1959.

Lucretius, *De rerum natura*. Trans. Cyrus Bailey. Oxford: Clarendon, 1947.

Lyotard, Jean-François. *L'Enthousiasme: la critique kantienne de l'histoire*. Paris: Galilée, 1986.

——— . *The Lyotard Reader*. Ed. Andrew Benjamin. Oxford: Blackwell, 1989.

Maimon, Solomon. "Über die Theodicee," *Deutsche Monatsschrift* (1791): 190–212.

Makkreel, Rudolf. *Imagination and Interpretation in Kant: The Hermeneutical Import of the "Critique of Judgment."* Chicago: University of Chicago Press, 1990.

Marx, Karl and Friedrich Engels. *Marx-Engels Werke*. 41 vols. Berlin: Dietz, 1968–85.

Mendelssohn, Moses. *Gesammelte Schriften: Jubiläumsausgabe*. 24 vols to date. Ed. Ismar Elbogen, Julius Guttmann, Eugen Mittwoch, Alexander Altmann. Reprinted, 1929–32, 1938. Stuttgart: Frommann. Holzboog, 1974–.

Michalson, Gordon. *Fallen Freedom*. Cambridge: Cambridge University Press, 1990.

Molnár, Géza von. "'Die Wette biet' ich': Der Begriff des Wettens in Goethes 'Faust' und Kants Kritik." In *Geschichtlichkeit und Aktualität: Studien zur deutschen Literatur seit der Romantik*, ed. Hans Joachim Mähl and Klaus-Detlef Müller. 29–50. Tübingen: Niemeyer, 1988.

Nancy, Jean-Luc. *L'Impératif catégorique*. Paris: Flammarion, 1983.

Nietzsche, Friedrich. *Sämtliche Werke: Kritische Studienausgabe*. 15 vols. Ed. Giorgio Colli and Mazzino Montinari. Berlin: de Gruyter, 1967–77.

Osler, Margaret, ed. *Atoms, Pneuma, and Tranquillity: Epicurean and Stoic Themes in European Thought*. Cambridge: Cambridge University Press, 1991.

Paton, H. J. "Kant on Friendship." In *Friendship: A Philosophical Reader*, ed. Neera Kapur Badhwar. 133–49. Ithaca and London: Cornell University Press, 1993.

Pera, Marcello. *The Ambiguous Frog: The Galvani-Volta Controversy on Animal Electricity*. Trans. Jonathan Mandelbaum. Princeton: Princeton University Press, 1992.

Petuchowski, Elizabeth. "'Von der Menschlichkeit in finsteren Zeiten': A Post-World War II Address," *Lessing Jahrbuch* 20 (1988): 29–43.

Pope, Marvin, ed. *The Anchor Bible: Job*. New York: Doubleday, 1965.

Prauss, Gerold. *Kant, zur Deutung seiner Theorie von Erkennen und Handeln*. Cologne: Kiepenheuer & Witsch, 1973.

Rasch, Wolfdietrich. *Freundschaftskult und Freundschaftsdichtung im deutschen Schrifttum des 18. Jahrhunderts*. Halle: Niemeyer, 1936.

Raymond, Janice. *A Passion for Friends: Toward a Philosophy of Female Affection*. Boston: Beacon Press, 1986.

Reimen, Pia. "Struktur und Figurenkonstellationen in Theodor Gottlieb von Hippels Komödie 'Der Mann nach der Uhr.'" In *Königsberg: Beiträge zu einem besonderen Kapitel der deutschen Geistesgeschichte*. 199–263. Frankfurt am Main: Lang, 1994.

Richter, Simon. "The Ins and Outs of Intimacy: Gender, Epistolary Culture, and the Public Sphere," *The German Quarterly* 69 (Spring, 1996): 111–24.

Rink, Friedrich Theodor. *Ansichten aus Immanuel Kant's Leben*. Königsberg: Göbbels & Unzer, 1805.

Ritzel, Wolfgang. "Kant über den Witz und Kants Witz," *Kant-Studien* 82 (1991): 102–09.

Ronell, Avital. *Stupidity*. Urbana and Chicago: University of Illinois Press, 2002.

Rorty, Amélie. "Akrasia and Pleasure: *Nicomachean Ethics* Book 7." In *Essays on Aristotle's Ethics*, ed. Amélie Rorty. 267–84. Berkeley: University of California Press, 1980.

Rosenkranz, Karl. *Geschichte der Kant'schen Philosophie*. 1840. Reprinted, Berlin: Akademie, 1987.

Saine, Thomas. *The Problem of Being Modern: The German Pursuit of Enlightenment from Leibniz to the French Revolution*. Detroit: Wayne State University Press, 1997.

Saner, Hans. *Kants Weg vom Krieg zum Frieden*. Munich: Piper, 1973.

——. "Die Negative Bedingungen des Friedens." In *Zum ewigen Frieden*, ed. Otfried Höffe. 150–75. Berlin: Akademie, 1995.

Schelling, Friedrich. *Ideen zu einer Philosophie der Natur*. Leipzig: Breitkopf and Härtel, 1797.

——. *Von der Weltseele: Eine Hypothese der höheren Physik zur Erklärung des allgemeninen Organismus*. Hamburg: Perthes, 1798.

——. *Werke nach der Originalausgabe in neuer Anordnung*. 6 vols. Ed. Manfred Schröter. Munich: Beck, 1927–54.

Schestag, Thomas. "Komische Authentizität." In *Theorie der Komödie – Poetik der Komödie*, ed. Ralf Simon. 139–53. Bielefeld: Aisthesis, 2001.

Schiller, Friedrich. *On the Aesthetic Education of Man*. Ed. and trans. Elizabeth Wilkinson and L. A. Willoughby. Oxford: Clarendon Press, 1982.

——. *Über das Schöne und die Kunst: Schriften zur Ästhetik*. Munich: Hanser, 1975.

Schmidt, Eberhard. "Rechtssprüche und Machtsprüche der preussischen Könige des 18. Jahrhunderts," *Berichte über die Verhandlungen der Sächsischen Akademie der Wissenschaften zu Leipzig* 95 (1943): 3–48.

Schmitt, Carl. *Verfassungslehre*. Munich and Leipzig: Duncker & Humblot, 1928.

——. *Der Nomos der Erde im Völkerrecht des jus publicum Europaeum*. Cologne: Greven, 1950.

——. "Nomos, Nahme, Name." In *Der beständige Aufbruch*. Ed. Siegfried Behn. 92–105. Nürnberg: Glock & Lutz, 1959.

——. *Der Leviathan in der Staatslehre des Thomas Hobbes: Sinn und Fehlschlag eines politischen Symbols*. 1938. Reprinted, Cologne: Hohenheim, 1982.

——. *Die Diktatur: Von den Anfängen des modernen Souveränitätsgedankens bis zum proletarischen Klassenkampf*. 1924. Reprinted, Berlin: Duncker & Humblot, 1989.

Schöndorfer, Otto. "Zur Entstehungsgeschichte des 'Streit der Fakultäten,'" *Kant-Studien* 24 (1920): 389–93.

Schopenhauer, Arthur. *Werke*. 5 vols. Ed. Ludger Lütkehaus. Zürich: Haffmans, 1994.

Schulte, Christoph. "Zweckwidriges in der Erfahrung: Zur Genese des Misslingens aller philosophischen Versuche in der Theodizee bei Kant," *Kant-Studies* 82 (1991): 371–96.

Shell, Marc. *Children of the Earth: Literature, Politics, and Nationhood*. Oxford: Oxford University Press, 1993.

Shell, Susan M. *The Rights of Reason: A Study of Kant's Philosophy and Politics*. Toronto: University of Toronto Press, 1980.

——. "Bowling Alone: On the Saving Power of Kant's 'Perpetual Peace,'" *Idealistic Studies* 26 (Spring, 1996): 153–73.

——. *The Embodiment of Reason: Kant on Spirit, Generation, and Community*. Chicago: University of Chicago Press, 1996.

——. "Cannibals All: The Grave Wit of Kant's Perpetual Peace." In *Violence, Identity, and Self-Determination*, ed. Hent de Vries and Samuel Weber. 150–61. Stanford: Stanford University Press, 1997.

Silber, John. "The Ethical Significance of Kant's *Religion*." In *Religion within the Limits of Reason Alone*, trans. Theodore Greene and Hoyt Hudson. lxxix–cxxxiv. New York: Harper, 1960.

Spalding, G. L. "Über die Quellen, aus welchen eine Theodicee zu fließen pfleget," *Berlinische Monatsschrift* (1791): 526–34.

Spalding, Keith. *Historical Dictionary of German Figurative Usage*. Oxford: Blackwell, 1952.

Spangenberg, August Gottlieb. *Leben des Herrn Nicolaus Ludwig Grafen und Herrn von Zinzendorf und Pottendorf*. 1773–75. Reprinted, Hildesheim: Olms, 1971.

Sterne, Laurence. *The Life and Opinions of Tristram Shandy, Gentleman*. Ed. James Aiken Work. Indianapolis: Bobbs-Merrill, 1940.

Stölzel, Adolf. *Carl Gottlieb Svarez. Ein Zeitbild aus der zweiten Hälfte des achtzehnten Jahrhunderts*. Berlin: Vahlen, 1885.

——. *Brandenburg-Preußens Rechtsverwaltung und Rechtsverfassung, dargestellt im Wirken seiner Landesfürsten und Obersten Justizbeamten*. Berlin: Vahlen, 1888.

——. *Fünfzehn Vorträge aus der Brandenburglich-Preußischen Rechts- und Staatsgeschichte*. Berlin: Vahlen, 1889.

Swift, Jonathan. *Satyrische und ernsthafte Schriften von Dr. Jonathan Swift*. 6 vols. Trans. Salomon Gessner and Johann Heinrich Waser. Hamburg, 1756–66.

——. *The Writings of Jonathan Swift*. Ed. Robert Greenberg and William Bowman Piper. New York: Norton, 1973.

Tagliapietra, Andrea. *La verità e la menzogna: dialogo sulla fondazione morale della Politica*. Milan: Mondadori, 1996.

Tatar, Maria. *Spellbound: Studies in Mesmerism and Literature*. Princeton: Princeton University Press, 1978.

Verweyen, Hansjürgen. "Social Contract Among Devils," *Idealistic Studies* 26 (Spring 1996): 201.

Viesel, Hansjörg. *Jawohl, der Schmitt: Zehn Briefe aus Plettenberg*. Berlin: Support, 1988.

Voegelin, Eric. *Die Rassenidee in der Geistesgeschichte von Ray bis Carus*, 3 vols. Berlin: Junker & Dünnhaupt, 1933.

Vorländer, Karl. *Die älteste Kant-Biographie: Eine kritische Studie*. Berlin: Reuther & Reichard, 1918.

——. *Immanuel Kant. Der Mann und das Werk*. 2 vols. Leipzig: Meiner, 1924.

——. *Kants Leben*. Ed. Rudolf Malter. Hamburg: Meiner, 1986.

Vuillman, Jules. "On Lying: Kant and Benjamin Constant," *Kant-Studien* 73 (1982): 413–24.

Warda, Arthur. "Der Streit um den 'Streit der Fakultäten,'" *Kant-Studien* 23 (1919): 385–405.

——. *Kant's Bücher*. Berlin: Breslauer, 1922.

Watson, Stephen. *Tradition(s): Refiguring Community and Virtue in Classical German Thought*. Bloomington: Indiana University Press, 1997.

Weis, Norbert. *Königsberg: Immanuel Kant und seine Stadt*. Braunschweig: Westernmann, 1993.

Wieland, Christoph Martin. *Gesammelte Schriften*. 26 vols to date. Ed. Deutsche Kommission der Königlich preussischen Akademie der Wissenschaften, Fritz Homeyer *et al*. Berlin: Weidmann, 1909–.

Zammito, John. *Genesis of the "Critique of Judgment."* Chicago: University of Chicago Press, 1992.

——. *Kant, Herder, and the Birth of Anthropology*. Chicago: University of Chicago Press, 2002.

Ziolkowski, Theodore. *The Mirror of Justice*. Princeton: Princeton University Press, 1997.

Žižek, Slavoj. *Tarrying with the Negative*. Durham, NC: Duke University Press, 1993.

SOURCES

"Out of the Blue" is an expanded version of the central section of a longer essay that appeared under the same title in *Futures: Of Jacques Derrida*, ed. Richard Rand (Stanford: Stanford University Press, 2001), 99–129.

An earlier version of "In the Name of Friendship" was published under the title "Politics of Friendship – Once Again," *Eighteenth-Century Studies* 32 (1999): 133–55.

A significantly shorter version of "Under the Sign of Failure" appeared in *Idealistic Studies* 26 (1996): 135–51.

Thanks to Martin Klebes for preparing the index.

INDEX